Private Women, Public Meals: Social Conflict in the Synoptic Tradition

PRIVATE WOMEN

PUBLIC MEALS

*Social Conflict in the
Synoptic Tradition*

KATHLEEN E. CORLEY

HENDRICKSON
PUBLISHERS
PEABODY, MASSACHUSETTS 01961-3473

ISBN 1–56563–003–3

Library of Congress Cataloging-in-Publication Data

Corley, Kathleen E., 1960–
    Private women, public meals: social conflict in the synoptic
    tradition / Kathleen E. Corley.
        p. cm.
    Includes bibliographical references and index.
    ISBN 1–56563–003–3
    1. Dinners and dining in the Bible. 2. Women in the Bible.
3. Social conflict in the Bible. 4. Bible. N.T. Gospels—
Criticism, interpretation, etc. I. Title.
BS2555.6.D56C67 1993
226'.095'082—dc20   93-5702
                                                                   CIP

for Bailey

Table of Contents

Acknowledgments

This book is the culmination of a long process of thought and research which began years ago during preparations for my doctoral exams at The Claremont Graduate School. It was in the midst of that hectic time that it suddenly occurred to me that the issue of women and their place in ancient Christian groups had less to do with Christian ideology itself than it did with larger cultural, social and economic forces which ebbed and flowed over a span of several centuries. As I struggled with how to place the New Testament in the context of these forces as I understood them, I came upon the work of Dennis Smith and Mary Douglas which focused my attention upon a seemingly simple social convention which could be used as an indicator of social change: the meal. The study of women in the context of ancient meal conventions has since then proven to be a remarkably fruitful avenue of research on ancient attitudes about women generally, and for understanding New Testament perspectives about women more particularly. This book, which grows out of research for my doctoral dissertation, examines the Synoptic Gospels, but its ramifications for other areas of New Testament research, particularly Pauline studies, are obvious.

Since the original submission of this manuscript in January of 1992, I have not endeavored to address additional scholarly work that may have appeared since that time, but rather tried to fine tune my overall presentation and argument. I am grateful to the editors at Hendrickson Publishers who have aided me in this regard, particularly Patrick Alexander. My friend Harold Gray prepared the manuscript for publication, for which I am grateful. I would also like to thank others who read earlier versions of the manuscript in whole or in part, including Burton Mack, Karen Torjesen, James M. Robinson, Ronald Hock, Howard Jackson, Lee Klosinski and Diana Bailey. They no doubt saved me from many mistakes. Moreover, I would also like to thank my earlier mentors for their continuing interest and encouragement, including Bernadette J. Brooten, Robert Gundry and Moisés Silva. As good research is not accomplished in a void, I would like additionally to thank my colleagues Shawn Carruth and Sterling Bjorndahl for our many conversations about this project. Finally, I wish to acknowledge my best friend and most cherished partner in scholarly discourse, Diana Bailey, who has worked tirelessly to help me meet publication deadlines. In gratitude for our many years of lively discussion and close friendship, I dedicate this endeavor to her.

Kathleen E. Corley
University of Wisconsin-Oshkosh
August 1993

Abbreviations

Books and Periodicals

AER	*American Ecclesiastical Review*
ANF	Ante-Nicene Fathers
ATR	*Anglican Theological Review*
BAGD	W. Bauer, W. F. Arndt, F. W. Gingrich and F. W. Danker, *Greek-English Lexicon of the New Testament and Other Early Christian Literature*
Bib	*Biblica*
BT	*Bible Today*
BTB	*Biblical Theology Bulletin*
BVC	*Bibel et Vie chrétienne*
BZ	*Biblische Zeitschrift*
CBQ	*Catholic Biblical Quarterly*
CH	*Church History*
ChrT	*Christianity Today*
CJ	*Classical Journal*
ConservJudaism	*Conservative Judaism*
CP	*Classical Philology*
CQ	*Classical Quarterly*
CW	*Classical World*
EstEcles	*Estudios Eclesiásticos*
ETL	*Ephemerides theologicae lovanienses*
ExpTim	*Expository Times*
FoiVie	*Foi et Vie*
GeistLeb	*Geist und Leben*
GRBS	*Greek, Roman, and Byzantine Studies*
HR	*History of Religions*
HTR	*Harvard Theological Review*
IndJTh	*Indian Journal of Theology*
Int	*Interpretation*

ISBE	*International Standard Bible Encyclopedia*
JBL	*Journal of Biblical Literature*
JFSR	*Journal of Feminist Studies in Religion*
JJS	*Journal of Jewish Studies*
JRS	*Journal of Roman Studies*
JSNT	*Journal for the Study of the New Testament*
JThSoAfrica	*Journal of Theology for Southern Africa*
JTS	*Journal of Theological Studies*
LCL	Loeb Classical Library
LSJ	Liddell-Scott-Jones, *Greek-English Lexicon*
LV	*Lumen Vitae*
MM	J. H. Moulton and G. Milligan, *The Vocabulary of the Greek Testament*
NovT	*Novum Testamentum*
NTS	*New Testament Studies*
PerRelSt	*Perspectives in Religious Studies*
PL	J. Migne, *Patrologia latina*
RArch	*Revue archéologique*
RelSRev	*Religious Studies Review*
RTL	*Revue théologique de Louvain*
SBLMS	Society of Biblical Literature Monograph Series
ScEs	*Science et Esprit*
StLukeJ	*St. Luke's Journal of Theology*
Str-B	[H. Strack and] P. Billerbeck, *Kommentar zum Neuen Testament aus Talmud und Midrasch*
StudPat	*Studia Patristica*
TD	*Theology Digest*
TDNT	G. Kittel and G. Friedrich, eds., *Theological Dictionary of the New Testament*
TQ	*Theologische Quartalschrift*
TS	*Theological Studies*
TToday	*Theology Today*
TZ	*Theologische Zeitschrift*
ZNW	*Zeitschrift für die neutestamentliche Wissenschaft*

Ancient Writers

Aeschines	
In Tim.	*In Timarchus*
Anth. Graec.	*Anthologia Graeca*
Athen. *Deipn.*	Athenaeus, *Deipnosophistae*
Cicero	
Cael.	*Pro Caelio*
Fam.	*Epistula ad familiares*
Sen.	*De Senectute*
Verr.	*In Verrum*

Clement of Alexandria
    Paed.   *Paedagogus*
Cornelius Nepos
    praef.   *praefatio*
Demosthenes
    In Neaer.   *In Neaeram*
Dio Cass.   Dio Cassius
Dio Chrysostom
    Or.   *Orationes*
Diod. Sic.   Diodorus Siculus
Diog. Laert.   Diogenes Laertius
Dion. Hal.   Dionysius of Halicarnassus
Epictetus
    Ench.   *Enchiridion*
Eunapius
    V.S.   *Vitae sophistarum*
Herodotus
    Hist.   *Historicus*
Josephus
    Ant.   *Antiquitates Judaicae*
    J.W.   *Bellum Judaicum*
Lucian
    Asin.   *Asinus*
    Cyn.   *Cynicus*
    Dial. Meret.   *Dialogi meretricii*
    Men.   *Menippus*
    Symp.   *Symposium*
Macrobius
    Sat.   *Saturnalia*
Martial
    Epigr.   *Epigrammata*
Ovid
    Amor.   *Amores*
    Met.   *Metamorphoses*
Philo
    Vit. Cont.   *De vita contemplativa*
    Flacc.   *In Flaccum*
    Sacr.   *De sacrificiis Abelis et Caini*
    Spec. Leg.   *De specialibus legibus, I-III*
Plato
    Symp.   *Symposium*
Plutarch
  Vitae
    Art.   *Artoxerexes*
    Comp. Lyc. et Num.   *Comparatio Lycurgi et Numae*
    Demetr.   *Demetrius*
    Rom.   *Romulus*

Mor.	*Moralia*
Apophth. Lac.	*Apophthegmata Laconia*
Aud. Poet.	*Quomodo adulescens poetas audire debeat*
De Cup. Div.	*De cupiditate divitiarum*
De Gen.	*De genio Socratis*
Praec. Conjug.	*Praecepta conjugalia*
Quaest. Conv.	*Quaestiones convivalies*
Quomodo Adul. Amic.	*Quomodo adulatur ab amico inter noscatur*
Sept. Sap. Conv.	*Septem sapientum convivium*
Pseudo-Lucian	
Am.	*Amores*
Sallust	
Cat.	*Catilina*
Seneca (the Elder)	
Controv.	*Controversiae*
Seneca (the Younger)	
Epist.	*Epistulae*
Statius	
Silv.	*Silvae*
Strab.	Strabo
Suetonius	
Claud.	*Claudius*
Tib.	*Tiberius*
Tacitus	
Ann.	*Annales*
Germ.	*Germania*
Theophrastus	
Char.	*Characteres*
Val. Max.	Valerius Maximus
Vitruvius	
De Arch.	*De Architectura*

Introduction

For at least a decade, scholars have discussed the presence and position of women in the early Christian communities. The presupposition has long been that the earliest group around Jesus was an inclusive one, and that Jesus' teaching was one that encouraged the full participation of women. Hence, Paul's rehearsal of an early baptismal creed, "in Christ there is neither Jew nor Greek, neither slave nor free, neither male nor female" (Gal 3:28) was consistent with a uniquely Christian message, a message which superseded an earlier and more restrictive Jewish code. Eventually, it is assumed, the uniquely Christian inclusivity and equality were obliterated by the influence of Hellenistic patriarchalism. This work challenges this assumption and its resultant historical reconstruction of the controversy regarding the place of women in early Christianity.

The controversy over the inclusivity of many Christian groups is rather the result of an Empire-wide social innovation beginning in the Late Republican era, whereby women began to have increased access to the "public" sphere and took on "public" roles previously denied to them. This social innovation was the result of larger economic changes and fluctuations in the market economy which placed economic and social power in the hands of women. By the Augustan era, the political and economic threat of this social innovation was felt, and legislative measures were undertaken to restrict the newer freedoms of Roman women. The interest in the patriarchal family as a means of insuring the political stability of the Empire then caused a shift (backwards) in the social consciousness which reemphasized ideal women's roles. Thus, scholars of this era of

Greco-Roman history detect a domestication of morals from the first through the third centuries which is independent of Christian teaching.

These fluctuations in Greco-Roman society and social ideology may be conveniently charted by analyzing one of the most conservative aspects of any society, the meal. Social anthropologists have suggested that the sequence of meals, their cuisine, and the elements of their preparation resist innovation, since such customs reflect and symbolize a culture's social and political relationships. Greco-Roman women's meal etiquette may be shown to reflect changes in the larger social system during this period. In greater numbers, aristocratic women began to attend public meal functions, a behavior associated with their lower-class counterparts who had long enjoyed more freedom in the public realm. However, innovations in meal practice generally undermine the basic social constructs and relations of a society. Innovations in the meal practice of aristocratic Greco-Roman women undermined the gender and class-based social hierarchy of Greco-Roman society. The reaction to these innovations and the rhetoric leveled against women who practiced them were therefore harsh. Absence from public meals became part of a complex of ideas which defined a woman's social classification and restricted her participation in the public sphere. Women who ventured out into the public in this manner were labeled "slaves" and "prostitutes." By the time of Justinian it became grounds for divorce if a freewoman attended a public meal without the escort of her husband. It appears that many segments of Hellenistic society, including Hellenistic Jewish society, were affected by both the innovation of meal practice and the conservative social ideology which persisted and eventually curtailed this innovation.

The inclusive table practice of early Christianity is therefore not the result of a uniquely Christian ideology which encouraged convivial inclusivity; rather it reflects an Empire-wide social innovation that affected all Greco-Roman society at a basic level, that of the meal. One would expect to find early in the first century that certain groups of free association would have reflected these changes in public meal practice and would have allowed the social mixture of men and women as well as slaves and free in public meals. This would be particularly true in the case of groups with a large membership of freedpeople and slaves. As the first century proceeded, one might also expect to find a continued objection to such meal innovation and a renewed emphasis on ideal women's roles and behavior. Moreover, among slaves and the free poor, one would probably not find an exaggerated concern for meal propriety and "ideal" women's roles. Thus, neither the inclusion of women in meal settings nor the accusations of licentiousness leveled against them necessarily differentiate early Christian groups from their Hellenistic context or from other religious or philosophical movements of the early Roman Empire.

Since early Christian groups most often gathered together at meals during public worship and discourse, early Christian ideas about meals should reflect early Christian ideas about the place of women in Christian communities. For example, Pauline churches seem to have been peopled with men, women, slaves, and freed-people, all gathering together for public meals. Yet, Galatians 3:28, however bravely pronounced in the early 50s, is never repeated with the "neither male and female" pair as part of the creed. In fact, in 1 Corinthians (in which the "neither male nor female" pronouncement is absent) we find Paul urging the "veiling" of women as they make public religious pronouncements as well as calling for the traditional "silence" of women in public assemblies (1 Cor 11—14). Later in the century, the Deutero-Pauline letters use traditional Hellenistic "household codes" to encourage ideal Greco-Roman behavior on the part of women and slaves. First Peter heightens this interest in traditional household structures and further emphasizes the proper and obedient behavior of women and slaves (1 Pet 2:18—3:7).

The Gospel tradition also reflects both the fluctuation in Greco-Roman meal etiquette and an emphasis on ideal women's roles. That the early Jesus movements attracted women converts is confirmed by the Gospels themselves. At an early level of the tradition, Jesus is slandered for his table practice, one that includes "tax-collectors and sinners" and features "wine-bibbing" and "gluttony." Such characterizations reflect typical literary depictions of those known for banqueting with "promiscuous" women. Similar epithets can be found in the context of Greco-Roman philosophical debate, as rhetorical slander was leveled against philosophical groups who featured women among their members. The "Children in the Marketplace" pericope from Q highlights servants who acknowledge Jesus and John by "wailing" and "piping," both activities of women and slaves hired for funerals and banquets. Furthermore, within the narratives found in the Gospels, such as the stories of the Syro-Phoenician woman who requests "crumbs" and the woman who anoints Jesus at a meal, one can detect stereotypical depictions of women who would have been categorized as "promiscuous" or "improper." By incorporating these kinds of materials, the evangelists reveal the roots of their communities in earlier groups whose gatherings incorporated a slave/free social mixture of both genders. All of the Synoptics show an awareness that such scenes were at odds with Greco-Roman propriety.

Of the Synoptics, Mark shows the least concern for the material about women that he incorporates into his Gospel. This may reflect either his earlier date or his interest in other matters. The women do appear as members of the group, "disciples" as it were, and their presence is firmly embedded in the narrative. Their primary function in the community is one of simple service, particularly "service" at table. The women accompany the men and in particular are identified as Jesus' personal servants. However, this feminine accompaniment arouses little comment on Mark's part. As Mark tells the story, the woman's anointing of Jesus and her presence at the meal are not objected to on account of their impropriety, but on account of the cost of the ointment. Likewise, the Syro-Phoenician woman is rejected at first by Jesus not because she is "promiscuous," but rather because she is a Gentile. Jesus is known for dining with "tax-collectors and sinners," which would include women, but the presence of the women among Jesus' dining company is not emphasized; however, as servants, particularly as "table-servants," the women exemplify Markan discipleship. Thus, in Mark, the freemen are encouraged to take on the role of the women or lower-class servants.

Nevertheless, Mark does give a nod to the social conservatism of the Hellenistic world. It is highly unlikely that Mark portrays women as "leaders," as many have suggested. Moreover, women are never clearly depicted as eating with or reclining with men. Women are rarely portrayed as speaking in public, the hemorrhaging woman being the one exception. Even the anointing scene is set in a private home, as are the scenes with the Syro-Phoenician woman and Peter's mother-in-law. When Jesus "eats and drinks with tax-collectors and sinners" it is in the private home of a tax-collector. Furthermore, although it may be argued that such slander assumes the presence of women, Mark does not comment on it. The only woman in the Gospel clearly depicted as a "courtesan" is the daughter of Herodias, who in a stereotypical scene requests the head of John the Baptist in the context of a banquet. All the women around Jesus are in contrast to Herodias and her daughter: they may be present for meals, but they are not promiscuous or prostitutes.

Luke also acknowledges the ample presence of women in both the early stages of the Jesus movement and the Hellenistic mission. Luke, however, has two categories of women which are accepted into the messianic community. As in Mark, Jesus is known for his acceptance and forgiveness of "tax-collectors and sinners," but in Luke these include women. Thus, the woman who anoints Jesus becomes a "woman known in the city," one of the repentant "sinners" Jesus is accused of socializing with. She is also likened to one of the "children/servants" of the marketplace who accept Jesus' message, in contrast to the Pharisees who do not. However, this woman "sinner" does not join Jesus at the table. Thus, in Luke, even the "sinners" are never explicitly portrayed as actually eating with Jesus as they are in Mark. Jesus is accused of "eating and drinking with tax-collectors and sinners," but he is also depicted as eating with one tax-collector and visiting another. The woman "sinner" does not join Jesus at the table, and she is never called πόρνη. If the term πόρνη occurred in Q, Luke omits it from his narrative. Moreover, as part of a larger omission, Luke does not repeat the odd story of the Syro-Phoenician woman. He also omits Mark's contrasting story of Herod's birthday symposium with a courtesan. Luke probably keeps the tradition that Jesus socialized with women and "sinners" because of its antiquity.

The second category of women in Luke are those women who are most often around Jesus. Luke is careful to protect their reputations. In fact, rather than being prostitutes, the women most often with Jesus include a married woman, and all follow Jesus out of gratitude for their healings. These women even support his movement financially. They are no longer simple table servants as in Mark, but are a more respectable group akin to patronesses. Likewise, Mary and Martha join Jesus for a respectable private meal, where Mary takes the traditional submissive stance seated at Jesus' feet (Luke 10:39). Furthermore, women do not speak in public in Luke's Gospel, and they are discouraged from participating in διακονία, a leadership role reserved for men. Therefore, in spite of the many women in his narrative, Luke portrays a conservative meal practice as well as emphasizes a private role for the women in his community.

Surprisingly, only Matthew does not follow the general pattern of recasting his traditional material with a concern for Greco-Roman propriety. This is surprising because Matthew has been characterized as being written to a predominantly Jewish-Christian community, and Jewish groups have often been characterized as overly patriarchal during this period. However, only Matthew adds women and children to both of his Feeding narratives, meals which he portrays as Eucharistic feasts. This is undoubtedly related to his version of the Feast parable which now, as a wedding, has become a family affair. Thus, the party to welcome the Messiah is a wedding for which even young unmarried women prepare. In his rendition of Herod's birthday party, Matthew not only implies that both Herodias and her daughter are present throughout the banquet, but subsequently shifts the blame for John's death from Herodias to Herod. Matthew not only includes the story about the Syro-Phoenician woman, but sets it more naturally outside, not in a private dwelling. He also rewrites the story to focus on the woman's faith. In his story of the anointing of Jesus, Matthew omits the direct criticism of the woman and emphasizes the objection to the costliness of the perfume. The women who follow Jesus at the end of Matthew's narrative are not simply servants, but are examples of true discipleship. It is not the women who are alarmed at the tomb but the guards. Unlike the women in Mark, Matthew's women do as they are told and report the resurrection to their fellow disciples.

Furthermore, only Matthew is not reluctant to use the term πόρνη. Not only do "tax-collectors and courtesans" enter the kingdom of God (and the Jesus movement via John's baptism), but even Jesus' genealogy features four women with sexually suspicious histories. If the term "courtesans" occurred in Q, Matthew keeps it. Of all the Synoptics, only Matthew delights in portraying an egalitarian inclusive community of "little ones" in which men, women, and children gather together for meals. This is in contrast to Mark and Luke. Although Matthew shifts to a family image of the Christian community, this shift does not seem to result in an emphasis on traditional Greco-Roman gender roles, as it does in the Deutero-Pauline or Petrine Epistles. Matthew and Luke, then, go in very different directions with the traditional material they adopt. Luke, anxious to convert an increasingly conservative Hellenistic world, exhibits the most concern for traditional Greco-Roman propriety. Matthew's community is more class-inclusive, and the call to convert "all nations" still manifests a lack of concern for gender or class. This is all the more surprising given the recent consensus that the Matthean community is urban and wealthy.

In order to substantiate my reconstruction of the place of women in early Christian groups, this study will investigate the changing social patterns in Greco-Roman society which affected women's participation in formal meals or banquets. Meal customs were undergoing change during the Roman period, so that women from various social strata began to attend public meals—a behavior formerly associated with lower-class women, prostitutes, and slaves. Thus, women who attended public meals, whatever their social status, were labeled "promiscuous" or "prostitutes." This means that the presence of women in meetings of free association in Jesus movements and the language used to describe them, though noteworthy, are neither extraordinary nor unique.

However, certain Synoptic Gospels betray a concern for traditional Greco-Roman meal propriety. As a collection, the Synoptic Gospels show several positionings on the issue of women and inclusive table practice. Mark is aware of Greco-Roman propriety and literary banquet themes, but evidences little concern for the impropriety of other stories about women in his narrative. Luke, however, is concerned to portray the women around Jesus as respectable and maintains in his narrative scenes the Greco-Roman gender-based division of public and private spheres. Only Matthew allows women a place at the table and portrays them as reclining at meals with men. The labeling of the women around Jesus as "courtesans," avoided by Mark and Luke, is embraced by Matthew. Of the Synoptics, it is Matthew who is more in line with earlier Jesus movements, insofar as his table etiquette is concerned. Thus, it will be seen that Greco-Roman ideas about meal propriety helped shape the identity of the Synoptic communities and helped determine the place of women in these early Christian groups.

Part I

Women in Early Christianity and Early Christian Communal Meals

Women in Early Christianity and Early Christian Communal Meals 1

History of Scholarship on Women in Early Christianity

Scholarship on Women and the New Testament

In recent decades, the scholarly literature on women in early Christianity and the New Testament has proliferated. There is no need to review entirely this mass of literature; numerous articles attempt this task.[1] Following Carolyn Osiek's general approach, it is most helpful to categorize scholarship on women and the New Testament according to their various perspectives on biblical authority and use of biblical texts.[2] The challenge of this branch of biblical scholarship has been to develop a consistent perspective on the patriarchal social structure reflected in New Testament texts. Each of the four positions discussed below represents a kind of response to that patriarchal structure, whether it be to affirm it as normative for the modern church, or to reinterpret New Testament texts as no longer applicable for today.

Some scholars still seek to *reaffirm* the patriarchal tradition found in New Testament texts. From this perspective the gender-

---

[1] Carolyn Osiek, "The Feminist and the Bible: Hermeneutical Alternatives," in *Feminist Perspectives on Biblical Scholarship*, ed. Adela Yarbro Collins (Chico, Calif.: Scholars Press, 1985), 93–105; and even more recently, a series of articles in *Interpretation* 42 (1988), ed. P. J. Achtemeier; Katherine Doob Sakenfeld, "Feminist Perspectives on Bible and Theology: An Introduction to Selected Issues and Literature," 5–18; George W. Stroup, "Between Echo and Narcissus: The Role of the Bible in Feminist Theology," 19–32; Pheme Perkins, "Women in the Bible and Its World," 33–44; Elizabeth Achtemeier, "The Impossible Possibility: Evaluating the Feminist Approach to Bible and Theology," 45–57.

[2] Osiek, "The Feminist and the Bible." Osiek is followed by Sakenfeld, "Feminist Perspectives."

based social hierarchy found in the Bible is considered a divinely ordained structure having its roots in creation. Hence, the headship of the man and the subordination of the woman as outlined in texts like Ephesians 5 should not be abandoned. Neither should churches move to include women in teaching offices, since Paul prohibits this in 1 Timothy 2. Written arguments for this position may be found in James B. Hurley, *Man and Woman in Biblical Perspective*[3] as well as in Robert Culver's more recent defense of a traditional view of women in the church.[4] This perspective is best exemplified by the recently formed Council on Biblical Manhood and Womanhood, a cross-denominational Protestant committee that now uses one's position on women in ministry and marriage as the test of one's adherence to biblical inerrancy.[5]

A second position seeks to *reinterpret* materials about women found in the Bible which previously have been interpreted to require women's subordination in the home and church.[6] New Testament texts such as those found in Ephesians, 1 Corinthians, and the Pastorals have received renewed attention by scholars interested in maintaining a high view of biblical authority. These scholars contend that many texts concerning women have been misunderstood and therefore misapplied over the centuries. For example, Paul did not advocate the subordination of women to their husbands, but rather mutual submission between spouses. Scholars of this perspective often advocate the admission of women to all ministerial orders of the church. Such scholars could also be identified as "evangelical" or "biblical feminist." An excellent source for this perspective is the collection of articles in *Women, Authority and the Bible*, edited by

---

[3] Grand Rapids, Mich.: Zondervan, 1981.

[4] Robert D. Culver, "A Traditional View: Let Your Women Keep Silence," in *Women in Ministry: Four Views*, ed. Bonnidell Clouse and Robert G. Clouse (Downers Grove, Ill.: InterVarsity Press, 1989), 25–52. A similar view is presented by Susan T. Foh, "A Male Leadership View: The Head of the Woman is the Man," also found in *Women in Ministry*, 69–105.

[5] The CBMW was formed following the 1987 meeting of the International Council on Biblical Inerrancy, since that organization could not come to an agreement on the place of women in the church and home. See Kenneth S. Kantzer, "Problems Inerrancy Doesn't Solve," *ChrT* 31 (Feb. 20, 1987): 14–15. The CBMW distributes its views in a document called the "Danvers Statement" (Wheaton, Ill.: Council on Biblical Manhood and Womanhood, November 1988). Members of the CBMW include James B. Hurley, George W. Knight III and Beverly LaHaye.

[6] Osiek calls these scholars "loyalists" ("The Feminist and the Bible," 99); Sakenfeld, "Feminist Perspectives," 9–10.

Alvera Mickelsen.[7] Scholars of this perspective also attempt to identify those biblical texts and stories which show women in a "positive" light, as in Leonard Swidler's *Biblical Affirmations of Woman*.[8] Another conservative scholar who seeks to promote a more equitable approach to male-female relations in the context of the modern church is Ben Witherington. Witherington sees the Jesus movement as one reform movement within a culture that was primarily patriarchal.[9] The feminist scholar Phyllis Trible, though not identified with the term "evangelical," also seeks to reinterpret biblical texts in order to retrieve a more positive tradition which has been lost.[10]

A third trajectory in recent studies on women in the New Testament is one which *reconstructs* a new history of women in New Testament times. The forerunner of this approach is Elisabeth Schüssler Fiorenza, whose book *In Memory of Her: A Feminist Reconstruction of Christian Origins*[11] exemplifies this progressive current in feminist New Testament studies. Rather than taking at face value the picture of early Christianity as presented in certain New Testament texts, Schüssler Fiorenza seeks to reconstruct a new image of women's actual participation in early Christian communities. This reconstructed history serves as a point from which to critique other biblical

---

[7] Downers Grove, Ill.: InterVarsity Press, 1986. Contributors include Patricia Gundry, Catherine Kroeger, Marianne Meye Thompson, Clark Pinnock, David Scholer, Willard Swartley, and others.

[8] Philadelphia: Westminster Press, 1979. See Richard Boldrey and Joyce Boldrey, *Chauvinist or Feminist? Paul's View of Women* (Grand Rapids, Mich.: Baker Book House, 1976); Virginia Ramey Mollenkott, *Women, Men and the Bible*, rev. ed. (New York: Crossroad, 1988); Letha Scanzoni and Nancy Hardesty, *All We're Meant to Be: A Biblical Approach to Women's Liberation* (Waco: Word Books, 1974); Evelyn Stagg and Frank Stagg, *Woman in the World of Jesus* (Philadelphia: Westminster Press, 1978); and in *Women in Ministry: Four Views*, see Walter Liefeld, "A Plural Ministry View: Your Sons and Your Daughters Shall Prophesy," 127–53, and Alvera Mickelsen, "An Egalitarian View: There is Neither Male Nor Female in Christ," 173–206.

[9] *Women in the Ministry of Jesus: A Study of Jesus' Attitudes to Women and their Roles as Reflected in His Earthly Life* (Cambridge: Cambridge University Press, 1984); idem, *Women in the Earliest Churches* (Cambridge: Cambridge University Press, 1988); and his more recent and less technical, *Women and the Genesis of Christianity* (Cambridge: Cambridge University Press, 1990), based on his two earlier monographs.

[10] For example, Trible argues that Gen 1–3 presents men and women as being equally created in the image of God, both having "dominion." See *God and the Rhetoric of Sexuality* (Philadelphia: Fortress Press, 1978); *Texts of Terror: Literary-Feminist Readings of Biblical Narratives* (Philadelphia: Fortress Press, 1984); Osiek considers Trible a "revisionist." See Osiek, "The Feminist and the Bible," 101f.; Sakenfeld, "Feminist Perspectives," 9–10.

[11] New York: Crossroad, 1983.

texts that attempt to limit women's participation in church structures or to subordinate women in the household. Schüssler Fiorenza maintains that in earliest Christianity women were participants in the Jesus movement, which was a "discipleship of equals."[12] This reconstruction of Christian origins is done on the basis of reading New Testament texts with a "hermeneutic of suspicion." This approach holds that the New Testament was written from a culturally conditioned, androcentric position, and therefore its portrayal of the "way things were" is not to be trusted. On the basis of this hermeneutic, scholars like Schüssler Fiorenza feel free to reject as non-authoritative any biblical texts that do not support the "full humanity of women."[13] For Schüssler Fiorenza, authority lies not in the biblical texts themselves, but within the experience of "Women-Church."[14] This liberationist perspective is shared by Rosemary Radford Ruether[15] and Letty M. Russell.[16] Scholars like Bernadette J. Brooten also seek to reconstruct a new picture of women in early Christianity and the ancient world.[17] Several anthologies now demonstrate the growing breadth of feminist liberation theology and hermeneutical method.[18] Such feminist perspectives have not gone unchallenged.[19]

---

[12] Schüssler Fiorenza, *In Memory of Her*, 140ff.

[13] "The Will to Choose or Reject: Continuing Our Critical Work," in *Feminist Interpretation of the Bible*, ed. Letty M. Russell (Philadelphia: Westminster Press, 1985), 125–36; Elisabeth Schüssler Fiorenza, *Bread Not Stone: The Challenge of Feminist Biblical Interpretation* (Boston: Beacon Press, 1984).

[14] See Stroup, "Between Echo and Narcissus," 26ff.

[15] *Religion and Sexism: Images of Woman in the Jewish and Christian Traditions* (New York: Simon and Schuster, 1974); *Sexism and God-Talk: Toward a Feminist Theology* (London: SCM Press; Boston: Beacon Press, 1984); *Women-Church: Theology and Practice of Feminist Liturgical Communities* (New York: Harper and Row, 1985).

[16] *Household of Freedom* (Philadelphia: Westminster Press, 1987).

[17] Bernadette J. Brooten, "Early Christian Women and Their Cultural Context: Issues of Method in Historical Reconstruction," in *Feminist Perspectives on Biblical Scholarship*, 65–91; idem, *Women Leaders in the Ancient Synagogue: Inscriptional Evidence and Background Issues* (Brown Judaic Studies 36; Chico, Calif.: Scholars Press, 1982). See also Perkins, "Women in the Bible and Its World."

[18] Adela Yarbro Collins, ed., *Feminist Perspectives on Biblical Scholarship* (Chico, Calif.: Scholars Press, 1985); Ann Loades, ed., *Feminist Theology: A Reader* (London: SPCK; Philadelphia: Westminster, 1990); Russell, *Feminist Interpretation of the Bible* (Philadelphia: Westminster, 1985). For early reconstruction efforts, see articles in *Women of Spirit: Female Leadership in the Jewish and Christian Traditions*, ed. Rosemary Radford Ruether and Eleanor McLaughlin (New York: Simon and Schuster, 1979).

[19] Elizabeth Achtemeier, "The Impossible Possibility"; Jean C. Lambert, "An 'F Factor'? The New Testament in Some White, Feminist, Christian Theological Construction," *JFSR* 1 (1985): 93–113; Stroup, "Between Echo and Narcissus."

A fourth perspective on women in the New Testament and the Bible generally is one which *rejects* the Bible altogether as being unsavable. The primary proponent of this view is Mary Daly, whose books have become well known.[20] For Daly, both the Bible and Christian theology are hopelessly patriarchal; it is not possible to separate some kind of timeless Christian message from a book that is culturally and socially bound. As a post-Christian, Daly asserts that in the case of the Bible, the medium *is* the message, and the message is patriarchy and oppression for women. According to Daly, reinterpreting the Bible is not sufficient. The only hope for women is to leave the church entirely, taking on a post-Christian perspective which may transcend patriarchy.

Scholarship on women and the New Testament thus spans a variety of perspectives. Putting aside for the moment the most radical extremes, there is one criticism which has been leveled against Christian feminists and biblical feminists alike. In both of these perspectives, there is an interest in upholding the uniqueness of the Christian message. In particular, most Christian scholars attempt to credit Jesus of Nazareth with achieving some form of new egalitarian perspective. In doing so, most paint Judaism as an overly oppressive religion, one in which women had little or no place in the home or synagogue. This is particularly the case with biblical or evangelical feminists.[21] Although more sensitive to the concerns of Jewish feminists, even scholars like Schüssler Fiorenza have not escaped critique in this regard.[22] Scholars such as Ross Kraemer and Bernadette J. Brooten have continued to produce research which indicates that contrary to many Christian reconstructions, Hellenistic Judaism was in fact enormously appealing to many Hellenistic women, and that Jewish women were not overly oppressed during New Testament times.[23] In order to gain a better grasp of the experience of both Jewish and Christian women in the ancient world, many New Testament scholars have turned to the fields of classics and social history

---

[20] *Beyond God the Father: Toward a Philosophy of Women's Liberation* (Boston: Beacon Press, 1973); *Gyn/Ecology: The Metaphysics of Radical Feminism* (Boston: Beacon Press, 1978); *Pure Lust* (Boston: Beacon Press, 1984).

[21] Judith Plaskow, "Christian Feminism and Anti–Judaism," *Cross Currents* 28 (1978): 306–9; Perkins, "Women in the Bible and Its World," 34.

[22] Ross S. Kraemer, "Review: In Memory of Her," *RelSRev* 11 (1985): 1–9.

[23] See pp. 66–75.

to inform their efforts towards a historical reconstruction of women's roles in early Christianity.[24]

Scholarship on Women in Greco-Roman Antiquity

Like scholarship on the place of women in the Bible and early Christianity, scholarship on women in the ancient world has also flourished in recent years. A review article written by Susan Treggiari in 1975 details classical scholarship up until the early 1970s on various aspects of ancient social history, including slavery and the position of women in Roman society.[25] Treggiari cites as a primary resource for studying women in the Roman period, J. P. V. D. Balsdon's *Roman Women: Their History and Habits*.[26] Balsdon's work is still considered a standard source on women for this period. Also available from the 1970s is the issue of *Arethusa* that is devoted to the topic of "Women in Antiquity." Now in book form, this collection contains an extensive bibliography on women in antiquity compiled by Sarah B. Pomeroy.[27] Treggiari notes with satisfaction a trend in classical studies which weaves a more realistic picture of women's lives in ancient times, free of overly romanticized notions based on an uncritical reading of pious ancient epitaphs or an unsubstantiated Juvenal.[28] Although she considers them somewhat outdated, Treggiari still recommends works such as those by Freidländer,[29] Fowler,[30]

---

[24] Perkins, "Women in the Bible and Its World," 36ff. A more recent example of this method involving historical reconstruction is Antoinette Clark Wire's new book on women in Corinth, *The Corinthian Women Prophets: A Reconstruction through Paul's Rhetoric* (Minneapolis, Minn.: Fortress Press, 1990).

[25] "Roman Social History: Recent Interpretations," *Social History* 8 (1975): 149–64.

[26] London: Bodley Head, 1962; rev. ed. 1974.

[27] John Peradotto and J. P. Sullivan, eds., *Women in the Ancient World: The Arethusa Papers* (Albany, N.Y.: State University of New York Press, 1984).

[28] Apparently, many classics scholars in past decades have had a tendency to read modern morality and sensibilities back into the Roman period. For example, the idea that the consummation of marriages in antiquity occurred when the bride was between the ages of 9 and 12 has often been rejected as impossible by nineteenth- and twentieth-century scholars who found the notion of sex with minors abhorrent (Treggiari, "Roman Social History," 160f.).

[29] L. Freidländer, *Roman Life and Manners Under the Early Empire*, trans. A. B. Gough (London: Routledge, 1909).

[30] W. Warde Fowler, *Social Life at Rome in the Age of Cicero* (London: Macmillan & Co., 1909).

and Carcopino.[31] Since the writing of Treggiari's article, an English translation of the more recent *A History of Private Life from Pagan Rome to Byzantium*, edited by Paul Veyne, has also appeared.[32] This volume also betrays a more forthright attitude in its discussion of Roman private life. For example, Veyne is careful not to rewrite Roman social history in the image of the modern women's liberation movement, emphasizing instead the true limitations of Roman institutions such as slavery and marriage.

Treggiari's article anticipates Sarah B. Pomeroy's then forthcoming book, *Goddesses, Whores, Wives and Slaves: Women in Classical Antiquity*.[33] Pomeroy's work reflects an unromanticized approach to the place of women in the ancient world. Pomeroy limits her comments to the results of an analysis of archaeological data, documentary evidence, and the literature of Greece and Rome. Organizing her work into sections on Greek antiquity and Roman antiquity, Pomeroy carefully distinguishes between descriptions of women of the aristocratic class and those of the lower classes and slave populations. Her later book, *Women in Hellenistic Egypt*, also utilizes legal materials, documentary evidence, and inscriptions to develop a clearer picture of the daily lives of ancient women.[34] Pomeroy's work has become an important source for New Testament scholars interested in reconstructing the daily life of ancient Christian women.[35] Actual sources in translation concerning women's private lives in antiquity can also now be found in *Women's Life in Greece and Rome: A Source Book in Translation*, compiled by Mary R. Lefkowitz and Maureen B. Fant.[36]

Since the publication of *Goddesses, Whores, Wives and Slaves*, other books on women and ancient social life have appeared, such as the collections of articles in *Images of Women in Antiquity*,[37] *The*

---

[31] Jérôme Carcopino, *Daily Life in Ancient Rome*, trans. E. O. Lorimer (New Haven and London: Yale University Press, 1940). See Treggiari, "Roman Social History," 161.

[32] Arthur Goldhammer, trans. (Cambridge, Mass.; London: Belknap Press of Harvard University Press, 1987). Originally published as *Histoire de la vie Privée, vol. 1: De l'Empire romain à l'an mil* (Editions du Seuil, 1985). "The Roman Empire" by Paul Veyne; "Late Antiquity" by Peter Brown; "Private Life and Domestic Architecture in Roman Africa" by Yron Thébert.

[33] New York: Schocken Books, 1975.

[34] New York: Schocken Books, 1984.

[35] Perkins, "Women in the Bible and Its World," 36.

[36] Baltimore, Md.: Johns Hopkins University Press, 1982.

[37] Averil Cameron and Amélie Kuhrt, eds. (Detroit: Wayne State Univ., 1983).

Family in Ancient Rome: New Perspectives,[38] the more recently translated *Pandora's Daughters: The Role and Status of Women in Greek and Roman Antiquity* by Eva Cantarella,[39] and J. P. Hallett's *Fathers and Daughters in Roman Society: Women and the Elite Family.*[40] As in current research on women and the New Testament period, the trend in classical research on women in antiquity has been to focus more on the actual lives of women in antiquity, rather than to rely entirely on literary representations of women. Similarly, literary descriptions of women are now being read with a more critical or "suspicious" eye. For example, Hallett's book demonstrates that, in spite of the oft-mentioned power of the Roman father in the context of the family (*patria potestas*), many daughters in elite Roman families experienced inordinately close and loving relationships with their fathers. In fact, according to Hallett, it was a woman's identity as her father's daughter that determined the course of a Roman woman's life. Eva Cantarella's analysis of the place of women in ancient society is similar to that of Paul Veyne. She too is careful not to allow modern notions of "women's liberation" to color her presentation of ancient women's lives. For example, in her discussion of the freedoms gained by women under imperial Rome, Cantarella endeavors to stress that the freedom experienced by Roman women should be perceived as a relative freedom. The lives of many women during this period underwent little change. Thus, recent scholarship on women in antiquity strives above all else to achieve a balance in its reconstruction of ancient women's lives, so that a sharper picture of the actual lives of women may be determined once the relevant evidence has been fairly interpreted.

The availability of such studies on women in the Greco-Roman world has contributed to the efforts of New Testament scholars to reconstruct and understand the lives of women during the Hellenistic era. Many feminist New Testament scholars have begun to emphasize the importance of utilizing sources which illuminate actual ancient women's experience, such as legal materials, inscriptional evidence, visual art, and documentary papyri.[41] Scholars who have taken the lead in this area are Bernadette J. Brooten and Ross Kraemer, who are

---

[38] Beryl Rawson, ed. (Ithaca, N.Y.: Cornell University Press, 1986).

[39] Maureen Fant, trans. (Baltimore and London: Johns Hopkins University Press, 1987). Originally published as *L'ambiguo malanno* (Editori Riuniti, 1981).

[40] Princeton: Princeton University Press, 1984.

[41] Perkins, "Women in the Bible and Its World," 36.

primarily interested in developing a fairer picture of the lives of Hellenistic Jewish women.[42] In the utilization of such sources, scholars like Brooten and Kraemer attempt to balance descriptions of women's lives (written by men) with documentation of actual women's lives (from inscriptions, art, and papyri). In this regard, all ancient literature, along with the New Testament itself, is approached with a "hermeneutic of suspicion," since its documents might not give trustworthy evidence for historical reconstruction. Information regarding the actual participation of women in ancient public life is now used in possible explanations of the presence of women as patrons of early churches as well as among Paul's missionary friends.[43]

Categories of Women in Antiquity

Both classical scholars and New Testament scholars alike are now also more careful to distinguish between the different social classes that existed in the ancient world, because the lives of ancient women were determined by the class into which they were born. There are not necessarily corresponding categories in ancient society to modern notions of "upper class," "middle class," and "lower class." Studies focusing on the status of women in the aristocracy are not necessarily helpful in establishing the quality of life of women in non-aristocratic families.[44] Furthermore, being wealthy in the ancient world did not necessarily affect one's actual social status, which was determined by birth. Petronius' ridiculing of the upstart freedman Trimalchio in his *Satyricon* caricatures the wealthy, *nouveau riche*, who had no "class." There are several basic categories of social classes for women in Greco-Roman antiquity.

Aristocratic Women.[45] The class of the Roman elite made up a relatively small portion of the overall population of the Roman

---

[42] See pp. 66–75, esp. p. 75.

[43] So Wayne A. Meeks, *First Urban Christians. The Social World of the Apostle Paul* (New Haven: Yale University Press, 1983), 23–25; see Perkins, "Women in the Bible and Its World," 39. For a discussion of women's increasing participation in the public sphere during the Hellenistic era, see pp. 53–66.

[44] Perkins, "Women in the Bible and Its World," 36, n. 12.

[45] For information on upper-class Roman women, see Cantarella, *Pandora's Daughters*, 113–70; Hallett, *Fathers and Daughters*; Pomeroy, *Goddesses*, 149–89; Veyne, "Roman Empire," in *History of Private Life*, 1.9–49.

empire. Freeborn women of this class were from families of considerable wealth. Theoretically, during much of their lives these women were dominated by the presence of some male figure, whether it be a father, a husband, or a tutor. Young women of the aristocracy married young, often between the ages of nine and twelve, and to men considerably older than themselves.[46] According to ancient Roman law, women were to be under the guardianship of a man for the duration of their lives, although by the late Republic this tutelage was only a slight liability for Roman women.[47] Aristocratic women had the right to initiate divorce. Roman women could also own property in their own right, and inherit their father's estates.[48] In fact, laws such as the Lex Voconia were passed to limit the amount that women might inherit. In spite of such legislation, however, inscriptional evidence indicates that large amounts of money did pass into the hands of women, allowing their greater participation in public offices, public events, and building projects.[49] Riet Van Bremen has shown that, beginning with the late Republican era and increasingly throughout the first and second centuries CE, women throughout the Roman Empire used their wealth to build public buildings and temples, participate in city offices, and act as patrons.[50] Once married, a freewoman attained the status of matron. Although traditionally the respectable Roman matron was to limit herself to running her husband's estate or other domestic tasks such as spinning wool, by the imperial period many matrons became active in Roman society, religion, philosophy, and politics. The habits of the Roman elite had little effect on the large poorer classes, yet they did influence the aristocracy of other Roman subjects. Herod's sons, for example, were reared in aristocratic circles. Thus, Herodias' willingness to divorce her husband in order to marry his brother Antipas reflects an

---

[46] Although the legal age for a girl to be married was 12, there is evidence which suggests that marriages were arranged and consummated even when a girl was as young as nine years. See M. K. Hopkins, "The Age of Roman Girls at Marriage," *Population Studies* 19 (1965): 309–21.

[47] Pomeroy, *Goddesses*, 151.

[48] Kathleen E. Corley, "Women's Inheritance Rights in Antiquity and Paul's Metaphor of Adoption," unpublished paper, Claremont Graduate School, 1987.

[49] Riet Van Bremen, "Women and Wealth," in *Images of Women in Antiquity*, 223–42.

[50] Ibid.

aristocratic Roman sensibility.[51] Wealthy freedmen and freedwomen were also wont to ape the habits of their betters.[52]

Freedwomen.[53] Lower in status but often not lacking in actual wealth, many women born in slavery earned their purchase prices and their freedom. In terms of economics, freedwomen could be of various levels of economic means. Some were poorer and staffed the various businesses of the Greco-Roman world as shopkeepers, inn-keepers, weavers, artisans, actresses, musicians, butchers, or prostitutes. Many freedwomen worked in the textile industry; however, others became wealthy merchants in various trades and were often known for selling luxury items such as purple dye for the making of cloth. As a necessity, some of these women no doubt worked alongside their husbands in various trades and businesses. Other freedwomen remained attached to their former master's household, where they continued to contribute to household management as cooks, domestic servants, table waitresses, or hairdressers. Some freedwomen continued in prostitution or became madams of brothels, training younger women to ply their trade. After gaining their freedom, many freedwomen went on to marry their former masters or to become their master's formal concubine. Often chided for alleged promiscuity, freedwomen probably did exercise more freedom of movement in public places, their former slave status affording them a certain level of personal freedom.

Evidence suggests that some freedwomen earned their freedom by means of prostitution, contributing to the overall reputation of freedwomen as sexually "promiscuous." Consequently, moral standards were not as high for freedwomen as for matrons. In the period of the early Empire, however, matrons began to move about more freely in the public sphere, and became victims of slander which characterized them as baseborn freedwomen. Some freedwomen, along with freedmen, became members of the various trade guilds

---

[51] Hallett, *Fathers and Daughters*, 230–37; Perkins, "Women in the Bible and Its World," 36, n. 12.

[52] See A. M. Duff, *Freedmen in the Early Empire*, (New York: Barnes and Noble, 1958); Susan Treggiari, *Roman Freedmen During the Late Republic* (Oxford: Clarendon Press, 1969); Richard I. Pervo, "Wisdom and Power: Petronius' *Satyricon* and the Social World of Early Christianity," *ATR* 67 (1985): 307–25; idem, *Profit with Delight: The Literary Genre of the Acts of the Apostles* (Philadelphia: Fortress Press, 1987), 77–85.

[53] For documentation to this section, see pp. 32, n. 46; 48–52.

and burial societies in the ancient world. In these societies, freedmen and freedwomen would have enjoyed socializing in the context of corporate formal meals. Lydia, the purple-seller in Acts, should probably be understood as a freedwoman, since she is depicted as a merchant of luxury goods and is wealthy enough to have her own household. Priscilla and Aquila, leather workers or artisans, were also probably freed Jews from Rome.[54]

Free Women. Apart from the freeborn aristocracy, many women were also born into free families of various social means. Some freewomen, such as the small property owners, merchants, and tradespeople, would have lived lives indistinguishable from wealthier freedwomen. Similarly, the quality of life for many freeborn women was no doubt indistinguishable from the lives of many freedwomen.[55] Like freedwomen, the ranks of the free poor also staffed the businesses and trades in the ancient world. Free poor women could be shopkeepers, butchers, innkeepers, weavers, fishers, waitresses, shoemakers, or prostitutes. Like freedwomen, poor freewomen probably ran small businesses with their husbands; in rural areas they might have run farms with their husbands. Unlike slaves, women born free were allowed to enter into legal marriages, many of which endured far longer than those of their aristocratic counterparts. Freeborn women of different economic levels also no doubt mingled with their freedmen and women contemporaries, as they shared similar occu-

---

[54] A general consensus has formed that early Christian communities were mixed groups made up of slaves, freedpeople, and the lower-class freeborn, with leaders coming from a wealthier group, such as wealthier freedmen and women, and the wealthier freeborn. See Meeks, *The First Urban Christians*, ch. 2; E. A. Judge, *The Social Pattern of the Christian Groups in the First Century* (London: Tyndale Press, 1960), ch. 5. As Jewish tradesmen from Rome, Priscilla and Aquila were most likely freedpeople (Treggiari, *Roman Freedmen*, 169ff.). The wealthy purple-seller Lydia was also more than likely a freedwoman as she came from the East and sold luxury items (Pomeroy, *Goddesses*, 200; Schüssler Fiorenza, *In Memory of Her*, 178). See also G. H. R. Horsley, "The Purple Trade, and the Status of Lydia of Thyatira," in *New Documents Illustrating Early Christianity* (Macquarie University, Australia: The Ancient History Documentary Research Centre, 1982), 2.25–32. For the probable trade of Priscilla, Aquila, and also Paul, see Ronald F. Hock, *The Social Context of Paul's Ministry: Tentmaking and Apostleship* (Philadelphia: Fortress Press, 1980).

[55] For information on women in the lower classes, see Mima Maxey, "The Occupations of the Lower Classes in Roman Society," in *Two Studies on the Roman Lower Classes*, ed. M. F. Park and M. Maxey (New York: Arno Press, 1975); Pomeroy, *Goddesses*, 190–204; Beryl Rawson, "Family Life Among the Lower Classes at Rome in the First Two Centuries of the Empire," *CP* 61 (1966): 71–83; Susan Treggiari, "Jobs for Women," *American Journal of Ancient History* 1 (1976): 76–104.

pations, and also gathered together in guilds and burial societies for corporate banquets and socializing.

Slave women.[56] Slavery was one of the largest economic institutions in the Greco-Roman world. Large households employed numerous slaves, including many women. Female slaves were primarily domestic servants and served as food preparers, cooks, table servants, hairdressers, and the like. In the context of banquets, women slaves were also part of the entertainment, playing the cithara and flute, acting and dancing, as well as sometimes serving the food. Wealthy householders would also often hire out their banquet slaves to a third party on off days, sending them into the marketplace in the mornings to look for work. Owners of businesses might also use women slaves in factories, particularly in the textile industry. Most brothels were staffed with female slaves, and these women were often owned outright by brothel owners. Many prostitutes were slaves, although some women continued to ply this trade after earning their freedom. Some became brothel owners. As a matter of course, all slaves were sexually available to their masters or to others who might hire them. This sexual availability no doubt was a liability for women slaves or pretty young boys. Many men fathered children by their female slaves, and these children became the property of their fathers. Women might have the opportunity to purchase their freedom, as did men, but they were more often bound to their master's household following emancipation. Most households, even peasant ones, had at least one female slave. The institution of slavery was therefore something commonly known and understood throughout the Greco-Roman world.

The Public/Private Dichotomy

There was one major distinction, however, that governed all definitions of a woman's place in ancient society, regardless of her income or social class; namely, the distinction between "public" and "private" space. Michelle Zimbalist Rosaldo[57] and Jean Bethke Elsh-

---

[56] For documentation to this section, see pp. 48–52.

[57] "Women, Culture and Society: A Theoretical Overview," in *Women, Culture and Society*, ed. M. Z. Rosaldo and Louise Lamphere (Stanford: Stanford University Press, 1974), 17–42. See also Rosaldo, "The Use and Abuse of Anthropology: Reflections on Feminism in Cross-Cultural Understanding," *Signs* 5 (1980): 389–417.

tain.[58] have established that this separation of men and women according to public and private spheres has existed throughout much of Western history. A social anthropologist, Rosaldo demonstrates that an opposition of "public" and "domestic" "provides the basis of a structural framework necessary to identify and explore the place of male and female in psychological, cultural, social, and economic aspects of human life."[59] Elshtain traces this public/private distinction from traditional societal norms in ancient Greece through much of Western history. In ancient Greece, open places were traditionally reserved for men. Men moved freely about in the marketplace, the law courts, and openly attended public banquets, theatres, and lectures. Respectable women were limited to the domestic or "private" sphere, where they were expected to manage the affairs of the household. If respectable women ventured out of doors, they were heavily veiled and escorted by household slaves. Women who had freer access to the "public" realm were generally courtesans, household slaves, and prostitutes.

Although this public/private dichotomy begins in the West as a characteristic of ancient Greek society, Karen Jo Torjesen traces the continuing ideology of this gender-based dichotomy through the entire Greco-Roman period, using Rosaldo's social-anthropological model. Torjesen suggests that much of the controversy over women in leadership positions in the early church may be traced to conflicts over the traditional limitation of women to the private sphere.[60] For example, the controversy over women's leadership in the church reaches its crisis point during the third century, when Christian groups ceased meeting in private homes and met instead in public basilicas. Torjesen contends that it is at this point that leadership models began to reflect the characteristics of public offices. The replacement of the private roles of the household as models for Christian leadership with the public roles of governmental officials contributed to the removal of women from church leadership positions.[61]

---

[58] *Public Man, Private Woman: Women in Social and Political Thought* (Princeton, N.J.: Princeton University Press, 1981).

[59] Rosaldo, "Women, Culture and Society," 23.

[60] *When Women Were Priests* (Harper/Collins, forthcoming).

[61] "Reconstruction of Early Christianity," in *Searching the Scriptures: A Feminist-Ecumenical Commentary and Translation*, ed. Elisabeth Schüssler Fiorenza (N.Y.: Crossroad, forthcoming).

Torjesen has also shown how the categories of public and private contributed to the determination of ideal women's virtues. A virtuous woman, ideally, would be one who exemplified a "private" woman. Thus, an ideal woman was characterized by her domesticity and love for her husband, as well as her willingness to bear children, stay at home, or weave cloth. A traditional woman was quiet and submissive and did not go brazenly out in public or neglect to wear her veil. Women's vices became characteristics of a "public" woman, such as the type of woman most often seen on the streets of ancient Athens. Similarly, the characteristics of slaves, prostitutes, and courtesans became qualities of an unvirtuous woman.[62] In spite of the many actual social roles for women evidenced in the ancient world, this traditional ideology cast ancient women into two categories of social classification on the level of social ideology based on their sexual availability: free/matron or slave/whore. Torjesen is not alone in her analysis of the significance of this public/private dichotomy for Greco-Roman social ideology. A recent study on women in Hellenistic Judaism also utilizes the categories of public and private in an analysis of the place of women during the Mishnaic period.[63]

History of Scholarship on Early Christian Communal Meals

Communal Meals in Early Christianity

In recent years it has been determined that, like their Greco-Roman counterparts, early Christians gathered together for standardized meals. In this regard early Christian communities would fit well into the cultural milieu of their Greco-Roman contemporaries, for whom formal banquets were the most common context for the free association of both secular and religious groups.[64] This is the most likely setting in which followers of Jesus, the Pauline groups, as well as other developing Christian communities would have come together for the sharing of ideas, storytelling, and eventually ritual practice. Moreover, although the notion that Jesus himself also em-

---

[62] Karen Jo Torjesen, "Tertullian's Political Ecclesiology and Women's Leadership," *StudPat* 21, ed. E. A. Livingstone (Leuven: Peeters, 1989), 277–82; "Women's Virtues and Vices: Mechanisms for Social Control," in *When Women Were Priests*.

[63] Judith Romney Wegner, *Chattel or Person? The Status of Women in the Mishnah* (New York and Oxford: Oxford University Press, 1988), esp. 145–67.

[64] Burton L. Mack, *Myth of Innocence* (Philadelphia: Fortress, 1988), 81–83.

phasized gathering for meals is by no means clear, nevertheless it is not impossible to imagine that Jesus and his followers, like other Hellenistic peoples, found the meal setting to be a natural place for discourse.[65] Hence there has been a recent emphasis on "table fellowship" as the most important "generative matrix" for the social formation of the Jesus movements.[66]

The key study in this regard is the work of Dennis Smith, who in 1980 completed a Harvard dissertation comparing Greco-Roman meals to the meals described in 1 Corinthians.[67] A segment of his research is now available in his recent book with Hal Taussig, *Many Tables: The Eucharist in the New Testament and Liturgy Today*.[68] Smith first establishes the form of ancient banquets and then shows how this common Greco-Roman meal tradition was adapted to other settings, such as family gatherings, funerary banquets, philosophical society meetings, trade guild meetings, meetings of religious organizations, and Jewish festival meals.[69] Finally, in his analysis of First Corinthians, Smith shows that the early Corinthian Christians adapted this same common Greco-Roman meal tradition for their own religious meetings, which included a meal according to the Greco-Roman meal pattern.[70] Thus, early Christian meetings were patterned after a common Greco-Roman meal form.

In another article, Smith shows how literary representations of formal banquets (*symposia*) contributed to literary representations of Jesus' activities found in the Gospels. Smith suggests that this is particularly true in the Gospel of Luke, in which the banquet motif is part of a larger Lukan literary strategy.[71] In light of Smith's research, it is

---

[65] Ibid., 82.

[66] Ibid., 82–83, n. 4.

[67] Dennis E. Smith, "Social Obligation in the Context of Communal Meals: A Study of the Christian Meal in 1 Corinthians in Comparison with Graeco-Roman Communal Meals" (Th.D. diss., Harvard Divinity School, 1980). See also Mack, *Myth of Innocence*, 80–83; Lee E. Klosinski, "Meals in Mark" (Ph.D. diss., Claremont Graduate School, 1988); Scott Bartchy, "Table Fellowship with Jesus and the 'Lord's Meal' at Corinth," in *Increase in Learning: Essays in Honor of James G. Van Buren*, ed. Owens and Hamm (Manhattan, Kans.: Manhattan Christian College, 1979), 45–61.

[68] London: SCM Press; Philadelphia: Trinity International Press, 1990.

[69] See summary in Smith and Taussig, *Many Tables*, 21–35.

[70] D. Smith, "Social Obligation."

[71] D. Smith, "Table Fellowship as a Literary Motif in the Gospel of Luke," *JBL* 106 (1987): 613–38. In this regard Smith is now followed by Jerome Neyrey, "Ceremonies in Luke–Acts: The Case of Meals and Table Fellowship," in *The Social World of Luke–Acts: Models for Interpretation*, ed. Jerome H. Neyrey (Peabody, Mass.: Hen-

clear that the literary setting of philosophical discussions in the context of a banquet was popular in Greco-Roman literature and may have influenced the setting of much of Jesus' teaching activities in the context of a meal.[72] Such a setting would seem natural, as attested by other works, such as Plato's *Symposion*, Plutarch's *Symposiaca*, Xenophon's *Symposion* and Athenaeus' *Deipnosophistae*. Smith therefore doubts that any of the traditions linking Jesus' teaching activity to meal settings are historical.[73] However, the importance of meal settings in the Gospel tradition might still reflect the significance of actual meals in early Christian groups and various Jesus movements.[74] Burton Mack suggests, "If one looks for settings that could account for the Jesus movements, one sees that gathering for meals was the single most important 'generative matrix' for social formation."[75]

Social Anthropology of Food and Meal Innovation

In a recent Claremont dissertation, Lee Klosinski further establishes the importance of meals in the literary strategy of another Gospel, the Gospel of Mark.[76] According to Klosinski, food and meals are essential themes in the Markan narrative. The evangelist uses these themes as building blocks for parables, metaphors, descriptions of characters and discipleship, narrative settings, and plot devices.[77] Mark's placement of several meal scenes, the feeding narratives in particular, is central to Mark's overall narrative design.[78]

---

drickson, 1991), 361–87.

[72] David E. Aune, "Septem Sapientium Convivium," in *Plutarch's Ethical Writings and Early Christian Literature*, ed. Hans Dieter Betz (Leiden: Brill, 1978), 51–105; D. Smith, "Table Fellowship." Another dissertation done recently that may contribute to the discussion is Craig Thomas McMahan, "Meals as Type Scenes in the Gospel of Luke" (Ph.D. diss., Southern Baptist Theological Seminary, 1987). For a complete discussion of the literary genre, see Josef Martin, *Symposion: Die Geschichte einer literarischen Form* (Paderborn: Ferdinand Schöningh, 1931); Alessandra Lukinovich, "The Play of Reflections between Literary Form and the Sympotic Theme in the *Deipnosophistae* of Athenaeus," in *Sympotica: A Symposium on the Symposion*, ed. Oswyn Murray (Oxford: Clarendon Press, 1990), 263–71.

[73] Dennis E. Smith, "The Historical Jesus at Table," *SBL 1989 Seminar Papers* (Atlanta, Ga.: Scholars Press, 1989), 466–86.

[74] Mack, *Myth of Innocence*, 80–83.

[75] Ibid., 82–83, n. 4.

[76] Klosinski, "Meals in Mark."

[77] Ibid., 206.

[78] Ibid.

The Last Supper thus becomes the last of a series of meals, a scene in which the primary Markan themes of meals and discipleship intersect.[79] In light of Mark's interest in food and meals, Klosinski goes on to characterize the Markan community as a "community at table."[80] In light of Mark's social ethic of διακονία, "service at table," Klosinski further suggests that membership in the Markan table community entailed a "new assessment of status and a new social hierarchy."[81] He suggests this in light of the fact that "table service" in the Greco-Roman world was the activity of women and slaves. The women who follow and serve Jesus to the end are the true models of Markan discipleship.[82] Rank in the Markan community is based on one's ability to serve and not one's social prestige.[83]

Buttressing Klosinski's analysis is an extensive discussion of meals from the perspective of contemporary anthropological theory.[84] Descriptions of meals in Mark can be seen to reflect social values in the Markan community, because meals and parties, as highly structured events, mediate and symbolize "a matrix of social and political relationships which mediate status and power" as well as symbolize group boundaries.[85] Klosinski bases his conclusions on an analysis of anthropological studies which have determined the function of food in the socialization process of individuals and society.

Klosinski follows such scholars as Mary Douglas, who in her article "Deciphering a Meal"[86] suggests that food functions in society much like a language, as a code with a precoded message:

> If food is treated as a code, messages it encodes will be found in the pattern of social relations being expressed. The message is about different degrees of hierarchy, inclusion and exclusion, boundaries and transactions across the boundaries.[87]

---

[79] Ibid., ch. 6.

[80] Ibid., 211.

[81] Ibid., 212.

[82] Ibid.

[83] Ibid.

[84] Ibid., ch. 2. Klosinski overviews the work of such scholars as Claude Lévi–Strauss, Mary Douglas, Marcel Mauss, Sherry Ortner, and Raymond Firth. For an overview of scholarship in this field, see Jack Goody, *Cooking, Cuisine and Class: A Study in Comparative Sociology* (Cambridge: Cambridge University Press, 1982).

[85] Klosinski, "Meals in Mark," 55–56.

[86] In *Myth, Symbol and Culture*, ed. C. Geertz (New York: W. W. Norton and Co., 1971), 61–81.

[87] Douglas, "Deciphering a Meal," 61.

According to Douglas, the time of the sharing of food, the meal itself, is really an ordered system which represents those social systems it is associated with. A meal is therefore a structured social event which reflects social structures.[88]

Douglas has further established that as structured social events, the order of meals and their cuisine are extremely resistant to change. In another study with Michael Nicod,[89] Douglas establishes a way to distinguish between acceptable and unacceptable changes in cuisine. Nicod and Douglas determined that the less structured a meal was, the more people would be open to alterations in its cuisine. If the meal were highly structured, however, individuals were only open to having an improvement made on their traditional foods. The more structured a meal, the less likely it is to be changed or altered by dietary or other innovations. Other scholars have discussed the conservative nature of meals as structured social events. Food preparation and meal etiquette are learned in the home and are customs not easily changed.[90] Changes in meal patterns or cuisine may be a form of social protest against the societal structures those meal patterns and cuisine represent.[91] The Markan category of discipleship as "table service" therefore subverts the normal Greco-Roman categories of power, prestige, and rank. The lowest individual in a structured Greco-Roman meal, the male or female slave, is held up as the greatest role model for the Markan community to follow.[92]

The Direction of This Study

This study brings together these insights from the fields of Christian feminism, classical social history and social anthropology in order to create a new context within which to understand the portrayal of women in the Synoptic Gospels. Following recent feminist methodology, ancient sources, including the Gospels themselves, will be read with discernment in order to better reconstruct the actual situation of women during the New Testament period. An

---

[88] Ibid., 69.

[89] Mary Douglas and Michael Nicod, "Taking the Bisquit: The Structure of British Meals," *New Society* 30 (1974): 744–47.

[90] See Goody, *Cooking Cusine and Class*, 37, 44–48.

[91] Klosinski, "Meals in Mark," 37.

[92] Ibid., 212–13.

attempt will be made to balance descriptions of women, written from the perspective of traditional social ideology, against other documentation which would indicate the actual social practice of Greco-Roman women. Thus, I hope to contribute to the reconstruction of the position of women in the Synoptic communities and in early Christianity generally. This will be done by positioning the Gospel depictions of women in meal settings within the larger context of Greco-Roman meal ideology and Greco-Roman meal innovations. By analyzing women and meals in the Gospels, light will be shed on the evangelists' attitudes towards women and social change, as well as on the place of women in the Synoptic communities.

Following an investigation of the changes in the meal patterns of Greco-Roman women, an analysis of the Synoptic Gospels from a redaction-critical perspective will reveal that these early Christian texts show several positionings on the issue of women and mixed gender table practice. Mark, although aware of literary banquet themes involving women, exhibits little concern for the impropriety underlying the stories about women within his narrative. Luke, though, is not only aware of literary banquet themes, but is anxious to portray the women in his narrative as respectable. Of all the Synoptics, only Matthew clearly portrays women as reclining for meals in public with men and allows for the presence of women identified as "courtesans" in his narrative. Thus, concern for Greco-Roman meal customs and ideology underlie the portrayals of women in each of the Synoptic Gospels.

The intersection of insights from Christian feminism, classical social history, and social anthropology indeed provide intriguing new material which may inform our study of women in antiquity and the early Christian communities which produced the New Testament texts. "Table fellowship" and conviviality have been determined as central to the development of early Christian groups, communities which gathered together at formal meals for fellowship and worship. In this regard, early Christian groups would have fit well into the cultural milieu of their Greco-Roman contemporaries, for whom formal banquets were the most common context for the gathering of social, philosophical, or religious groups. As in many cultures, these structured meals symbolized and mediated social and political relationships in Greco-Roman society and delineated group boundaries. As a social practice tremendously resistant to change, standardized meals undoubtedly functioned to maintain and stabilize the class-based social hierarchy of Greco-Roman society. Innovations in meal practice would have undermined the basic social constructs and power relations in Greco-Roman society. Innovations in the meal practice of women and slaves, then, would undermine the gender and class-based hierarchy of Greco-Roman society, as well as the gender-based division of that society into "public" and "private" categories.

We will see that how Greco-Roman peoples ate their meals was indeed changing during the New Testament period. Unlike their Greek counterparts, free Roman women were joining men for formal, highly structured meals in social, religious, and philosophical settings. This was first suggested by Sterling Bjorndahl in his short study, "Gospel of Thomas 61: A Chreia Elaboration Pattern," in which he suggested that Salome was being depicted as joining Jesus on a dining couch, rather than a bed.[93] Such an innovation in meal practice threatened the class-based hierarchy of Greco-Roman society. In response to this threat, many objected to women's behavior during this period of social change in a way that segregated women into two classes: (1) the chaste, properly behaved freeborn matron and (2) the promiscuous, baseborn prostitute.

---

[93] Paper presented to the New Testament Seminar, Claremont Graduate School, Feb. 2, 1988. In a short appendix, Bjorndahl suggested that when a woman appears with a man at a public banquet in a Greco-Roman text, she is more than likely to be a courtesan or prostitute of some kind. See ch. 2. I am indebted to my friend and colleague for our many conversations since the presentation of his paper.

Women in the Context of   2
Greco-Roman Meals

Women's Table Etiquette: The Background

It has been established that the primary setting of early Christian dialogue and worship was a formal, public meal. Such meals were a standard feature of Greco-Roman social, religious, and philosophical life; however, during the late Republican and early imperial times, aspects of Greco-Roman meal etiquette were undergoing changes, changes which reflected larger cultural forces throughout Greco-Roman society. Just as women were moving into public roles and gaining rights previously denied them under a more restrictive Greek social code, Roman women were attending public meals. From Hellenistic sources of the second century BCE through second century CE we can conveniently chart these fluctuations in Greco-Roman society by analyzing changes in the meal etiquette of Greco-Roman women. The presence of women in public meals during the Roman period has been identified as a sign of the shift in the status of women during the Roman period.[1] As Roman matrons would have been free to accompany their husbands to public banquets, and in particular would have been allowed in religious meal settings, the inclusion of women in Christian meals would have been noteworthy but not unique.[2] This position is in part supported by assertions made

---

[1]D. Smith, "Social Obligation," 34ff., 209ff.; Klosinski, "Meals in Mark," 67ff.
[2]First suggested by D. Smith, "Social Obligation," 209ff.; see also Aune, "Septem," 72, esp. n. 45.

24

by scholars both of women's history[3] and Greco-Roman social history.[4]

The sequence of meals, their cuisine, and the elements of their preparation, however, are very resistant to innovation. Meal practices are among the most conservative aspects of society; they often maintain and stabilize social systems, rather than change them. For this reason, we will see that, although women's meal etiquette was certainly undergoing change, the ideology surrounding women's roles and their proper behavior was not. Social ideology concerning women's behavior in the public sphere was not advancing at the same rate as the actual behavior of women. Hence, even though there is evidence that women were beginning to participate in the public sphere and in public meals, opinions concerning the propriety of such changes were mixed. Thus, from the second century BCE through the second century CE, alongside evidence that women were attending public meals, we can also chart harsh criticism of this practice. Many Greco-Roman writers slander those women overstepping ideal womanly roles by accusing them of sexual misconduct or unchastity. This is no different in the case of proper table etiquette for women. Women, if matrons, were expected to be present for certain portions of the meal, such as the δεῖπνον, but they were also to be somewhat circumscribed in the sort of meal that they attended lest they be criticized by those with more idealistic views. Such social criticism attempted to limit women's meal practice and restrict their dining companions. Therefore, women dining or reclining with those outside of their immediate family would still elicit a degree of social criticism even during the Roman period.

Women's Table Etiquette in Ancient Greece

The roots of this social ideology governing women's participation at meals can be found in the meal customs of ancient Greece. Women seldom dined with men, even in private; rather, they remained secluded in the women's quarters of the household where

---

[3] Balsdon, *Roman Women*, 271–72; Cantarella, *Pandora's Daughters*, 134; Pomeroy, *Goddesses*, 189; Leonard Swidler, "Greco-Roman Feminism and the Origin of the Gospel," in *Traditio-Krisis-Renovatio aus theologischer Sicht: Festschrift für Winfried Zeller zum 65. Geburtstag*, ed. Bernd Jaspert and Rudolf Mohr (Marburg: N. G. Elwert, 1976), 46.

[4] Carcopino, *Daily Life in Ancient Rome*, 265ff.; Freidländer, *Roman Life*, 94, 239.

they often took their meals alone. The dining room of a house properly belonged to the area of the house reserved for men. As a rule, the wife of a family would dine only with her husband and children, or with others of the intimate family circle. If guests were invited, the wife and children would dine alone in the women's quarters, with exceptions made for family festivals such as weddings or other religious celebrations with a limited guest list. In family meals the man would recline and the woman of the house would sit at his feet. Because unexpected guests were a common occurrence, however, it is not clear how frequently husbands and wives actually ate together in ancient Athenian households.[5]

Public meals or large banquets held in private homes were also reserved for men, except for those women classified as prostitutes or hetaerae, women present to enhance the entertainment of the men. The flute girls, dancers, and other entertainers present were certainly prostitutes, and the presence of such women was often considered essential for the συμπόσιον, or drinking party, following the δεῖπνον, or meal.[6] There were symposia that were more sedate, such as those dedicated to more philosophical pursuits, in which case the necessity of the presence of such women was questionable.[7] Also commonly

[5]Wilhelm Adolf Becker, *Charicles, or Illustrations of the Private Life of the Ancient Greeks* (London: Longmans Green and Co., 1895), 488ff., 490ff.; Hugo Blümner, *The Home Life of the Ancient Greeks* (New York: Cooper Square Publishers, 1966), 202ff.; Cantarella, *Pandora's Daughters*, 46; Pomeroy, *Goddesses*, 80ff.; Michael Vickers, *Greek Symposia* (London: The Joint Association of Classical Teachers, n.d.), 5.

[6]Lucian, *Symp.* 46; *Dial. Meret.* 1, 3, 6, 12, 15; Athenaeus, *Deipn.* 4.129, 131, 150; 8.349; Plutarch, *Sept. Sap. Conv.* 150D. See also Aune, "Septem," 72; Becker, *Charicles*, 241–50; 344ff; Blümner, *Home Life of the Ancient Greeks*, 171; 216–17; Vern Bullough and Bonnie Bullough, *Prostitution: An Illustrated Social History* (New York: Crown Publishers, 1978), 35ff.; Hans Licht, *Sexual Life in Ancient Greece* (New York: Barnes and Noble, 1953), 172ff.; J. Martin, *Symposion*, 255ff.; Vickers, *Greek Symposia*, 5. D. Smith argues that these women were not necessarily in attendance for the sexual sport of the men ("Social Obligation," 20–21, also nn. 49–50); but see more recently Eva C. Keuls, *The Reign of the Phallus: Sexual Politics in Ancient Athens* (New York: Harper and Row, 1985), 160ff. and Oswyn Murray, "The Greek Symposion in History," in *Tria Corda: Scritti in onore di Arnaldo Momigliano*, ed. E. Gabba (Biblioteca di Athanaeum 1; Como: New Press, 1983), 257–72. Murray suggests that the symposium served as a central cultural organization throughout ancient Greek and Hellenistic periods which in part derived its strength from its function as a fraternal or "brotherhood" social grouping. In such a setting, women were merely slaves and sexual objects (see 264). See also more recently Burkhard Fehr, "Entertainers at the *Symposion: The Akletoi* in the Archaic Period," 185–95; and Ezio Pellizer, "Outlines of a Morphology of Sympotic Entertainment," 177–84, in *Sympotica*, ed. O. Murray.

[7]Plato, *Symp.* 176E; Plutarch, *Quaest. Conv.* 616A; see also D. Smith, "Social

present were those women of the higher class of prostitutes, the hetaerae, who were present for conversation as well as sexual sport.[8] The hetaerae, unlike men's wives, were allowed to recline next to the men at a meal, rather than being seated at their feet.[9] Therefore, if a woman were present at such a gathering, whether or not it was held in a public or private dining room, she was most certainly some sort of prostitute. Hence, the mere fact that a woman was known for eating and drinking with men would be enough for her to be so labeled.[10] For this reason respectable women usually took their meals in the women's quarters, lest they be surprised by unexpected male guests and thought to be hetaerae.[11]

As well as providing entertainment and sex, certain of these women present at banquets were also known for their ability to participate in the conversation of the men, and some were even known for their wit and rhetorical skills in philosophical repartée.[12] This would have been a secondary characteristic for such women, whose primarily social role assumed sexual availability.[13] Thus hetae-

---

Obligation," 20–21.

[8] Becker, *Charicles*, 317–18; Blümner, *Home Life of the Ancient Greeks*, 171–74; Bullough and Bullough, *Prostitution*, 36ff.; Keuls, *Reign of the Phallus*, 160ff., Licht, *Sexual Life in Ancient Greece*, 339ff.

[9] Becker, *Charicles*, 317; Blümner, *Home Life of the Ancient Greeks*, 203; Vickers, *Greek Symposia*, 5.

[10] See Demosthenes, *In Neaer.*, 24; 48; Aune, "Septem," 72, n. 44; Becker, *Charicles*, 490; Blümner, *Home Life of the Ancient Greeks*, 203; Keuls, *Reign of the Phallus*, 160ff.

[11] Demosthenes, *In Neaer.* 24; Isaeus 13–14; Becker, *Charicles*, 490.

[12] Chreiai attributed to courtesans are quite numerous. See Athenaeus, *Deipn.* 13.584a and *Deipn.* 13, passim. See Licht, *Sexual Life in Ancient Greece*, for the romantic notion of educated hetaerae, 339ff.; as well as Sterling Bjorndahl, "Thomas 61–67," "Appendix A," 7–9; Bullough and Bullough, *Prostitution*, 41–42; Cantarella, *Pandora's Daughters*, 49ff., Ronald F. Hock, "The Will of God and Sexual Morality: I Thessalonians 4:3–8 in its Social and Intellectual Context" (unpublished paper presented at the Annual Meeting of the SBL, New York, 1982), 9; Pomeroy, *Goddesses*, 89; William W. Sanger, *The History of Prostitution* (New York: Arno Press, 1972), 55ff.

[13] That this was an actual social reality for Athenian courtesans has been questioned. See Keuls, *Reign of the Phallus*, 194ff. where she critiques the romantic notion of these hetaerae. She writes: "It appears that Athenian men were at pains to construct an image of witty, prosperous hetaerae in order to gloss over the fact that their principal sex objects were debased and uneducated slaves, who were at the mercy of their profit-hungry owners, and who were almost certain to end their lives in misery" (199–200). She also suggests that many of these recorded "witticisms" of hetaerae collected in the post-classical world are not sophisticated at all, but are rather male-generated jokes, relying heavily upon sexual innuendo (199). Although Keuls may overstate her point, it is certainly important to keep in mind that many of the

rae, flute girls, and the like were part and parcel of the banquet scene, remaining central to the literary symposia tradition and as a banquet τόπος in the literature of both the Greek and Roman periods. Moreover, prostitutes, flute girls, and hetaerae also abound in artistic representations of banquets from ancient Greece.[14] The most characteristic feature of vase paintings from ancient Greece is the banquet context as a setting for erotic scenes.[15] The social condition of the women pictured in these vase paintings cannot easily be discerned, yet it is clear that they all represent prostitutes of some sort.[16]

Women's Table Etiquette in Ancient Rome

Much of the ideology surrounding women's table etiquette found in polite society of the Roman period reflects earlier Greek meal practices. It has been demonstrated that the Romans by and large adopted Greek meal practices, including the custom of reclining and the dividing of the meal into two parts: the δεῖπνον, or meal proper, followed by the συμπόσιον, the portion of the banquet reserved for drinking, entertainment, and conversation, or in some cases, philosophical discourse or religious ritual.[17] However, the one major exception to Greek practice was the inclusion of wives in some formal banquet settings. Wives were eventually allowed to recline at the table with their husbands.[18] This is a development of the late Republican and early imperial periods. Before the time of Augustus, women, if present at a meal, still sat beside their husbands' couch, rather than reclining.[19] Cornelius Nepos, writing around 34–35 BCE,

---

legends of these women were collected and passed on by men, who certainly had a stake in painting a picture of their own behavior that was in some way defensible.

[14] D. Smith, "Social Obligation," 20; Keuls, *Reign of the Phallus*, 160ff.

[15] Otto J. Brendel, "The Scope and Temperament of Erotic Art in the Greco-Roman World," in *Studies in Erotic Art*, ed. T. Bowie and C. V. Christenson (New York and London: Basic Books, 1970), 19.

[16] Brendel, "Scope and Temperament," 32.

[17] D. Smith, "Social Obligation," 24ff.; See also more recently, Annette Rathje, "The Adoption of the Homeric Banquet in Central Italy in the Orientalizing Period" and Jon D'Arms, "The Roman *Convivium* and the Idea of Equality," 279–88, in *Sympotica*, ed. O. Murray.

[18] D. Smith, "Social Obligation," 33ff.; Klosinski, "Meals in Mark," 67; Freidländer, *Roman Life*, 239, nn. 8, 9.

[19] Balsdon, *Roman Women*, 272; Becker, *Charicles*, 317; Carcopino, *Daily Life in Ancient Rome*, 265; Fowler, *Social Life at Rome*, 277ff.

notes this as a sign of the cultural superiority of the Romans over the Greeks:

> Many actions are seemly according to our code which the Greeks look upon as shameful. For instance, what Roman would blush to take his wife to a dinner party? What matron does not frequent the front rooms of her dwelling and show herself in public? But it is very different in Greece; for there a woman is not admitted to a dinner party unless relatives only are present, and she keeps to the more retired part of the house called "the woman's apartment," to which no man has access who is not near of kin.[20]

Other primary texts indicate that it became more common for Roman women to partake of meals privately with their husbands and to attend public banquets as their husbands' escorts.[21] Weddings and other family celebrations were also traditionally attended by women.[22] Seating practices at such occasions, however, were not uniform. It appears that some women did recline next to their spouses, but not always.[23] There is evidence that some women kept the habit of sitting,[24] and even in the second century CE Lucian still calls sitting "womanish and weak."[25] Women and men also commonly reclined separately, men with men, women with women, couch by couch. Women were sometimes given a couch or section of couches completely set apart from the men. This was particularly the case at weddings.[26] Unmarried women, that is, young maidens, were still excluded from public banquet settings other than weddings,

---

[20] Cornelius Nepos, *praef.* 6–7 (trans. J. C. Rolfe).

[21] Private meals: Plutarch, *Praec. Conjug.* 140A; *De Cup. Div.* 528B; Achilles Tatius 1.5. Public meals: Dio Chrysostom, *Or.* 7.67–68; Plutarch, *De Gen.* 594D-E; *Otho* 3.5–6; Dio Cass. 57.12; Statius, *Silv.* 1.6.43–5 and the banquet of Trimalchio in Petronius' *Satyr.* I am greatly indebted to my colleague Sterling Bjorndahl for several of these references he originally collected in "Appendix A," of "Thomas 61–67." See more recently, D'Arms, "Roman *Convivium*," 308–20, in *Sympotica*, ed. O. Murray.

[22] Lucian, *Symp.* 8–9; Athen. *Deipn.* 9.376ff.; Balsdon, *Roman Women*, 181ff.; Becker, *Charicles*, 488ff.; Freidländer, *Roman Life*, 234ff.; D. Smith, "Social Obligation," 210ff.

[23] Bjorndahl, "Thomas 61–67," 7; Carcopino, *Daily Life in Ancient Rome*, 265; 317, n. 121. In addition to references in Bjorndahl, see also Ovid, *Amor.* 1.4.

[24] Dio Chrysostom, *Or.* 7.76ff., which depicts a rural household meal where wife and daughter sit, but there is a stranger present; note that in Plutarch, *Sept. Sap. Conv.* 150B, whereas Melissa reclines on a couch, Eumetis sits.

[25] *Symp.* 13.

[26] Lucian, *Symp.* 8–9; Petronius, *Satyr.* 67–69; Ovid, *Met.* 12.210–20; Athen., *Deipn.* 14.644D; D. Smith, "Social Obligation," 210.

although they may have been allowed to be present at a private meal even if a stranger were present.[27] One assumes that if present, daughters would be seated at their parents' feet, as all children were, until they came of age and married.[28]

It was also not thought proper for matrons to remain for the συμπόσιον, and many left after the completion of the δεῖπνον.[29] In any case, proper matrons and young children alike would probably not have participated in the after-dinner frivolity which characterized many of the huge banquets of the late Republic and early Empire.[30] The one exception seems to be in Plutarch, *Banquet of the Seven Sages*, where Melissa and Eumetis remain for a short while after the conclusion of the δεῖπνον, but leave well before the end of the συμπόσιον. They never say a word during the time they are there.[31] This is undoubtedly a more sedate affair. In spite of the behavior of Melissa and Eumetis, Plutarch still gives a traditional remark concerning women's proper behavior: "Philosophy should no more have a part in conversation over wine than should the matron of the house."[32] Furthermore, although the reference in Cornelius Nepos is to a *convivium*,[33] the two references to matrons' attending official banquets seem to be formal δεῖπνα not συμπόσια.[34] It is therefore unclear just how widespread or acceptable the new Roman practices were. Paul Veyne, in his discussion of Roman private life, remarks:

> When a man was invited out to dinner, was it proper to invite his wife as well? From the few indications in the sources I have not been able to arrive at any firm answers. . . . [35]

---

[27] Dio Chrysostom, *Or.* 7.76ff.; Clement of Alexandria, *Paed.* 2.7; Freidländer, *Roman Life*, 236; Hock, "Will of God and Sexual Morality," 11.

[28] Suetonius, *Claud.* 32; Tacitus, *Ann.* 13.16; Carcopino, *Daily Life in Ancient Rome*, 265; Fowler, *Social Life at Rome*, 278; D. Smith, "Social Obligation," 34. As surprising as it may seem, Roman girls were married between the ages of 9 and 12 years. See M. K. Hopkins, "Roman Girls at Marriage," 309–27.

[29] Aune, "Septem," 72–73; Bjorndahl, "Thomas 61–67," 9–11; Vickers, *Greek Symposia*, 5; Plutarch, *Quaest. Conv.* 612F–613A; 653A–D; *Sept. Sap. Conv.* 150–55 (here two women remain for a small part of the discussion, but leave long before the συμπόσιον is over).

[30] Balsdon, *Roman Women*, 271–72.

[31] *Sept. Sap. Conv.* 150–55; In Petronius, *Satyr.* 67–69, the wife of Trimalchio chats, but she is not discussing philosophy. See D. Smith, "Social Obligation," 210.

[32] *Quaest. Conv.* 612F–613A, 8–9.

[33] *praef.* 6–7.

[34] Plutarch, *Otho* 3.5–6; Dio Cass. 57.12.

[35] Veyne, "Roman Empire," in *History of Private Life*, 1.39; see also Balsdon,

Despite the changes occurring in meal practices during this time, then, earlier and more conservative meal ideology may have continued to limit the meal etiquette of certain Greco-Roman women.

Women in Greco-Roman Club Meals

For many of the lower classes, various voluntary associations provided a place for social, religious, and philosophical interaction. Again, the primary focus for such interaction centered around the sharing of a communal meal. Although it is not clear that women were members of collegia and other associations, evidence indicates that women attended club meals, both secular and religious.[36] By the Roman period, women even sponsored such organizations financially.[37] Since women were not excluded from specifically religious gatherings, women would have been present at various cult meals, particularly if they held an official cult position.[38] However, given the ever present ideology governing women's attendance at meals, particularly the συμπόσιον, even the presence of women at certain cultic συμπόσια would certainly have been innovative.[39] Again, the seating pattern of such meals is difficult to determine, and it may well be that women, if present at all, would have been seated together as a group, or perhaps in a separate room.[40] From archaeological sites it is

---

Roman Women, 271–72.

[36] G. H. R. Horsley, "Invitation to the *kline* of Sarapis," *New Documents Illustrating Early Christianity*, vol. 1 (Macquarie University, Australia: The Ancient History Documentary Research Centre, 1981), 5–9; Ramsay MacMullen, "Women in Public in the Roman Empire," *Historia* 29 (1980): 212; D. Smith, "Social Obligation," 109ff.

[37] MacMullen, "Women in Public," 212; Pomeroy, *Goddesses*, 200–201; Van Bremen, "Women and Wealth," 223–42; Elizabeth Lyding Will, "Women in Pompeii," *Archaeology* (Sept./Oct. 1979), 34–50.

[38] Aune, "Septem," 71–73; Schüssler Fiorenza, *In Memory of Her*, 176ff.; D. Smith, "Social Obligation," 209–10; Klosinski, "Meals in Mark," 62.

[39] Aune, "Septem," 73, n. 45; D. Smith, "Social Obligation," 209.

[40] See D. Smith, "Social Obligation," 109ff. Smith bases his assumption that the women are actually present at this meal on the basis of a reconstruction of a lacunae in the "Decree of Oregones" inscription (251ff.). However, if reconstructed according to either Fergusen or Sokolowski, as cited by D. Smith, it would seem that the women might not be immediately present because the men are instructed to take the women's portion to them; they may only be entitled to a portion of the sacrifice, and not be present at all. As on some occasions members were entitled to take their portions of sacrificial meat home with them, this may not be an impossible suggestion (Wendell Lee Willis, *Idol Meat in Corinth: The Pauline Argument in*

difficult to determine where exactly women sat in dining rooms full of couches. Veiling at some functions may also have been required, as may have been the case for weddings.[41]

It must be remembered that although trade guilds and other societies had religious functions, they were primarily fraternities; their central meals and celebrations would have had fraternal overtones, being "brotherhood" gatherings.[42] The rules of banquet behavior established for many of these club meals are meant to keep the frivolity to a minimum, which becomes explicable in light of the kinds of men's entertainment that was hired for a banquet.[43] If members of a club participated in the dramas and miming, the close contact with the slave women and young men hired to perform in these presentations might have pressed the need to curtail excesses.[44] Rules such as staying off a neighbor's couch would be appropriate if a neighbor's wife were present (although none are explicitly mentioned).[45]

It may also be helpful to reflect on the social class of those usually present for guild and burial society dinners during the Roman period. Many of these associations were central to the lives of slaves, freedmen and women, and the lower class freeborn.[46] As we shall see,

---

1 Corinthians 8 and 10 [SBLDS 68; Chico, Calif.: Scholars Press, 1985], 64). Furthermore, as the food is to be presented to the women (who are listed as a group), this may imply that if they are present, they may be seated either off to themselves or in the second dining room apart from the men (D. Smith, "Social Obligation," 113). Finally, I would suggest that the ἐλευθέραι present are probably freedwomen, not "independent women" (D. Smith, "Social Obligation," 110).

[41] Lucian, *Symp.* 8; Clement of Alexandria, *Paed.* 2.7; 1 Cor 11:1–16; D. Smith, "Social Obligation," 210.

[42] Veyne, "Roman Empire," in *History of Private Life*, 1.189–90. Veyne goes so far as to say that women were not admitted at all into these confraternities; they were created precisely as a place for men to associate away from their women. See also Murray, "Greek Symposion in History," 264; Willis, *Idol Meat in Corinth*, 49ff.

[43] D. Smith, "Social Obligation," 170ff.; Willis, *Idol Meat in Corinth*, 54ff., 61; see above, pp. 25–28.

[44] D. Smith, "Social Obligation," 167ff. Note that after a dramatic presentation in Xenophon's banquet, the men run off to make love to their wives (Xenophon, *Symp.* 9.7).

[45] D. Smith, "Social Obligation," 170.

[46] R. H. Barrow, *Slavery in the Roman Empire* (New York: Barnes and Noble; London: Methuen and Co., 1928), 200; L. Wm. Countryman, "Patrons and Officers in Club and Church," *SBL 1977 Seminar Papers*, ed. P. J. Achtemeier (Missoula, Mont.: Scholars Press, 1977), 136–37; Duff, *Freedmen in the Early Roman Empire*, 69; Treggiari, *Roman Freedmen*, 169ff.; Orlando Patterson, *Slavery and Social Death: A Comparative Study* (Cambridge, Mass. and London: Harvard University Press, 1982), 69. This has significance for the early Christian communities in general, if the

many women in this class already held the social and sexual classification of being "available to all." Therefore, their presence at such
meals would not have been circumscribed. Freedwomen did not have
to adhere to as high a standard of morality as did higher class
matrons.[47] Hence, only the behavior of the patroness, should she be
freeborn (i.e., not a wealthy freedwoman herself), would have been
restricted in such a setting.

Ramsay MacMullen has shown that women were included in
public meals, even in Italy. The numbers, however, may have been
small, since people were invited to such events by rank. He writes:

> Not only were women, more often than not, excluded altogether from
> these occasions, however, and from apparently all inclusive phrases like
> "all citizens" or "the entire people"; beyond that, if they were indeed
> invited, they were generally put at the bottom of the pecking order, as
> the sequence of mention indicates, and as is sometimes made mathe-
> matically clear in differential distributions: largesses might be given
> out in the ratio 30 : 20 : 3 to town senators, Augustales and women.[48]

---

consensus forming about the actual social make up of the early communities is correct,
i.e., that these were predominantly mixed groups of slaves, freedpeople, and lower-
class freeborn, with leaders coming from a wealthier group (not necessarily "upper
class," but wealthy freedmen and women) particularly in urban areas (Judge, *Social
Pattern*, ch. 5; Meeks, *First Urban Christians*, ch. 2; John E. Stambaugh, "Social
Relations in the City of the Early Principate: State of Research," *SBL 1980 Seminar
Papers*, ed. P. J. Achtemeier (Chico, Calif.: Scholars Press, 1980), 75–99). As Jewish
tradespersons or leatherworkers from Rome, Priscilla and Aquila were most likely
freedpeople (see Treggiari, *Roman Freedmen*, 169ff.). As a wealthy purple-seller, Lydia
is also a likely candidate for a freedwoman (Schüssler Fiorenza, *In Memory of Her*,
178; Pomeroy, *Goddesses*, 200). Luke, a physician, and Tertius, the amanuensis, would
also be good candidates for freedmen. Even Paul, who predominantly uses metaphors
that would have appealed to slaves or former slaves, was a leatherworker of some sort
and called Phoebe his "patroness" (Rom 16:1a; Ambrogio Donini, "The Myth of
Salvation in Ancient Slave Society," *Science and Society* 15 [1951]: 57–60; Dale B.
Martin, *Slavery as Salvation: The Metaphor of Slavery in Pauline Christianity* [New
Haven and London: Yale University Press, 1990]; Patterson, *Slavery and Social Death*,
70–72). Being a freedman would not have excluded one from being a citizen or from
having a degree of education (Clarence A. Forbes, "The Education and Training of
Slaves in Antiquity," *Proceedings of the American Philological Association* 86 (1955):
321–60). For Paul's trade, see also Hock, *Social Context of Paul's Ministry*. It is
interesting that the observation about Paul's source of metaphors is often made, but
usually leads to the conclusion that his audience included slaves and freedpeople, not
that Paul himself might have been baseborn, or the son of freedpeople. The possibility
that these groups were similar to Greco-Roman clubs might also explain the social
mixture of the early Christian groups, i.e., "slaves and free," "men and women."

[47] See below, pp. 48–52.

[48] MacMullen, "Women in Public," 212–13.

MacMullen also indicates that patronesses were included in the banquets of those associations they sponsored. Still, male patrons of collegia and associations outnumbered female patrons about 14 to 1.[49] Women were indeed included, but only in far smaller numbers.[50] In spite of these small numbers, the attendance of respectable free Roman women in any public meal was still a major innovation.

There are also a few descriptions of private meals in Hellenistic texts with a mixed guest list. Dio Chrysostom preserves one picturesque, rustic scene of a family meal (not a public banquet) at which a stranger is present. The wife sits beside her husband, though, rather than reclining; and the shy (and embarrassed) daughter helps with the serving before sitting quietly next to her mother. This picture is probably idealized, but it may reflect something of the everyday Roman meal practice of the lower classes in the country.[51] In Achilles Tatius' tale of *Clitophon and Leucippe*, several family meals occur. The wives are present and recumbent. Nonetheless, the wives recline not beside their husbands but next to each other.[52]

The Continuing Influence of Greek Meal Ideology

The Erotic Scene of the Banquet

During the Roman period, some respectable women attended public meals, yet people also resisted this change for various reasons. First of all, many Hellenistic people who had inherited Greek meal customs would not necessarily have adopted the newer Roman practice of including women at public meals.[53] Furthermore, the Empire that had embraced the Greek form of the meal had also inherited the social ideology that governed such meals. For example, the erotic Greek image of the banquet replete with prostitutes is paralleled in

---

[49] Ibid., 211–12.

[50] Ibid., 213. Caution against using such evidence to reflect the actual experience of Greco-Roman women may therefore be in order. Change in the practice of the wealthy might not indicate a change for all. See Averil Cameron, "Neither Male Nor Female," *Greece and Rome* 27 (1980), 60–68; Freidländer, *Roman Life*, 264ff.

[51] Dio Chrysostom, *Or.* 7.64–77. In a conversation, Ron Hock suggested that this may also reflect an ideal scene of a Cynic utopia.

[52] This novel was probably written in Alexandria in the late second century CE, but the time it is meant to depict is still unclear. See Bjorndahl, "Thomas 61–67," 8–9.

[53] D. Smith, "Social Obligation," 210.

Roman art.[54] Moreover, an erotic bacchanal scene survives on an Etruscan ash urn that includes women,[55] and in the ruins of Pompeii can be found an erotic mosaic of an open-air banquet scene.[56] Erotic banquet scenes are a characteristic motif of Arretine art.[57] Otto Brendel, in his discussion of the pervasive influence of the banquet scene in erotic art of the Roman period, comments that such allusions to Greek banquets became a "reconstruction of a romantically viewed past," and that the convivial setting itself as the occasion of erotic goings-on acquired a fictitious rather than realistic quality.[58] This is in contrast to earlier Greek representations, which probably reflected actual social practice.[59] In general, then, when women appear in artistic representations of banquets from the Roman period, particularly recumbent women, they are most likely to be prostitutes of some kind.[60] Respectable women appear only with their husbands in a meal setting in funerary reliefs. In such contexts, the women are not recumbent, but seated.[61]

---

[54] Brendel, "Scope and Temperament,"50ff.; 58ff.; J. M. C. Toynbee, *Death and Burial in the Ancient World* (London: Thames and Hudson, 1971), 12.

[55] Ibid., 28, plate 21.

[56] Ibid., 50–51, plate 31.

[57] Ibid., 58ff, plates 37–41.

[58] Ibid.

[59] Ibid., 31–32; see also Keuls, *Reign of the Phallus*, 160ff.

[60] The evidence of one Etruscan painting is therefore an anomaly. Becker, *Charicles*, 317; on the Etruscan piece, see Cantarella, *Pandora's Daughters*, 104; Jean-Marie Dentzer, "Aux origines de l'iconographie du banquet couché," *RArch*. 2 (1971), 252ff. See also plates in Becker, *Charicles*, 319 (wife seated), 338, 344 (reclining hetaerae/flute girl); Keuls, *Reign of the Phallus*, 161, plate 134; 169, plates 143, 144; 166, plate 140 (reclining hetaerae); 166, plate 138 (women at banquet in theatrical costume); 175, plates 152, 154; 177, plate 155; 213, plate 185 (hetaerae in the context of banquet revelry); 216, plates 189, 190 (funerary relief with wife seated); Toynbee, *Death and Burial*, 24, plate 1 (men and women at banquet); plate 2 (wife seated); Veyne, "Roman Empire," in *History of Private Life*, 1.184 (wife seated); 188 (well-clothed women seated at banquet with four men); Vickers, *Greek Symposia*, fig. 4 (wife seated); fig. 12 (hetaerae at banquet); fig. 19 (flute girl on couch with man in sexual pose). In *Daily Life in Ancient Rome*, p. 317, n. 121, Carcopino suggests that seating practices in Gaul had no fixed custom. For evidence he cites Émile Espérandieu, *Recueil général des bas-reliefs, statues et bustes de la Gaule romaine* (Paris: Imprimerie Nationale), vol. 6 (1915), nos. 5154, 5155; vol. 8 (1922), nos. 6449, 6489. However, looking over these plates I would say that the women are all well-clothed and seated, and are therefore wives. For a group of seated women, see also plate 6 in *Sympotica*, ed. O. Murray. This plate is discussed by Frederick Cooper, "Dining in Round Buildings," in *Sympotica*, ed. O. Murray, 66–85, esp. 79–81.

[61] Becker, *Charicles*, 317–19; Carcopino, *Daily Life in Ancient Rome*, 317, n. 121; Toynbee, *Death and Burial*, 12, 268.

Secondly, literature from the Roman period also amply illustrates that Greek meal ideology remained influential during the Roman period, particularly in areas of the Empire strongly influenced by Greek ideals. Even Cornelius Nepos seems to be comparing current Roman practice with current Greek practice, rather than with ancient Greek practice.[62] Moreover, Roman books on architecture distinguish between Roman and Greek floorplans and include the difference in the placing of dining rooms. Vitruvius writes:

> In these halls men's banquets are held. For it was not customary for women to join men at dinner. Now these peristyles are called the men's block, for in them men meet without interruption from the women.[63]

The editors of this text assume that Vitruvius is describing the Alexandrian age rather than the actual building plans of Greeks during the early imperial period. The following story, related by Cicero not much earlier, however, belies the assumption that Greek families and others influenced by Hellenistic meal customs automatically embraced newer, Roman customs.

In his orations against Gaius Verres, Cicero relates stories intended to call into question the moral character of the former governor of Sicily, as well as to point out this man's inability to govern properly a Roman territory. In *Against Verres* Cicero opens his tale by asking his audience, "Are you aware of the number of freeborn persons, of respectable married women, to whom he [Verres] offered violence during his foul and disgusting career as governor?"[64] He then goes on to relate a story of Verres' conduct while he was traveling in the province of Asia, where he stops at a town called Lampsacus. The inhabitants in this area are described by Cicero as well-behaved Greeks, but also as being "ready to oblige all Roman citizens." Verres, whom Cicero also describes elsewhere as one wont to carouse, chase disreputable women, and hold wild, drunken dinner parties,[65] arrives

---

[62] *praef.* 6–7.

[63] *De Arch.* 7.4. For a further discussion of dining facilities in antiquity, see Birgitta Bergquist, "Sympotic Space: A Functional Aspect of Greek Dining-Rooms," 37–65; Frederick Cooper, "Dining in Round Buildings," 66–85; Nancy Bookidis, "Ritual Dining in the Sanctuary of Demeter and Kore at Corinth: Some Questions," 86–94; and John Boardman, "*Symposion* Furniture," all in *Sympotica*, ed. O. Murray.

[64] For this quote and the entire narrative that follows, see Cicero, *Verr.* II.1.24.63ff.

[65] *Verr.*, II.3.68.159–60; II.5.12.30–13.31; II.5.13.34; II.5.32.83; II.5.36.94.

in this quiet Greek town, and immediately asks his men to inquire as to the availability of a woman to make his stay more pleasurable. One of Verres' staff, Rubrius, discovers that a well-known, respected town official, Philodamus, has an unmarried daughter. She is described as "a woman of exceptional beauty, but accounted entirely chaste and modest." Verres, whom Cicero jibes as never even having seen such a woman, plots with Rubrius as to how he might procure this woman for the evening. Verres has Rubrius installed in the house of Philodamus, and being a good host, Philodamus arranges a dinner party, encouraging Rubrius to invite whomever he wishes; all of Verres' staff become the dinner guests of Philodamus. Now the stage is set:

> The guests assembled in good time, and took their places. Conversation began; they were invited to drink in the Greek fashion; their host urged them to drink; they asked for bumpers, and the party became a general buzz of talk and merriment. As soon as Rubrius thought the ice was sufficiently broken, he said, "Tell me, Philodamus, why not send for your daughter to come in and see us?" The respectable and already elderly father received the rascal's suggestion with astonished silence. As Rubrius persisted, he replied in order to say something, that it was not the Greek custom for women to be present at a men's dinner party. At this someone in another part of the room called out, "But really, this is intolerable: let the woman be sent for!" At the same moment, Rubrius told his slaves to shut the front door and stand on guard at the entrance. Philodamus, seeing that their purpose was the violation of his daughter, called his slaves and told them not to trouble about himself, but to save his daughter.[66]

After this, the whole house explodes in an uproar, the son returns to help guard the virtue of his sister, and the plan to abduct the daughter of Philodamus (who is never named) is thwarted. The town is so shocked by this outrage against their first citizen that they gather in the streets to protest. Verres realizes he had better get out of town.[67]

Several things become clear in this story about Verres. First of all, Greeks under Roman rule at the close of the Republic (ca. 70 BCE), even those outside of Greece, could still adhere to Greek meal customs, which included the exclusion of respectable women from men's dinner parties. Moreover, even the Romans that Cicero ad-

---

[66] Cicero, *Verr.* II.1.26.66–67 (trans. C. H. G. Greenwood).
[67] *Verr.* II.1.26.65–27.68.

dresses are expected to be shocked and outraged by this sort of behavior on the part of a Roman assistant governor. Verres' behavior is intolerable, not only because it is insensitive to local customs, but because by his conduct Verres is treating a modest and chaste woman like a courtesan by having a member of his staff request her presence at a men's banquet. It is not unreasonable to assume that many Greeks throughout the Empire kept, or at least respected, the old-fashioned custom of excluding women both from the public meal proper (δεῖπνον) and from the drinking party (συμπόσιον).[68]

Cicero's invective against Verres reveals, apart from artistic representations, that the Greek ideology connecting courtesans and prostitutes to banquet settings remained constant during the Roman period. Furthermore, knowledge of Greek customs regarding hetaerae reached all the way to Rome, as many courtesans of the "Greek type" were purchased by Romans in Italy, after merchants and slave traders from the East flooded into Rome.[69] This continued connection of courtesans to banquet settings, often depicted in Roman art, may also be found in Hellenistic texts throughout the late Republican and early imperial periods. I will review further evidence for this connection from texts dating roughly from the second century BCE through the mid-second century CE.

Banquet Courtesans and Their Procurers

In the *Greek Anthology* at least two epigrams reflect the continued connection of courtesans to banquets. The first comes from Meleager's collection of epigrams that was compiled sometime in the early part of the first century BCE, but many of the epigrams go back to an earlier period:

> I know your oath is void, for they betray your wantonness, these locks still moist with scented essences. They betray you, your eyes all heavy for want of sleep, and the garland's track all round your head. Your ringlets are in unchaste disorder all freshly touzled, and your limbs are tottering with the wine. Away from me, public woman (or, "common

---

[68] D. Smith also suggests that "undoubtedly many Greeks clung to the old ways throughout the empire" ("Social Obligation," 210).

[69] Pierre Grimal, *Love in Ancient Rome* (Norman and London: University of Oklahoma Press, 1986), 121.

whore"); they are calling you, the lyre that loves the revel and the clatter of the castanets rattled by the fingers.[70]

First of all, it is clear that the woman here described has been out drinking wine and participating in banquets. On account of her behavior she is called "wanton" (φιλάσωτος), and she is described as a "public woman" (γύναι πάγκοινε). This was a euphemism for the more indelicate term, "whore" (πόρνη).[71] The identification of the woman as "public" or "common to all" is not surprising, given the demarcation between the realms of "public" and "private" according to gender in antiquity. Public and open areas were the sphere of men and not of respectable women, who were relegated to the private sphere of the household.[72] For this reason, prostitutes were often associated with the marketplace and other open-air areas that were usually reserved for men and closed to women of good reputation.[73] A prostitute was then, as now, characterized as a "streetwalker." The woman in this epigram is obviously being described as a prostitute, a woman associated with public places, drunkenness, and the revelry of banquets.

The second epigram found in the *Greek Anthology* dates from the time of Augustus and concerns a procurer, that is, a pimp:

> Psyllus, who used to take to the pleasant banquets of the young men the venal ladies that they desired, that hunter of weak girls who earned a disgraceful wage by dealing in human flesh, lies here. But cast not stones at his tomb, wayfarer, nor bid another to do so. He is dead and buried. Spare him; not because he was content to gain his living so, but because as keeper of common women he dissuaded young men from adultery.[74]

---

[70] *Anth. Graec.* 5.175 (trans. with emendations, W. R. Paton).

[71] See Licht, *Sexual Life in Ancient Greece*, 330–32 for the many colorful euphemisms for "prostitute."

[72] That the separation of men and women throughout history as well as in antiquity on the basis of a public/private dichotomy is a meaningful vehicle for understanding gender inequities has been suggested by Elshtain, *Public Man, Private Woman*. Torjesen has recently outlined the significance of this public/private distinction for the place of women in the early church. See "Reconstruction of Early Christianity" in *Searching the Scriptures*, Schüssler Fiorenza (forthcoming), as well as her forthcoming book *When Women Were Priests*. See above, pp. 15–17.

[73] Balsdon, *Roman Women*, 224ff.; Becker, *Charicles*, 464–65; Bullough and Bullough, *Prostitution*, 34–35; Cantarella, *Pandora's Daughters*, 49–50; Keuls, *Reign of the Phallus*, 163; Licht, *Sexual Life in Ancient Greece*, 330ff.; Pomeroy, *Goddesses*, 201; Sanger, *History of Prostitution*, 48–49.

[74] *Anth. Graec.* 7.403.

This describes someone responsible for the procuring of prostitutes (ἑταῖραι) for young men's banquets (συμπόσια). Presumably this man hired the sorts of women necessary for a party: musicians, actresses, and the like, as well as those needed for conversation. Again these women are called "common," i.e., shared by all (κοινή). Male procurers were common in antiquity (πορνοβοσκοί, *lenones*);[75] however, many procurers were women (*lenae*), particularly older established hetaerae who became madams and trained young girls in order to make a profit from the girls' amours.[76] All procurers were classed as particularly despicable for trafficking in slavery and prostitution.[77] Moreover, procurers were also associated with tax-collectors (πορνοτελῶναι), particularly those tax-collectors who collected the state revenue on prostitutes and therefore kept lists of licensed harlots.[78] Although prostitutes in Rome were not formally taxed until the reign of Gaius Caligula (37–41 CE), "lewd" women and prostitutes had been called upon in Rome's past for special contributions, particularly in times of war.[79] Before being formally taxed, prostitutes in Roman areas had to be licensed and registered in order to practice their trade.[80] In his fourth *Discourse on Kingship*, Dio Chrysostom, describes a false king as being like a despicable procurer:

> So let him be a man insignificant in appearance, servile, unsleeping, never smiling, ever quarreling and fighting with someone, very much

---

[75] F. Hauck and S. Schulz, "πόρνη, κτλ," *TDNT* 6.582; Blümner, *Home Life of the Ancient Greeks*, 171ff.; Bullough and Bullough, *Prostitution*, 34–35; Grimal, *Love in Ancient Rome*, 121ff.; Otto Kiefer, *Sexual Life in Ancient Rome* (New York: Barnes and Noble, 1953), 61ff.; Licht, *Sexual Life in Ancient Greece*, 334; Aline Rousselle, *Porneia: On Desire and the Body in Antiquity*, trans. Felicia Pheasant (Oxford: Basil Blackwell, 1988), 78. A good example of a brothel-keeper is Battaros in Herodas, *Mime* 2.

[76] Blümner, *Home Life of the Ancient Greeks*, 171; Bullough and Bullough, *Prostitution*, 40; Grimal, *Love in Ancient Rome*, 129ff.; Keuls, *Reign of the Phallus*, 196ff.; Kiefer, *Sexual Life in Ancient Rome*, 61ff.; Pomeroy, *Goddesses*, 89; Sanger, *History of Prostitution*, 48. Gyllis in Herodas, *Mime* 1 is a good example of an older courtesan who has become a procurer.

[77] Aeschines, *In Tim.* 117–20; Cicero, *Verr.* II.1.39.101; Dio Chrysostom, *Or.* 4.97–98; *Or.* 14.14; Lucian, *Men.* 11; Plutarch, *Apoph. Lac.* 236 B-C; Theophrastus, *Char.* 6.5–6; see also Grimal, *Love in Ancient Rome*, 121ff.; Hock, "Will of God and Sexual Morality," 24; Pomeroy, *Goddesses*, 201; Sanger, *History of Prostitution*, 48.

[78] See n. 77 above; Hauck and Schulz, "πόρνη, κτλ," 582; see also Licht, *Sexual Life in Ancient Greece*, 334 and further references there, as well as Bullough and Bullough, *Prostitution*, 48.

[79] Bullough and Bullough, *Prostitution*, 48.

[80] Suetonius, *Tib.* 35.; Bullough and Bullough, *Prostitution*, 52–53.

like a pander [πορνοβοσκός] who in garb as well as in character is shameless and niggardly, dressed in a coloured mantle, the finery of one of his harlots. A foul and loathsome spirit is this, for he brings every possible insult and shame upon his own friends and comrades, or, rather, his slaves and underlings, whether he find them in the garb of private citizens or that of royalty. Or is it not plain to see that many who are called kings [βασιλεῖς] are only traders, tax-gatherers [τελῶναι], and keepers of brothels [πορνοβοσκοί]?[81]

This reference from Dio typifies the sort of reputation procurers had throughout the Greco-Roman period. In spite of the bad reputation held by procurers, in the second epigram the procurer Psyllus is defended for keeping young men from adultery (i.e., sex with other men's wives) by making prostitutes available. Thus, prostitution was often defended as providing a service to society. The virtue of respectable women was highly prized, and prostitution was seen as a means of insuring it.[82] Such a defense did not usually extend to the procurers themselves. As in the first epigram, however, women brought by men to a dinner party would still be associated with prostitution.

The association of prostitutes with banquets was such a common cultural theme that one of the elder Seneca's *Declamations* concerns a situation in which a whore asks a favor of a proconsul while dining:

Flamininus, when proconsul, was once asked a favor by a whore while dining. She said she had never seen a man's head being cut off. He had a condemned criminal killed.[83]

Such declamations, or controversies as they were also called, were intended to be used in the training of lawyers. They therefore are thought to reflect the form of real-life speeches made by rhetoricians.[84] The themes of these declamations, however, were often the object of derision, since they were not thought to reflect real situa-

---

[81] *Or.* 4.96–98 (trans. J. W. Cohoon).

[82] Bullough and Bullough, *Prostitution*, 53; Hock, "Will of God and Sexual Morality," 24–25; Pomeroy, *Goddesses*, 91; Sanger, *History of Prostitution*, 79; Hauck and Schulz, "πόρνη, κτλ," 582–83. See also Rousselle, *Porneia*, chs. 5 and 6 on concubinage as an alternative to marriage.

[83] *Controv.* 9.2 (trans. M. Winterbottom). Two versions of this story concerning L. Quinctius Flamininus are given in Livy 39.42–3. See also Cicero, *Sen.* 42; Val. Max. 2.9.3.

[84] M. Winterbottom, trans., *The Elder Seneca* (LCL; Cambridge, Mass.: Harvard University Press; London: William Heinemann, 1974), xi.

tions. In fact, many of the declamation themes in Seneca's collection derive from the Greek schools and reflect rather implausible situations with the stock characters of New Comedy, such as "rich man," "poor man," "prodigal son," and the like.[85] Banquet scenes with courtesans were also a stock setting of New Comedy,[86] which may perhaps explain the choice of the setting here. Such a scene would certainly have been recognized as stereotypical.

New Comedy plays and their stock characters were immensely popular during the Republican and imperial periods.[87] Terence's *The Eunuch* serves as a good example of a popular New Comedy, and it also has a banquet as one of its settings. The plot centers on a young courtesan, Thais, who began her life of pleasure after she was seduced as an adolescent. Eventually she falls in love with one of her customers. In the end love triumphs. Thais ceases to ply her trade and becomes her lover's official concubine.[88] This play in particular is quoted by Cicero, alluded to by both Horace and Persius, and is also quoted by several church fathers. Moreover, it was still being produced during the reign of Claudius.[89] This attests to both the popularity of New Comedy in general and to the availability for the popular imagination of the banquet scene throughout the Roman period.[90]

Cicero, who also narrates the infamous story of Gaius Verres' attempted abduction of a respectable Greek girl, maligns Verres further by painting him as an irresponsible rascal whose conduct at table is less than exemplary. Cicero mentions time after time that Verres habitually consorts with lewd women at banquets.[91] Verres' own son has become corrupted by the atmosphere to which his father has subjected him and at a tender age has been influenced by the disreputable friends of his father, particularly by those women his father was known to consort with at revels. Verres' son "spent his adolescence feasting with unchaste women and intoxicated men."[92]

---

[85] Ibid., xii–xiii.

[86] Gordon Willis Williams, "Terence," *Oxford Classical Dictionary*, ed. N.G.L. Hammond and H. H. Scullard (Oxford: Clarendon Press, 1978), 1044.

[87] Tenney Frank, *Life and Literature of the Roman Republic* (Berkeley and Los Angeles: University of California Press, 1956), 65ff.

[88] Grimal, *Love in Ancient Rome*, 130ff.

[89] Williams, "Terence," 1044.

[90] See also Plautus, *The Casket Comedy*, passim.

[91] See pp. 34–38.

[92] *Verr.* II.3.68.160; II.5.12.30–13.31.

Many of the women at these parties were married women,[93] who therefore would have had the status of matrons. However, because of their conduct, in particular their attendance at Verres' dinner parties, Cicero maligns them as "unchaste."[94] Cicero describes these women with language usually reserved for prostitutes. For instance, he characterizes them as being available for the public like prostitutes, in that their names were easily spoken in public places:

> There were loud references to his [Verres'] days on the shore, to his carousals and debaucheries there; his women's names were heard on the lips of the crowd.[95]

Inasmuch as the names of respectable women traditionally were never mentioned in public (remember that the chaste Greek girl Verres insulted is never named), this comment further underscores Cicero's invective that the women around Verres were more like prostitutes than matrons. Only the names of prostitutes and deceased women were freely mentioned in public.[96] The women usually singled out for mention during this period, such as Cleopatra, Julia, Poppaea, Sempronia, and Messalina, were hardly those known by the Romans for their virtue. In contrast to their more famous forebears (who were also often famous for their sexual promiscuity),[97] little could be said about ideal Roman matrons, not even their names. Respectable women were to be seen, but not heard, and certainly not heard of. The silence expected of a woman was a sign not of her philosophical education, as it was for men,[98] but rather of her submissiveness to her husband and her lack of participation in the public sphere of men. A properly trained young woman, then, had been

---

[93] *Verr.* II.5.13.34–14.35; II.5.52.137.

[94] *Verr.* II.3.68.160.

[95] *Verr.* II.5.36.94 (trans. L. H. G. Greenwood).

[96] David Schaps, "The Women Least Mentioned: Etiquette and Women's Names," *CQ* 27 (1977): 323–30; Cantarella, *Pandora's Daughters*, 124–26.

[97] Marylin Arthur, " 'Liberated Women': The Classical Era," in *Becoming Visible: Women in European History*, ed. Renate Bridenthal and Claudia Koonz (Boston: Houghton Mifflin, 1977), 83–84; M. I. Finley, "The Silent Women of Rome," in *Aspects of Antiquity: Discoveries and Controversies* (New York: Viking Press, 1968), 129–42; Kathleen O'Brien Wicker, "Mulierum Virtutes," in *Plutarch's Ethical Writings and Early Christian Literature*, ed. H. D. Betz (Leiden: Brill, 1978), 106–34; Cantarella, *Pandora's Daughters*, 129–32.

[98] Kathleen E. Corley, "Silence in the Context of Ascent and Liturgy in Gnostic Texts" (unpublished paper presented in the New Testament Seminar of the Claremont Graduate School, Fall 1987), 17ff.

trained to keep her mouth shut.[99] Respectable women who do attempt to speak out in public and participate in debates are described by Plutarch as "putting on men's airs."[100] This is undoubtedly why Plutarch excludes women from discussions, instructs wives to be silent when their husbands are entertaining friends, and why Melissa and Eumetis remain silent while they attend Plutarch's *Banquet of the Seven Sages*.[101] This is in contrast to the reputation of courtesans, who were often expected to be witty, educated, and involved in conversations at dinner.[102] By his remark about the verbal availability of Verres' women friends, then, Cicero is further characterizing them as courtesans. Finally, Cicero likens one of the married women around Verres to a prostitute when he remarks that she was "one man's wife, but at all men's service."[103] Such a comment needs little elucidation. Cicero's personal letters are full of descriptions of such women of loose morals and "matrons" who acted like courtesans.[104]

Cicero's discomfort with those who chose a lifestyle like that of Verres is well-known. He disdained wild dinner parties and preferred more sedate gatherings.[105] In one personal letter he writes of his dismay after being seated at a dinner next to the notorious mistress of Antony, Cytheris. This occasion is frequently noted:[106]

> Next below Eutrapelus reclined Cytheris. At such a dinner party, then, you remark, was the famous Cicero. . . . Upon my oath I never suspected that *she* would be there.[107]

In any case, Cicero left early, as he had no idea that it was to be that sort of soirée.[108]

---

[99] Ibid., 18–20. See also Hock, "Will of God and Sexual Morality," 11; MacMullen, "Women in Public," 216.

[100] *Comp. Lyc. et Num.* 3.5.

[101] See pp. 28–31; also *Praec. Conjug.* 139C. Aune, "Septem," 72, n. 44.

[102] See pp. 28–31.

[103] *Verr.* II.5.13.34.

[104] Grimal, *Love in Ancient Rome*, 147.

[105] D. Smith, "Social Obligation," 31–32.

[106] Balsdon, *Roman Women*, 53; Bullough and Bullough, *Prostitution*, 51; Amy Richlin, "Sources on Adultery at Rome," in *Reflections of Women in Antiquity*, ed. Helene Foley (New York, London, and Paris: Gordon and Breach Science Publishers, 1981), 384; Treggiari, "Libertine Ladies," *CW* 64 (1971), 197; Treggiari, *Roman Freedmen*, 140–41, 224–25.

[107] Cicero, *Fam.* 9.26 (trans. W. G. Williams).

[108] Bullough and Bullough make the incorrect statement that "Cicero enjoyed the companionship of Cytheris" (*Prostitution*, 51), which is hardly the case. Balsdon

This association of disreputable women with banquets, evident in the literature and descriptions of the actual social world of the late Republic, likewise continues into the first century of the Common Era. In Plutarch's *How to Tell a Flatterer from a Friend*, we find that a flatterer has characteristics similar to those of a procurer:

> He is a faithful helper in a love affair, he knows exactly the price to be paid for a prostitute [πόρνη], he is not careless in checking up the charge for a wine supper, nor slow in making arrangements for dinners, he tries to be in the good graces of his mistresses.[109]

Here it seems clear that the hiring of prostitutes went along with the normal preparations for a banquet, like the purchase of wine. Moreover, in making these arrangements in a timely manner, one would be pleasing one's mistress (παλλακίς) rather than one's wife (γαμετή), whose concerns are mentioned in Cicero's next comment. Likewise, when Plutarch narrates a story concerning Larentia, a well-known courtesan, he relates her employment by a keeper of the temple of Herakles for his preparation of a feast for the god. After feasting with her on a couch, the keeper then locks her in a room, supposedly for Herakles to enjoy.[110]

The *Epigrams* of Martial also contain banquet imagery with courtesans, as in this picture of first-century Roman opulence:

> Whoever can endure to be the guest of Zoilus should dine among the wives by the walls and drink, though sober, out of Leda's broken jar. . . . Garbed in green, he lies on a couch he alone fills, and with his elbows thrusts off his guests on either side, propped up as he is on purple and on silken cushions. There stands a catamite by him and offers his belching throat red feathers, and slips of mastick [i.e., toothpicks], and a concubine [*concubina*], lying on her back, with a green fan stirs a gentle breeze to cool his heat.[111]

Martial introduces one of the seamier characters from his anonymous world of Rome. The name is fictitious.[112] Zoilus, the stereotypical party-goer, lies on a dinner couch, dressed in green (a sign of

---

remarks that Cicero was shocked by her presence (*Roman Women*, 53).

[109] Plutarch, *Quomodo Adul. Amic.* 64F (trans. F. C. Babbitt).

[110] *Rom.* 5.1–4.

[111] *Epigr.* 3.82.1–10 (trans. W. C. A. Ker).

[112] F. A. Wright, *Martial: The Twelve Books of Epigrams*, trans. J. A. Pott and F. A. Wright (London: George Routlege and Sons; New York: E. P. Dutton and Co., 1924), x–xi.

effeminacy), sprawled over silken cushions. He is surrounded by a recumbent concubine, a catamite, and (later on) a young boy, all of whom could be possible sexual objects for Zoilus; homosexuality was not uncommon in συμπόσια settings.[113] Besides the one clearly identified courtesan, Martial also mentions the presence of "wives by the walls." This surely refers to prostitutes, not only on account of Martial's language in other epigrams, where prostitutes stand beside walls and archways,[114] but also because the most common location of streetwalkers was under archways and leaning against the walls of buildings in public places.[115] It is not clear whether Martial is also intending to slander matrons who might be present at such a party, in that he calls these women *uxores,* which could mean either wife or consort. In another epigram, Martial also connects the images of loose women, *convivia,* and archways.[116]

The last reference to courtesans from the first century CE comes from the graffiti of Pompeii. In the ruins of Pompeii there are several references to a famous woman named Novellia Primigenia,[117] who was no doubt a high class courtesan of some sort. An early translation of one diptych addressed to Novellia found in a tomb reads:

> Would that I were the jeweled goblet from which you drink at dinner. Better still that I stayed with you alone! Then I should thus give you kisses which I now send you![118]

In this instance we have a reference to a real woman, a real courtesan who is being connected to the pleasures of the banquet. In Pompeii during the late first century, then, actual women who were courtesans were still associated with the scene of sexuality, the banquet.

This association continues into the second century, particularly in the writings of Lucian, well-known for his parodies of Greco-Roman culture. In *Dialogues of the Courtesans,* it becomes plain that even in the second century a key role of the courtesan in the Greco-

---

[113] Keuls, *Reign of the Phallus,* 274–99; Licht, *Sexual Life in Ancient Greece,* 449ff.

[114] *Epigr.* 1.34.6; 12.32.22.

[115] Ker, *Martial,* 50; also Bullough and Bullough, *Prostitution,* 50; Licht, *Sexual Life in Ancient Greece,* 332ff.; Pomeroy, *Goddesses,* 202.

[116] *Epigr.* 7. 79.

[117] Text and translation (with emendations) from Michele D' Avino, *The Women of Pompeii,* trans. M. H. Jones and L. Nusco (Napoli: Loffredo, 1967), 78.

[118] Ibid., 78.

Roman mind was to escort young men to dinner parties. Numerous comments in Lucian indicate that the courtesans spent much of their time drinking and eating with men as well as sleeping with them. These women are also described as reclining beside men on couches.[119] Several of the dialogues relate the women's frustrations with the men they dance and drink with. In two dialogues, women decry the way that their escorts dance and consort with other women at parties, particularly the flute girls, whom these higher class courtesans seem to see as beneath their station.[120] In this instance, one courtesan, Joessa, complains about her recent love, Phaon:

> But ever since you realized that I doted on you, and you had me under your thumb, you've been having jokes with Lycena, before my very eyes, to annoy me, or at other times praising Magidium, the harp-girl, when we were dining together. These things make me cry and feel insulted. Only the other day, when you were drinking with Thraso and Diphilus, the company also included the flute-girl Cymbalium, and Pyrallis, whom I loathe! As you know that, I didn't worry particularly about you kissing Cymbalium five times. To kiss a woman like that was an insult to yourself! But oh! the way you kept on making signs at Pyrallis, and would lift up your cup to her when you drank![121]

The scene is not unlike earlier images of Greek συμπόσια. Several women attend a drinking party with young men. Several are musicians, such as the harp and flute girls, and several are the companions of the men, the higher class ἑταῖραι, who have a stronger tie to the men than do the other women. There is no mention of wives, and the women described are obviously all prostitutes of some sort. The scene is sexual, particularly with all the kissing and other frivolity going on during the meal. Although the scene is fictitious, it undoubtedly seemed familiar and stereotypical to those who read Lucian in the second century CE.

Lucian's *Dialogues of the Courtesans* also contains a telling conversation between a mother, Crobyle, and her daughter, Corinna. Crobyle has decided to encourage her daughter to become a courtesan because they have been left without financial support upon the

---

[119] *Dial. Meret.* 1; 3; 6; 11; 12; 15.

[120] *Dial. Meret.* 3.12. See also R. O. A. M. Lyne, *The Latin Love Poets From Catullus to Horace* (Oxford: Clarendon Press, 1986), 8–10, who describes the two classes of professional "women of pleasure."

[121] *Dial. Meret.* 12.311 (trans. M. D. McLeod).

death of Crobyle's husband. Crobyle worked for awhile after his death, but now she wants her daughter to make money "by associating with young men, drinking and sleeping with them."[122] Crobyle also instructs Corinna to mind her manners when out, and exhorts her to not drink too much or talk too much while at a party.[123] By selling her daughter's body, then, Crobyle hopes to become rich. In a way, Corinna's mother is similar to a retired hetaera who switches to procuring to make a living, and so trains up a young girl to become a prostitute.

Courtesans, Prostitutes, Freedwomen, and Slaves

Another striking fact that is borne out by Greco-Roman sources is the unmistakable relationship between slavery and prostitution.[124] Many prostitutes were slaves,[125] and the lowest class of prostitutes were owned outright by their brothel-keepers.[126] Moreover, the many female prostitutes and young boys who staffed the banquets of the ancient world were also slaves, particularly the flute players, cithara players, and other musicians, dancers, actors, and actresses.[127] The table servants and preparers of food were also slaves, often slave women or pretty young boys.[128] Wealthy householders

---

[122] *Dial. Meret.* 6.293.

[123] *Dial. Meret.* 6.294.

[124] *Anth. Graec.* 7.403; Cicero, *Verr.* II.1.24.63ff.; Dio Chrysostom, *Or.* 4.96–98; Philo, *Sacr.* 26–27; *Spec. Leg.* 3.170–71.

[125] J. P. V. D. Balsdon, *Romans and Aliens* (Chapel Hill: University of North Carolina Press, 1979), 80; Keuls, *Reign of the Phallus*, 199–200; Pomeroy, *Goddesses*, 139ff.

[126] Bullough and Bullough, *Prostitution*, 34.

[127] Barrow, *Slavery in the Roman Empire*, 63; C. Forbes, "Education and Training of Slaves in Antiquity," 329; John Kells Ingram, *A History of Slavery and Serfdom* (London: Adam and Charles Black, 1895), 19–20, 41ff.; Milton Meltzer, *Slavery from the Rise of Western Civilization to the Renaissance* (Chicago: Cowles Book Co., 1971), 135, 138, 161; Veyne, "Roman Empire," in *History of Private Life*, 1.57–60; William Westermann, *The Slave Systems of Greek and Roman Antiquity* (Philadelphia: American Philosophical Society, 1955), 13, 24.

[128] See Barrow, *Slavery in the Roman Empire*, 22, 42–43, 56–57; Yvon Garlan, *Slavery in Ancient Greece*, trans. Janet Lloyd (Ithaca and London: Cornell University Press, 1988), 32–33; Lyne, *Latin Love Poets*, 8–13; Maxey, "Occupations," 12–30; Meltzer, *Slavery from the Rise of Western Civilization*, 136; Murray, "Greek Symposion," 264; Patterson, *Slavery and Social Death*, 179; Veyne, "Roman Empire," in *History of Private Life*, 1.79; Westermann, *Slave Systems*, 3; Thomas Wiedemann, *Greek and Roman Slavery* (Baltimore, Md.: Johns Hopkins University Press, 1981),

who owned many slaves would also hire out their banquet slaves to a third party, and on slow days they would send their slaves to the open marketplace to look for work.[129] As a matter of course, all slaves were sexually available to their masters, or to those who hired them. This was a heavy burden in particular for slaves who were women or attractive young boys.[130] This underscores the point already made, that the women who did attend public meals were often sexual accompaniments to the proceedings, whether or not they had additional talents in the area of music, dancing, or acting.[131] Much to their wives' displeasure, many men fathered children by their female slaves. A man who chased his servant women to excess could become known as a "maid chaser" (*ancillariolus*).[132] Since most households, even peasant ones, had at least one maidservant, this was probably a common experience in the ancient world.[133] Even the designated concubine of a slave household manager could be made available to the other male slaves or to visitors.[134] We may infer that the sale of slave women into actual prostitution must have been common, since a seller had the right to forbid a slave from being secondarily sold into prostitution.[135]

In ancient Greece it was a disgrace for a citizen to marry such a freedwoman.[136] However, in the Roman period, one result of this

---

233. See also Veyne, "Roman Empire," in *History of Private Life*, 1.55 where he notes that the concubine of the slave steward also was responsible for preparing meals for the other slave workers. Not all food preparation was performed by slave help, however; wives and daughters prepared meals especially in peasant or poor households. See Garlan, *Slavery in Ancient Greece*, 60; Rachel Sargent, "The Size of the Slave Population at Athens during the 5th and 4th centuries Before Christ" (*Studies in the Social Sciences* 12.3; University of Illinois, Urbana, September 1924), 46.

[129] Meltzer, *Slavery from the Rise of Western Civilization*, 72–75; Garlan, *Slavery in Ancient Greece*, 62, 68, 70; Ingram, *Slavery and Serfdom*, 21

[130] Garlan, *Slavery in Ancient Greece*, 32–33, 152; Ingram, *Slavery and Serfdom*, 10, 53; Meltzer, *Slavery from the Rise of Western Civilization*, 48; Patterson, *Slavery and Social Death*, 50, 173; Westermann notes that the sexual use of female slaves in particular becomes more marked after the late Republican period; see *Slave Systems*, 74.

[131] See previous discussion above, 25–28.

[132] Veyne, "Roman Empire," in *History of Private Life*, 1.77.

[133] A. H. M. Jones, "Slavery in the Ancient World," in *Slavery in Classical Antiquity*, ed. M. I. Finley (Cambridge: W. Heffer and Sons, 1960), 1.

[134] Veyne, "Roman Empire," in *History of Private Life*, 1.64; Wiedemann, *Greek and Roman Slavery*, 128.

[135] Barrow, *Slavery in the Roman Empire*, 47; Veyne, "Roman Empire," in *History of Private Life*, 1.68.

[136] Wiedemann, *Greek and Roman Slavery*, 45–46.

general sexual availability of slaves was that slave women were frequently freed to become either the wife or the legal concubine of their former master. Such a woman would have the status of a matron (a status denied slave women and most freedwomen), unless she left her patron to marry another. This was not the case for male slaves, who rarely married their patronesses.[137] For the senatorial classes in Rome, marriage with a freedwoman was discouraged, particularly under the reign of Augustus. Concubinage with freedwomen, however, was commonly practiced.[138] Moreover, male admirers of certain slave women may have contributed to their manumission price, even if they did not intend to marry them.[139] Many scholars have suggested that this kind of sexual relationship between slave women and masters may have contributed to the higher manumission rates for female slaves.[140]

In the light of research on the manumission inscriptions found at Delphi, however (ca. 200 BCE–100 CE), other factors have also contributed to the higher rate of manumissions among slave women. First of all, a woman's purchase price was usually lower, and she was also more likely to remain with her master's household following the purchase of her freedom.[141] The maternal ties between slave women and owners should also not be overlooked, and children more often redeemed their mothers from slavery than they did their fathers.[142] Strong evidence, however, suggests that slave women may have had more opportunities to raise their purchase price because they in fact had more to sell. Prostitution seems to have been a significant source

---

[137] Barrow, *Slavery in the Roman Empire*, 175–79, 195–6; Duff, *Freedmen in the Early Roman Empire*, 61–62; Keith Hopkins, *Conquerors and Slaves* (SSRH 1; Cambridge: Cambridge University Press, 1978), 168; Ingram, *Slavery and Serfdom*, 68–9; Patterson, *Slavery and Social Death*, 263; Pomeroy, *Goddesses*, 195; Rousselle, *Porneia*, 97; Treggiari, *Roman Freedmen*, 210–12.

[138] Duff, *Freedmen in the Early Roman Empire*, 62; Treggiari, *Roman Freedmen*, 84–86. Some scholars warn against exaggerating the influence on manumission rates from sexual relations between slaves and masters. See Garlan, *Slavery in Ancient Greece*, 74–75 and K. Hopkins, *Conquerors and Slaves*, 169, who suggests that marriage was not always in the minds of all men who paid for the release of a female slave.

[139] Garlan, *Slavery in Ancient Greece*, 75; K. Hopkins, *Conquerors and Slaves*, 169; Wiedemann, *Greek and Roman Slavery*, 45–46.

[140] Duff, *Freedmen in the Early Roman Empire*, 62; Treggiari, *Roman Freedmen*, 84–86.

[141] Gustave Glotz, *Ancient Greece at Work: An Economic History of Greece from the Homeric Period to the Roman Conquest* (New York: Knopf, 1926), 217; K. Hopkins, *Conquerors and Slaves*, 162–69; Patterson, *Slavery and Social Death*, 251, 263–64.

[142] Patterson, *Slavery and Social Death*, 263

of income for many slave women earning their freedom,[143] and it also seems probable that they raised money by selling their children as well.[144] As part of their manumission agreement, many slave women at Delphi were required to give one child to their former owner to take their place.[145] Some scholars hesitate to acknowledge this kind of practice by slave women.[146] In any case, if generalizations can be made on the basis of such evidence, this may explain the small numbers of children in freed individuals' families and the fact that many former slaves purchased their children from individuals other than their own patrons.[147]

A noteworthy example of a woman who not only purchased her freedom by means of prostitution and entertaining men at banquets, but one who furthermore went on to become the formal concubine of her former master, is the exotic dancer Telethusa. Quite famous in Rome for her dancing abilities, Telethusa is mentioned in several poems in the *Carmina Priapea*[148] as well as in two of Martial's *Epigrams*.[149] Telethusa most likely raised her purchase price by selling her services as a dancer and prostitute on busy market streets such as the Sacred Way in Rome, in red-light districts or in entertainment centers such as the Roman Circus Maximus.[150] Martial, in his *Epigrams*, chides her patron for being so smitten with his former slave that their positions are now reversed. He has become the slave, and she the master.[151] Also in the *Carmina Priapea*, Telethusa and other unnamed women give offerings to Priapus for helping them to earn large amounts from prostitution.[152] Telethusa, who has earned

---

[143] Ibid., 263, 441, n. 4; Pomeroy, *Goddesses*, 195; Westermann, *Slave Systems*, 13–14; Wiedemann, *Greek and Roman Slavery*, 45–46.

[144] C. Wayne Tucker, "Women in the Manumission Inscriptions at Delphi," *Transactions of the American Philological Association* 112 (1982): 225–36.

[145] Tucker, *Manumission Inscriptions*, 233–35.

[146] Garlan, *Slavery in Ancient Greece*, 74–75; K. Hopkins, *Conquerors and Slaves*, 168.

[147] Treggiari, *Roman Freedmen*, 214; Rawson, "Family Life," 78ff.

[148] *Carmina Priapea* 19 and 40.

[149] *Epigr.* 6.71 and 8.51.23.

[150] Howard M. Jackson and Susan A. Zenger, "*Carmina Priapea:* Roman Poems in Honor of Priapus: The Latin Text and English Translation with Text-Critical and Expository Commentary" (unpublished manuscript), 75–76. I am indebted to my colleague Howard Jackson for making this manuscript available to me.

[151] *Epigr.* 6.71.

[152] *Carmina Priapea* 40; text and translation by Jackson and Zenger, *Carmina Priapea*, 151. See also *Carmina Priapea* 34 and 27.

enough to buy her freedom, offers Priapus a gilded wreath in gratitude. That the wreath she left is gilded indicates that this young
woman earned great deal of money indeed.[153]

Women might also have had opportunities to earn extra money
by means other than prostitution, particularly by using skills learned
in their master's service. Following their emancipation, freedwomen
could either remain in the service of their masters or seek employment in areas in which they had received training while in their
master's household. Work in clothing and textiles was most common,
and many became weavers; however, one also finds freedwomen who
were cobblers, shoemakers, leatherworkers, waitresses, shopkeepers
of various sorts, innkeepers, amanuenses, butchers, fisherwomen,
musicians, courtesans, and procuresses.[154] Freedwomen were also
known for their trade in luxury items, such as purple dye or perfumes.[155] Some became quite wealthy, either as merchants or as
high-class courtesans and went on to become patronesses of men's
guilds.[156] Other freedwomen undoubtedly worked side-by-side with
their husbands in business.[157]

But in terms of their sexual classification, freedwomen, having
been sexually "available to all" as slaves, and possibly having earned
some of the purchase price for their freedom by means of prostitution, would also have been classified as "prostitutes." This would have
been the case even if such activity were long since in their pasts, and
they had gone on to other professions. Probably only a few freedwomen earned the classification of "matron" by marrying their higher-
class patron. Thus, the moral expectations of married freedwomen
were not as high as that of the married freeborn.[158] In any case,
freedwomen obviously had a reputation for promiscuity, whether or
not every freedwomen had in fact prostituted herself at some time or
deserved such a reputation.[159]

---

[153] Jackson and Zenger, *Carmina Priapea*, 151.

[154] Barrow, *Slavery in the Roman Empire*, 63; Duff, *Freedmen in the Early Roman Empire*, 105–6, 148–49; Forbes, "Education and Training of Slaves in Antiquity," 328ff. Glotz, *Ancient Greece at Work*, 217; K. Hopkins, *Conquerors and Slaves*, 162; Meltzer, *Slavery from the Rise of Western Civilization*, 161; Patterson, *Slavery and Social Death*, 266; Pomeroy, *Goddesses*, 198ff.; Treggiari, *Roman Freedmen*, 138–42.

[155] Pomeroy, *Goddesses*, 200.

[156] Ibid., 198–201.

[157] Cameron, "Neither Male Nor Female," 60–68.

[158] Westermann, *Slave Systems*, 41.

[159] Treggiari, *Roman Freedmen*, 142. See pp. 53–59.

Women in Public in the Late Republic and Early Empire

Greco-Roman Matrons: "Liberated" or "Libertine"?[160]

The association of prostitutes and slave women with public meal settings in Greco-Roman literature can therefore be charted well into the second century CE. Such representations recall earlier Greek banquets scenes and carry sexual connotations. It is no wonder, then, that during the Roman period, the sight of women at public meals continued to elicit a certain degree of social criticism, depending on the type of meal a woman attended and her companions. It was not unreasonable to expect the presence of matrons at a dinner party, albeit in small numbers, but should they remain for the συμ-πόσιον or participate in frivolous or drunken behavior they could be characterized as prostitutes, women known for eating and drinking with men. It is no wonder that foreign meal practices were often commented on for the inclusion of daughters and mothers in these activities.[161] Many of the matrons of the late Republic and early Empire elicited precisely such criticisms; their critical contemporaries likened them to prostitutes. These women are usually noted by modern scholars for their "liberated" behavior during that time period. It is not coincidental that the first accusations of immorality leveled against Roman women date at the same time that their "emancipation" began.[162]

The outrageous behavior characterizing the late Republic and early Empire is well-known, particularly the flamboyant behavior of the women of the Roman aristocracy.[163] These accounts may be exagger-

---

[160]This play on words was first used by Treggiari in her article, "Libertine Ladies," 196–98.

[161] For foreign meal practices that the Romans thought surprising see Livy 1:57 (Etruscans); Macrobius, *Sat.* vii; Herodotus, 5.18; Plutarch, *Art.*; Quintius Curtius, 5.1 (Persians); Athen. *Deipn.* 1.23 (Tyrrhenians); Tacitus, *Germ.* 18–19 (Germans).

[162]Kiefer, *Sexual Life in Ancient Rome*, 45.

[163] Balsdon, *Roman Women*, 16; Grimal, *Love in Ancient Rome*, 146ff.; Judith Hallett, "The Role of Women in Roman Elegy: Counter-Cultural Feminism," in *Women in the Ancient World: The Arethusa Papers*, ed. John Peradotto and J. Sullivan (Albany, N.Y.: State University of New York Press, 1984), 245ff.; Kiefer, *Sexual Life in Ancient Rome*, 39ff.; Anna Lydia Motto, "Seneca on Women's Liberation," *The Classical World* 65 (1972), 156; Pomeroy, *Goddesses*, 189; Sanger, *History of Prostitution*, 82ff.; Treggiari, "Libertine Ladies," 196–98; Veyne, "Roman Empire," in *History of Private Life*, 1.75–76.

ated,[164] yet many during the Roman period harshly criticized the behavior of certain women.[165] Historians generally see this as a reaction against the partial freedom of women that developed during the late Republic and early Empire.[166] Freedom for women was seen as leading swiftly into debauchery and sexual licentiousness.[167] The writings of Virgil, Livy, Tacitus, and Juvenal indicate that during this period there occurred in Rome a reevaluation of the attitude toward women that caused a shift in the general outlook of women's roles.[168] Marylin Arthur concludes that this shift in outlook can be correlated with both political and social developments during these years, particularly the new focus on the importance of the nuclear family for the good of the state.[169] Rome tolerated the new independence of women only as long as it did not interfere with the real world of male politics.

But just how "free" were Roman women? Eva Cantarella argues that there were women who claimed greater freedom and enjoyed a certain degree of privilege at Rome, and that the number of these women increased between the first and second centuries. The majority of these women, however, belonged to a single social class, the aristocracy, and their "emancipation" was limited.[170] Peter Brown calls this "emancipation" of women during the early Empire a "freedom born of contempt," allowed only as long as it had no political impact, and restricted when it was seen as destructive to the male political order.[171] This "emancipation" should therefore be seen as relative, and not as akin to the sweeping "liberation" of the "Women's Liberation" movement of the 1960s.[172] This change in women's activities in the public sphere generated by economic and social currents does not necessarily indicate a change in the social ideology about women's proper behav-

---

[164] Balsdon, *Roman Women*, 271–72; Kiefer, *Sexual Life in Ancient Rome*, 47ff.; Pomeroy, *Goddesses*, 189.

[165] Arthur, "Liberated Women," 84–85; Cantarella, *Pandora's Daughters*, 142ff.; Kiefer, *Sexual Life in Ancient Rome*, 45ff; Van Bremen, "Women and Wealth," 234ff.

[166] Arthur, "Liberated Women," 84–85; Cantarella, *Pandora's Daughters*, 142ff.; Motto, "Seneca," 156ff; Van Bremen, "Women and Wealth," 234–35.

[167] Kiefer, *Sexual Life in Ancient Rome*, 45ff.; Motto, "Seneca," 234.

[168] Arthur, "Liberated Women," 84–85.

[169] Ibid., 85.

[170] Cantarella, *Pandora's Daughters*, 142–43. See also Cameron, "Neither Male Nor Female," passim.

[171] "Late Antiquity," in *History of Private Life* 1.247–48.

[172] Cantarella, *Pandora's Daughters*, 140–41.

ior or their social status.[173] Once the political ramifications of women's changing behavior were recognized, Roman men sought to restrict women's liberties and put them back "under their thumbs."[174]

This limitation of women's new behavior was accomplished in several ways: first through legislation limiting the partial freedoms that women had begun to exercise, and second by a new insistence on the importance of women's traditional virtues.[175] Aline Rousselle suggests that the true purpose of the Augustan marriage laws was to limit the new sexual freedom of Roman women.[176] The new laws restricting adultery therefore set out to prevent free respectable women, such as daughters of good families, wives, widows, and divorcees, from having casual sexual relationships. These laws also prevented husbands from allowing their wives any degree of sexual freedom or from keeping a wife that had committed infidelities.[177] Should a woman be convicted of misconduct, she would lose her status as matron[178] and be forced to wear the clothing of a prostitute.[179] Husbands who did not repudiate errant wives for adulterous behavior could be prosecuted for *lenocinium*, "procuring."[180]

Concurrent with this legislation was the development in the literature of the Augustan period of a contrast between the ideal wife and the immoral assertive woman.[181] Women were characterized as "wanton" and in need of control, and more significantly, they were maligned as "prostituting" themselves.[182] To protest against this new restrictive legislation, many Roman women actually registered as prostitutes in order to avoid being accused of adultery,[183] a practice which was forbidden under Tiberius.[184] In description then, the dis-

---

[173] See Van Bremen, "Women and Wealth," 236–37.

[174] Cantarella, *Pandora's Daughters*, 143.

[175] Cantarella hints at this in *Pandora's Daughters*, 143.

[176] Rousselle, *Porneia*, 87. On Augustan marriage laws see Balsdon, *Roman Women*, 217; Pal Csillag, *The Augustan Laws on Family Relations* (Budapest: Academiai Kiado, 1976); Kiefer, *Sexual Life in Ancient Rome*, 36ff.; Pomeroy, *Goddesses*, 159ff.; Richlin, "Sources on Adultery at Rome," 379–404.

[177] Rousselle, *Porneia*, 85–87.

[178] Ibid., 81.

[179] Ibid., 94.

[180] Ibid., 82ff.; 103ff.

[181] Arthur, "Liberated Women," 84.

[182] See for example, Tacitus, *Ann.* 2.85; Suetonius, *Tib.* 35.2.

[183] Rousselle, *Porneia*, 94; Pomeroy, *Goddesses*, 160.

[184] Pomeroy, *Goddesses*, 160.

tinction between many Roman matrons and prostitutes was slight[185] or at least uncertain,[186] and these women were seen as imitating the hetaerae of Greek fame.[187]

Insulting language used to describe such women reflects imagery usually connected to prostitutes. Although it is obvious that many women of the upper class were known for their education and pursuit of philosophy,[188] descriptions of liberated (considered libertine)[189] ladies characterize these women as being overly talkative and chatty, particularly at meals.[190] Juvenal's well-known invective against matrons who are barely seated at the dinner table before they begin to pour out their knowledge of the classics and Greek grammar is certainly explicable in light of the tradition linking these skills to courtesans in banquet settings.[191] Another prime example of such language is Sallust's description of Sempronia, wife of the consul in 77 BCE. Tacitus later uses this to describe Poppaea:

> She was well-read in Greek literature as well as in Latin; her singing and dancing were rather too professional for a lady, and she had many other accomplishments which made for dissipation. Self-restraint and chastity ranked lowest in her scale of values, and it was hard to say which she thought less of squandering, her money or her reputation. . . . Yet she had a good brain; she wrote verses; she was amusing; and whether in the language of the drawing room or the brothel, she was a good talker, full of wit, even of charm.[192]

Note that Sempronia manifests all the qualities of a courtesan: charm and wit, as well as skills in singing and dancing. She is learned

---

[185] Sanger, *History of Prostitution*, 77.

[186] Kiefer, *Sexual Life in Ancient Rome*, 59. Kiefer is therefore careful to distinguish between matrons and real prostitutes, i.e., women who consciously sought to earn a living from selling their bodies and new, "free living" women.

[187] Cantarella, *Pandora's Daughters*, 131; Grimal, *Love in Ancient Rome*, 146ff.; Kiefer, *Sexual Life in Ancient Rome*, 44; Lyne, *Latin Love Poets*, 13ff.

[188] Balsdon, *Roman Women*, 272–73; Edward Best, "Cicero, Livy and Educated Roman Women," *Classical Journal* 65 (1970): 199–204; Susan G. Cole, "Could Greek Women Read and Write?" in *Reflections of Roman Women*, ed. Helene Foley, 219–45; Freidländer, *Roman Life*, 251; Pomeroy, *Goddesses*, 172ff.

[189] See Treggiari, "Libertine Ladies," 196–98.

[190] Freidländer, *Roman Life*, 253; Kiefer, *Sexual Life in Ancient Rome*, 43ff. Pomeroy, *Goddesses*, 172.

[191] Juvenal, *Sat.* 6.

[192] Sallust, *Cat.* 24.3–25.5 (trans. J. P. V. D. Balsdon). See Tacitus, *Ann.* 13.45; Balsdon, *Roman Women*, 47–48; see also Kiefer, *Sexual Life in Ancient Rome*, 43–44; Pomeroy, *Goddesses*, 171.

and quite capable of carrying on a conversation about literature and philosophy; however, she is also "unchaste," has a bad reputation, and uses the vocabulary of brothels right alongside that of the drawing room. This is not as biting a description as that of Juvenal, but its intent becomes plain in light of other invectives against liberated/libertine women of the time.

"Liberated" women were also known for their drinking habits. Traditionally, respectable women in the Republican period were not allowed to drink alcohol.[193] Later, such prohibitions were relaxed, but proper women still drank moderately, if they drank at all.[194] Even well trained courtesans were to watch their alcohol consumption.[195] Roman women who did drink to excess were likened to the lowest of prostitutes.[196] Moreover, the religious rituals that many Roman women attended were also suspect,[197] and women who participated in other "strange" religions like Christianity were accused of prostitution, particularly those involved in the Isis cult. Grimal asserts that the Isis cult triumphed in Rome precisely at the time when there was more of an acceptance of emancipated behavior on the part of women.[198] It is interesting that both women participants in the Isis cult and women proselytes of Judaism were also eventually accused of meretricious behavior.[199]

The social background of the women described by Roman writers is disputed. Perhaps these women were not matrons, but rather wealthy freedwomen, who would have been classified as pros-

---

[193] Cantarella, *Pandora's Daughters*, 118.

[194] Balsdon, *Roman Women*, 272.

[195] Ibid., 272; Lucian, *Dial. Meret.* 6.

[196] Cantarella, *Pandora's Daughters*, 144. See above, pp. 38–39.

[197] Balsdon, *Roman Women*, 247; Cantarella, *Pandora's Daughters*, 151ff.; Pomeroy, *Goddesses*, 217ff.

[198] Grimal, *Love in Ancient Rome*, 305.

[199] On Poppaea, who was possibly a convert to Judaism, see Balsdon, *Roman Women*, 125ff. and Tacitus, *Ann.* 13.45, which is based on Sallust's description of Sempronia (see p. 56 above); Balsdon, *Roman Women*, 247; Cantarella, *Pandora's Daughters*, 148; See esp. David L. Balch on the criticisms leveled against eastern cults which were eventually inherited by Judaism and later by Christianity. A key criticism of both the Isiac religion (and the Dionysiac religion before it), and Judaism was the supposed opportunity for sexual promiscuity on the part of women participants, particularly in the context of nocturnal wine feasts. Balch also shows that, like Christian writers, Jewish writers utilized the Haustafeln in order to argue that their women were in their proper place, and therefore were no threat to the politeia (*Let Wives Be Submissive: The Domestic Code in 1 Peter* [SBLMS 26; Chico, Calif.: Scholars Press, 1981], chs. 5 and 6).

titutes anyway.[200] This suggestion, however, has been challenged; these women could have been from any class: courtesans, freed-women, or upper-class wives, widows, or divorcees.[201] Treggiari argues forcefully that there is no evidence that Roman freedwomen were more licentious than Roman matrons. She also asserts that most writers focused on the sexual immorality of the upper classes, rather than on those not born free.[202] Given the additional connection between slavery and prostitution, though, and given that many women may indeed have prostituted themselves in order to earn their freedom, such characterizations of Roman freedwomen are not un-expected. If this connection is accurate, then part of the characterization of these "liberated/libertine" freeborn women is that they were also acting like slaves.

Perhaps a lesson may be learned from recent study of the etiology behind fluctuations in the slave market during this same period. The causes of these fluctuations are rooted in the changing economic and political situation of the early Empire, whatever cultural rationalizations for the practice of freeing slaves eventually developed.[203] Examining the span of this historical period, Orlando Patterson has argued that religious and philosophical developments in ideology concerning slavery did not cause, influence, or determine the continuance of slave manumissions. Far from resulting from a humanitarian impulse, freeing slaves benefitted the owner. Owners were more than recompensed by the purchase price paid by the slave. Children were often left by parents as a replacement. Furthermore, the patronage system insured the continued service of the freed slave to the master for many years to come.[204]

---

[200] See discussion above, pp. 48–52. It has often been argued that the women men took to banquets during the Roman period were freedwomen who were often actresses and the like (Veyne, "Roman Empire," in *History of Private Life*, 1.187). The well-known "libertine ladies" and subjects of the erotic Roman elegies of the early imperial period would therefore be freedwomen rather than upper-class matrons. Treggiari has argued against this assumption ("Libertine Ladies," 196–98; *Roman Freedman*, 142).

[201] Treggiari, "Libertine Ladies," 196–98; Pomeroy, *Goddesses*, 172.

[202] Treggiari, "Libertine Ladies," 198.

[203] Patterson, *Slavery and Social Death*, 273–93. See also comments by Veyne, "Roman Empire," in *History of Private Life*, 1.64 and economic factors charted by K. Hopkins, *Conquerors and Slaves*, 1–100.

[204] Duff, *Freedmen in the Early Roman Empire*, 43–44; Patterson, *Slavery and Social Death*, 247; Treggiari, *Roman Freedmen*, 15–16.

By the first century, the government regarded these burgeoning numbers of manumissions as damaging to the state, as was also the case with the increasing "freedoms" enjoyed by women. Under the reign of Augustus legislation was passed that limited slave manumissions, just as legislation was implemented to limit the new freedoms of women.[205] In spite of the Augustan laws, slave manumissions almost certainly continued to increase during the first century. Increased manumissions were probably due not to any major ideological shift on the part of ancient people, but because of the economic benefit to the owner. The social ideology which supported the institution of slavery in actuality changed little. During this period both Jews and Christians continued to own slaves and tacitly supported the institution itself.[206] The presence of both slave and free in Jewish and Christian communities would therefore reflect the changing complexion of society brought about by the high manumission rates during the late Republic and on into the imperial period.[207] The same economic and political factors that precipitated the change in "status" for many slaves, obviously also precipitated a similar change in "status" for women, and at approximately the same time.[208]

Women of Virtue and Women of Vice

It is not surprising that the attendance of women at banquets was suspect during this period, given the association of drinking and revelry with slavery and prostitution. Women known for their forwardness in other areas were also known for their attendance at men's banquets, as were the women who consorted with Gaius Verres.[209]

---

[205] Duff, *Freedmen in the Early Roman Empire*, 190–91; Meltzer, *Slavery from the Rise of Western Civilization*, 184–85.

[206] Patterson, *Slavery and Social Death*, 275–78.

[207] Rawson, "Family Life," 82.

[208] Averil Cameron wrote an article over a decade ago which prompted the beginning of this research. She wrote: "Did the Church offer a better chance to women as something new and distinctively Christian, or was it itself profiting from an existing trend in the late Hellenistic world?" ("Neither Male Nor Female," 61). Cameron also suggested that "the notable number of women mentioned in this early phase is more likely to reflect their real and unsurprising status in these classes than to indicate a new or special role being offered to them" (65).

[209] See pp. 42–43 above; Balsdon, *Roman Women*, 272; Cantarella, *Pandora's Daughters*, 161; Freidländer, *Roman Life*, 247. See also D. Smith, "Social Obligation," 31–32 concerning the flamboyance of Roman banquets.

Such settings were considered enticing, since traditionally meal settings were associated with sexual promiscuity.[210] So, although wives
might be expected to attend a meal, guests were to stay away from
the wife of their host and were warned against reclining next to
married women, lest they be tempted to accost them.[211] Married
women were also cautioned against dining with strangers, and attending banquets without their husbands or without their husband's
permission was frowned upon. By the time of Justinian, a freewoman
who attended a public dinner without the escort of her husband
could be divorced.[212]

An early invective against this type of behavior occurs in Cicero.
In 56 BCE M. Caelius Rufus was tried for various charges brought
against him by his former lover, the infamous Clodia, also called
"Lesbia" by the poet Catullus.[213] Clodia was a wellborn woman from
a highly respected Republican family and recently widowed at the
age of 35.[214] Following her husband's death and her affair with
Catullus, she became enamored of the young Caelius, then twenty-
three. When their two-year liaison soured, it is thought that Clodia
instigated the fantastic charges brought against him.[215] Cicero defended Caelius with one of his more persuasive speeches; his primary
line of defense was to highlight the licentious behavior of Caelius'
accuser. Cicero portrays her as having lived like a prostitute and
depicts her as the antithesis to the ideal Roman matron. Her behavior
is "meretricious," and Cicero's speech emphasizes her sexual promis-

---

[210] More could be written on the banquet as a sensual setting, which of course
has its roots in the image of the symposium as a scene for erotic happenings. For the
sensual atmosphere of meal settings, see Achilles Tatius, 1.4.4–5; 5.4–6; 6.2–5; where
Clitophon sits near Leucippe at dinner, sees her beauty, and after falling in love with
her has lustful dreams (Hock, "Sexual Morality," 14); In Musonius Rufus, frg. 3,
women who take up philosophy must exercise sexual self control (Hock, "Sexual
Morality," 32); Pseudo-Lucian, *Amor.* 42–43, in which a woman's day includes flirting
with men at dinner and then indulging in adulterous unions (Hock, "Sexual Morality,"
16); Ovid. *Met.* 12.185–220, where a guest at a wedding banquet becomes consumed
with lust for the bride; Ovid, *Amor.* I, 4, where a husband and wife who recline
together on a couch are described in a most sexual way. Even cookbooks contained
sexual imagery (Hock, "Sexual Morality," 29).

[211] Lucian, *Asin.* 5; graffiti at Pompeii, D' Avino, *Women of Pompeii*, 73; Clement
of Alexandria, *Paed.* 2.7; Sir 9.9ff.

[212] Cantarella, *Pandora's Daughters*, 161.

[213] Cicero, *Pro Caelio*, Introduction, 398ff. Balsdon, *Roman Women*, 54ff.; Cantarella, *Pandora's Daughters*, 131–32; Grimal, *Love in Ancient Rome*, 148–56.

[214] Balsdon, *Roman Women*, 54.

[215] Ibid.

cuity.[216] Included in her meretricious behavior is her habit of eating with strangers:

> If a woman without a husband opens up her house to all men's desires, and publicly leads the life of a courtesan; if she is in the habit of attending dinner parties with men who are perfect strangers; if she does this in the city, in her park, amid all those crowds at Baiae; if, in fact, she so behaves then not only her bearing but her dress and her companions, not only the ardour of her looks and the licentiousness of her gossip but also her embraces and caresses, her beach parties, her water parties, her dinner-parties, proclaim her to be not only a courtesan, but also a shameless and wanton courtesan.[217]

Again the dichotomy between the categories of public and private come into play. Cicero explicitly names Clodia, an insult to any Roman matron, and describes her "public" behavior. She attends dinner parties with strange men in open-air places ("in the park," "in the city," "amid crowds") and invites men into her home for revels, as would the wealthy hetaerae of ancient Athens.[218] She dresses the part of a courtesan, which would mean that she wore the toga, or dressed in bright colors as did prostitutes.[219] Her conversation is also "licentious," as was Sempronia's, whose language was that of the brothel.[220] Cicero also compares Clodia to one of her own ancestors, Claudia, for whom the famous epitaph was written.[221] Claudia was also beautiful, but unlike Clodia she was the ideal Roman matron. She kept house, worked in wool, bore children and loved her husband.[222] Cicero describes Clodia as fulfilling none of these criteria. Her children are not mentioned and she roams public places rather than being at home. Her behavior betrays that her true vocation is prostitution.

The enumerating of women's virtues and vices in this manner is not at all uncommon in literature and inscriptions from the Greco-

---

[216] Ibid., 54–55; Mary R. Lefkowitz, "Invective Against Women," in *Heroines and Hysterics* (New York: St. Martin's Press, 1981), 32–40.

[217] Cicero, *Cael.* 20.44–49 (trans. R. Gardner). Gardner, *Cicero,* 466–67.

[218] Blümner, *Home Life of the Ancient Greeks,* 172ff.

[219] Ibid., 173; Kiefer, *Sexual Life in Ancient Rome,* 63. Sanger, *History of Prostitution,* 75.

[220] See pp. 56–57.

[221] Lefkowitz, "Invective," 32ff.; Cantarella, *Pandora's Daughters,* on Clodia, 131–32, on Claudia, 132–33.

[222] Cantarella, *Pandora's Daughters,* 133; Lefkowitz, "Invective," 32.

Roman world.[223] What is interesting is that during the imperial period, women's absence from banquets becomes one of the characteristics of the ideal woman. Similarly, dining without one's husband becomes a vice. Livy compares two women in this manner, one who attends a banquet without her husband, and another who remains home spinning wool alone.[224] Tacitus praises the chastity of German women, and comments that they have "no dinner tables with their provocations to corrupt them." Compared to licentious Roman matrons, these Germans also have fewer instances of adultery.[225] Athenaeus records the surprising practice of the Etruscans, whose women "dine, not with their own husbands, but with any men who happen to be present, and they pledge with wine any whom they wish."[226] Finally, Friedländer cites an epitaph of the wife of an imperial slave (unfortunately without a source) from Lower Moesia whose husband gives her the highest praise:

> She was the patron-saint of my home, my hope and my life. Her wishes were mine; her dislikes mine. None of her secret thoughts was concealed from me. She was a busy spinner, economical, but generous to her husband. She did not delight in eating, save with me. She was a good counsellor, prudent and noble.[227]

It would seem that a woman's dining habits revealed her true character, as did the other ideal virtues enumerated in epitaphs, such as devotion to home, motherhood, and modesty. Such glorifications of women in the Augustan age characterize the conservative emphasis on ideal roles for women during this period.[228]

---

[223] Arthur, "Liberated Women," 83–84; Cantarella, *Pandora's Daughters*, 129ff.; Friedländer, *Roman Life*, 264ff.; R. Lattimore, *Themes in Greek and Latin Epitaphs* (Illinois Studies in Language and Literature 28; Urbana: University of Illinois Press, 1942), 290ff.; Marjorie Lightman and William Zeisel, "Univira: An Example of Continuity and Change in Roman Society," *CH* 46 (March 1977): 19–32; Pomeroy, *Goddesses*, 161ff.; Torjesen, "Tertullian's 'political ecclesiology,' " 277–82; idem, "Women's Virtues and Vices," passim; Wicker, "Mulierum Virtutes," passim; idem, "First-Century Marriage Ethics: A Comparative Study of the Household Codes and Plutarch's Conjugal Precepts," in *No Famine in the Land. Studies in Honor of John L. McKenzie*, ed. James W. Flanagan and Anita Weisbrod Robinson (Missoula, Mont.: Scholars Press, 1975), 141–53.

[224] Livy, 1.57–60.

[225] Tacitus, *Germ.* 19.

[226] *Deipn.* 12.517D.

[227] Freidländer, *Roman Life*, 266.

[228] Arthur, "Liberated Women," 84–85.

"Prostitute" as a Topos in Greco-Roman Rhetorical Slander

Women associated with banquet settings were seen in the popular imagination as prostitutes. Certain Greco-Roman women did in fact attend dinners with their husbands. Yet areas influenced by Greek ideals and practices might exclude women from some meals, and certainly from those meals characterized as συμπόσια. Women who did attend such parties would have engendered a great deal of social criticism, particularly after the time of Augustus, when interest in maintaining the nuclear family as a means of insuring the political stability of the Empire shifted the social consciousness and reemphasized ideal women's roles. Absence from public banquets became part of that complex of ideas which eventually determined a woman's social status. This emphasis on women's traditional virtues eventually limited their ability to participate in the public sphere.

For obvious reasons, the term "prostitute" can be seen as the ultimate term in antiquity for maligning any woman, whatever her social status or occupation. The term "prostitute," or the accusation of meretricious behavior, could be leveled against women of all classes and vocations and does not seem to have been limited to describing lower-class freewomen, slave women, or actual prostitutes. Furthermore, the term had strong connections with the public behavior of women, particularly their unorthodox table etiquette or their free association with men in the public sphere.

In light of these observations, it is not surprising to find the term "prostitute" used in the context of philosophical repartee, in particular among philosophical schools that directed rhetorical slander at opponents during debates over philosophical systems.[229] Moreover, the use of this kind of slander by philosophical schools reveals the presence of women in philosophical groups. The Cynic school in particular was notable for including women, such as Hipparchia, and for defending women's ability to study philosophy and achieve moral virtue.[230] Epicureans practiced a communal lifestyle which included

---

[229] Luke T. Johnson, "The New Testament's Anti–Jewish Slander and the Conventions of Ancient Polemic," *JBL* 108 (1989): 419–41; esp. 431–32.

[230] *The Cynic Epistles*, esp. the Letters of Crates addressed to Hipparchia, illustrate non-traditional Cynic ideas on women's roles. In Lucian's *Fugitivi*, a female Cynic leaves her husband and runs away with two slaves. See F. Gerald Downing, *Jesus and the Threat of Freedom* (London: SCM Press, 1987), 115–21; idem, *Christ and the Cynics: Jesus and other Radical Preachers in First-Century Tradition* (JSOT Manuals 4; Sheffield: Sheffield Academic Press, 1988), 1–5.

women.[231] The women in Epicurean circles had diverse social backgrounds; many were slaves and courtesans, but many were also respectably married.[232] The Stoic philosopher Musonius Rufus also encouraged teaching women philosophy, albeit for the purpose of making them better wives and mothers.[233]

Since having a philosophical education was a characteristic of ancient Greek hetaerae, women in these groups were called "prostitutes" by rival philosophical sects. For example, Colotes, a follower of Epicurus, insults several of Plutarch's heroes by calling them names like "buffoon" (βωμολοχικός), "assassin" (ὁ ἀνδροφόνος), "nincompoop" (βαρυκέφαλος), and "prostitute" (ἑταίρη).[234] The "prostitute" Colotes refers to is undoubtedly Hipparchia,[235] who was from a noble family. Nevertheless, Hipparchia became enamoured with Cynic philosophy, married the noted Cynic philosopher Crates against her parents' wishes, and then traveled with him in public, attending public banquets at his side. Known for participating in philosophical discussions, she thought that her life was better spent in the pursuit of a philosophical education than wasted at the loom.[236] Likewise, in his sharp reply to Colotes, Plutarch repeats the evil gossip that Epicureans had prostitutes among their community; he also regularly accuses the Epicureans of sexual promiscuity.[237]

The term "prostitute," besides being viewed as an accusation of sexual promiscuity on the part of women in a group, was one of the standard charges of Hellenistic rhetoric and should be numbered among the polemical τόποι of Greco-Roman rhetorical slander. Slander indicated primarily that the other members of a philosophical group were in fact opponents; it might have little to do with the

---

[231] Wayne Meeks, "The Images of the Androgyne: Some Uses of a Symbol in Earliest Christianity," *HR* 13 (1974): 165–208, esp. 172.

[232] Catherine J. Castner, "Epicurean Hetairai As Dedicants to Healing Deities?" *GRBS* 23 (1982): 51–57; D. Smith, "Social Obligation," 57.

[233] William Klassen, "Musonius Rufus, Jesus and Paul: Three First-Century Feminists?" in *From Jesus to Paul. Studies in Honor of Francis Wright Beare*, ed. P. Richardson and J. Hurd (Ontario: Wilfred Laurier University Press, 1984), 185–206. See also Motto, "Seneca on Women's Liberation," for Seneca's encouragement of women in Stoic discipline and knowledge, and remarks by Wicker, "Mulierum Virtutes," 114.

[234] *Mor.* 1086E; Johnson, "Anti–Jewish Slander," 431.

[235] B. Einarson and P. DeLacey, *Plutarch's Moralia*, 14.16.

[236] Diog. Laert. 6.96–98.

[237] *Mor.* 1129B; Johnson, "Anti–Jewish Slander," 431.

actual character of the opponents so described. Such slander was a standard feature of sectarian debate.[238] This further buttresses the notion that identifying a woman as a "prostitute" did not necessarily indicate her actual social status or true vocation. This is also the case for such appellations as "tax-collector" or "prostitution tax-collector," the latter being an insult alternatively paired in various Hellenistic texts with "procurer," "pimp," or "brothel-keeper."[239] This holds true, moreover, for the term "sinner," which is paired with "tax-collector" in the Gospel accounts,[240] and the term "slave,"[241] both of which occur in the context of Jewish Hellenistic sectarian polemic.

David Balch has also determined that certain religious groups from the Roman era received the stereotypical criticism that their women were known for sexual immorality and that their organizations would contribute to the break-down of the state, the subversion of the household, and the destruction of the πολιτεία. Among these cultic communities were the Dionysus cult, the Egyptian Isis cult, and Judaism. Balch attributes this criticism to the continuation into the first century of earlier Aristotelian and Platonic concerns, which led to the rehearsal of the classical τόποι on household management on the part of Middle Platonists, Peripatetics, Stoics, Epicureans, Hellenistic Jews, and Neopythagoreans. The behavior of women participating in these religious groups, particularly aristocratic Roman women, was regarded as threatening not only to basic Roman household structures but also to the power of the state. This was a common conception of many Greco-Roman writers.[242]

Ancient myths of origins also reflect Greco-Roman fears that disruption of Hellenistic social hierarchy led ultimately to disaster and social revolution.[243] In response to such accusations of anti-social

---

[238] Johnson, "Anti-Jewish Slander," 432–33.

[239] See above, pp. 38–41.

[240] James D. G. Dunn, "Pharisees, Sinners and Jesus," in *The Social World of Formative Christianity and Judaism. Essays in Tribute to Howard Clark Kee*, ed. J. Neusner et al. (Philadelphia: Fortress Press, 1988), 274–80; D. Smith, "Jesus at Table," 466–86, esp. 474–84; Kathleen E. Corley, "Were the Women Around Jesus Really Prostitutes?" *SBL 1989 Seminar Papers*, 487–521, esp. 519–520. Increasingly, such terms are being recognized for their function as rhetoric and not historical description.

[241] Johnson, "Anti-Jewish Slander," 436.

[242] Balch, *Let Wives be Submissive*, chs. 5–6.

[243] Pierre Vidal-Naquet, "Slavery and the Rule of Women in Tradition, Myth and Utopia," in *Myth, Religion and Society*, ed. R. L. Gordon (Cambridge: Cambridge University Press, 1981), 187–200.

behavior, Hellenistic Jews like Josephus and Philo utilized the classical τόποι of Hellenistic household management to affirm that, rather than being sexually promiscuous, Jewish women did obey their husbands, nurture their children, and stay at home. To assert that Jewish women obeyed their husbands implied that they accepted the authority of Roman governors and the Emperor,[244] just as the accusation of promiscuity or the label of "prostitutes" indicated that the behavior of women in philosophical or religious groups was seen as threatening to Greco-Roman society. Such criticisms are therefore best understood as slander and not social description.

Jewish Meal Practice and Ideology in the Greco-Roman Era

Balch's research has established that Hellenistic writers also accused Jewish women of sexual promiscuity. Jewish inclusive table etiquette may have contributed to Jewish women's being labeled as promiscuous. Some scholars have doubted that Jewish women were included in community meals, using a restrictive table etiquette as a point of comparison between Hellenistic Judaism and inclusive early Christianity. Leonard Swidler automatically concludes that women in formative Judaism were simply excluded from all meals with men, and moreover were not even allowed to serve men at table.[245] However, the sources he uses to prove this are very late and may not be helpful in determining actual earlier Jewish practice.[246] Swidler's portrait of Jewish women's table customs fits in well with popular Christian generalizations concerning Jewish women's "low" status in the Greco-Roman world;[247] however, keeping in mind Bernadette J.

---

[244] Balch, *Let Wives be Submissive*, chs. 5–6.

[245] Leonard Swidler, *Women in Judaism. The Status of Women in Formative Judaism* (Metuchen, N.J.: Scarecrow Press, 1976), 125.

[246] Swidler uses third-century rabbinic texts and modern Palestinian practice to underscore his point.

[247] See for example, Lèonie J. Archer, "The Role of Jewish Women in the Religion, Ritual and Cult of Greco-Roman Palestine," in *Images of Women in Antiquity*, ed. Cameron and Kuhrt (Detroit: Wayne State University Press, 1983), 273–87; Swidler, *Women in Judaism*, passim. Archer's new book also follows this trend: *Her Price is Beyond Rubies: The Jewish Woman in Graeco-Roman Palestine* (JSOT Suppl. 60; Sheffield: JSOT Press, 1990). Barbara H. Geller Nathanson also complains about the anti–Judaic bias of many Christian interpreters in "Reflections on the Silent Woman of Ancient Judaism and Her Pagan Counterpart," in *The Listening Heart. Essays in Wisdom and the Psalms in Honor of Roland E. Murphy*, ed. K. G. Hoglund et al. (JSOT

Brooten's suggestions for a more sophisticated approach to recon-structing Jewish women's history,[248] it is more appropriate to allow for the possibility of diverse Jewish women's experience during these centuries.[249] Jewish women lived in the changing environment of the Greco-Roman world and were affected by the social developments around them. Jewish women also benefitted from the economic and legal changes of the Hellenistic world. There is evidence that some Jewish women had the right to divorce their husbands as did their Roman counterparts;[250] some were leaders and patronesses of their synagogues,[251] and some were educated in philosophy.[252] Some girls in Palestine even received a Greek education, though certain rabbis found this objectionable.[253] Moreover, many Greco-Roman women found Judaism, as well as Christianity and the Isis cult, attractive, as the evidence for female proselytes to Judaism attests.[254] We have also seen that Judaism, like the Isis cult, was accused for the sexual immorality of its women and that at least one Roman woman pros-elyte to Judaism was accused of meretricious behavior.[255] It is there-fore the case that Jewish women were also affected by the cultural undercurrents of the late Republic and early Empire, particularly as Palestinian Jews came under Roman domination during this period. Prior to the Augustan age, Palestinian Jews had been part of the

---

Suppl. 58; Sheffield: JSOT Press, 1987), 259–79.

[248] Bernadette J. Brooten, "Jewish Women's History in the Roman Period: A Task for Christian Theology," *HTR* 79 (1986): 22–30.

[249] Brooten, "Jewish Women's History," 25.

[250] See Brooten, "Jewish Women's History," 23, n. 3 for the literature on the debate over Jewish women's right to divorce in antiquity.

[251] Brooten, *Women Leaders in the Ancient Synagogue*; Shaye J. D. Cohen, "Women in the Synagogues of Antiquity," *ConservJudaism* 34 (1980): 23–29; Ross S. Kraemer, "Hellenistic Jewish Women: The Epigraphical Evidence," *SBL 1986 Seminar Papers* , ed. Kent Richards (Atlanta, Ga.: Scholars Press, 1986), 183–200.

[252] Philo describes women ascetics, the *Therapeutrides*, who dedicated their lives to the study of the Torah. See discussion below, pp. 70–71, and Brooten, "Jewish Women's History," 26; and more recently Ross S. Kraemer, "Monastic Jewish Women in Graeco-Roman Egypt: Philo Judaeus on the Therapeutrides," *Signs* 14 (1989): 342–70. Kraemer also mentions the Jewish women in Acts 16, apparently gathered at a synagogue for the study of the Torah when Paul finds them (367ff.).

[253] Saul Lieberman, *Greek in Jewish Palestine. Studies in the Life and Manners of Jewish Palestine in the II–IV Centuries C.E.* (New York: The Jewish Theological Seminary of America, 1942), 23–24.

[254] Brooten, "Jewish Women's History," 27; idem, *Women Leaders*, 144–47; Balsdon, *Roman Women*, 247.

[255] See pp. 56–57, esp. n. 199, and 65–67. above.

"Hellenistic" world for almost two centuries, as had Jews in the Diaspora.[256] Moreover, rabbinic literature reflects that, although rabbis continually warned townspeople not to adopt certain Hellenistic customs, they tolerated or even legalized many Hellenistic manners, customs, and superstitions.[257] We will see that Jewish women also attended public meals with men during the Hellenistic era.

Familiarity with banquet imagery may be assumed even in Palestine. Rabbinic literature from early Jewish Palestine shows a wide knowledge of the literature and cultures of the Hellenistic cultural world, including a knowledge of literary banquet motifs replete with male and female prostitutes.[258] It therefore should come as no surprise that Jewish meal customs during this period were quite similar in form to those in the rest of the Greco-Roman world.[259] Jewish formal meals were patterned after the Greco-Roman formal meal and included the normal order of a meal proper, followed in this case by a time for religious ritual.[260] Even the meal habits of the community of Qumran match those of the broader Greco-Roman world.[261] The literary form of the Passover Seder liturgy itself was greatly influenced by the traditions of symposium literature.[262] Moreover, the posture at the Passover meal was recumbent. Both the Mishnah and the Talmud indicate that the meal is to be taken reclining.[263] Although evidence from the Mishnah and the Talmud may not necessarily clarify first-century Jewish customs, there may be good reason to consider it more seriously in this instance. G. H. R. Horsley cites the comment of E. Ferguson, that

> It might be thought that this evidence is too late to confirm first-century practice; but the reason given for this posture in the Talmud,

---

[256] See Mack, *Myth of Innocence*, 45ff. for a solid discussion of the pervasive influence of Hellenic culture in Jewish communities at "all social levels."

[257] Lieberman, 91ff.

[258] Ibid., 47–50, 153ff.

[259] D. Smith, "Social Obligation," 178ff.; Klosinski, "Meals in Mark," 92.

[260] D. Smith, "Social Obligation," 178.

[261] Klosinski, "Meals in Mark," 92–93.

[262] Gordon J. Bahr, "The Seder of Passover and the Eucharistic Words," *NovT* 12 (1970): 181; S. Stein, "The Influence of Symposia Literature on the Literary Form of the Pesah Haggadah," *JJS* 8 (1957): 13–44; D. Smith, "Social Obligation," 178.

[263] m. *Pesaḥim* 10; b. *Pesaḥim* 108a; Bahr, *The Seder of Passover*, 190; G. H. R. Horsley, "Reclining at the Passover Meal," *New Documents Illustrating Early Christianity* 2 (Macquarie University, Australia: The Ancient History Documentary Research Centre, 1982), 75; Stein, "Symposia Literature," 17–18, 30–33.

namely as a sign of freedom, is such a thoroughly Greek reason that one should conclude that the practice dates from the Hellenistic period.[264]

Both the form of the meal and the recumbent posture of the Passover Seder meal may indeed reflect Greco-Roman meal customs.

It is noteworthy, therefore, that women are required to be present at the Passover meal and are also obliged to recline at their husband's side. This particularly applies to women of high standing (although one text makes reclining obligatory for ordinary house-wives as well).[265] Instructions concerning the distribution of gifts to women and children also make it clear that they were present for the proceedings.[266] That women began to recline at meals in the early imperial period adds further weight to Ferguson's suggestion that reclining at the Passover meal reflects an earlier Hellenistic practice and positions earlier Jewish customs squarely alongside those of their contemporaries. Archaeological evidence indicates that the fortress of Herod at Machaerus allowed for women at public meals. The fortress contains two dining rooms immediately alongside one an-other, one for women and one for men. That means that upper-class Jewish women attended public banquets with men but, like other Greco-Roman women, reclined separately.[267]

Although Jewish women may have been present and recumbent at the Passover Seder meal, there are instructions which exclude them from actual participation in the Seder liturgy.[268] Stein correctly compares this to the Greco-Roman practice of excluding women from the conversation portion of a banquet, the συμπόσιον.[269] Al-

---

[264] Horsley, "Reclining," 75.

[265] Stein, "Symposia Literature," 31, n. 71.

[266] Ibid., 29.

[267] See p. 29 above. For a description of Herod's fortress at Machaerus, see B. Schwank, "Neue Funde in Nabatäerstädten und ihre Bedeutung für die neutesta-mentliche Exegese," *NTS* 29 (1983): 429–35, esp. 434. Schwank suggests that this analysis of the fortress at Machaerus coheres with the description of Herod's sympo-sium in Mark 6:22 and 24, in that Herodias' daughter must "go out" from the men's company to speak to her mother. Mark's account, however, is highly fictionalized (See pp. 93–95 below). Schwank overviews recent studies on Nabatea and Petra in partic-ular, where archaeological finds suggest that long before Nabatea became a Roman province, it was heavily influenced by Roman and Hellenistic architecture and culture. Hence, Schwank suggests that Palestine may have been far more influenced by Hellenistic culture than has previously been supposed.

[268] Stein, "Symposia Literature," 32ff.; see also more recently Wegner, *Chattel or Person?* 156–57.

[269] Stein, "Symposia Literature," 31ff.

though women might be present for such proceedings, many were of the opinion that they should be quiet while there.[270] There is no way of knowing, however, just how strictly ancient Jewish communities adhered to this prohibition, particularly in the early part of the first century.

Evidence confirms, however, that Jewish men did encounter married women at a public banquet during the Hellenistic period, possibly even in Palestine. Sirach warns young men:

> Never dine with another man's wife, nor be in the habit of feasting with her with wine; lest your soul be inclined [ἐκκλίνω] to her and in your spirit you be plunged into destruction.[271]

Sirach also gives other instructions for banquet etiquette, such as avoiding overeating, watching one's wine consumption, speaking carefully, and not becoming too puffed up should one be given a high place at the table.[272] All such advice would fit in well with other Greco-Roman discussions of banquet etiquette. Notice, also, that sitting next to another man's wife in such a context might invite a sexual liaison.

Surprisingly, our best example of an inclusive dining community is Jewish. Philo discussed the dining habits of a first-century Alexandrian Jewish monastic community, the Therapeutic society, which consisted of both male (*Therapeutae*) and female (*Therapeutrides*) members.[273] In his discussion of their table customs, Philo contrasts their communal meals to Greek banquets. The pleasure derived from the meals of the Therapeutic society differs drastically from that of the Greeks, whose meals are known for their flute girls, jugglers, and other "unrestrained merrymaking," and for their focus on the passion for women—and even more shockingly—on the passion for men.[274] In contrast, the meals of the Therapeutic society transpire in quiet solemnity[275] and without alcoholic refreshment.[276] In place of theatrical or musical entertainment, these ascetics instead

---

[270] See pp. 30–31 above.

[271] Sir 9:9. Translation RSV with emendations from *The Oxford Annotated Apocrypha*, ed. Bruce M. Metzger (New York: Oxford University Press, 1965), 139–40.

[272] Sir 31:12—32:9.

[273] Here I am adopting the terminology of Ross Kraemer from her recent article, "Monastic Jewish Women," 343–44.

[274] Philo, *Vit. Cont.* 58.

[275] Ibid., 66.

[276] Ibid., 73.

join together in song and worship following their meal. Women, as well as men, fully participate in the after-dinner proceedings, which as we have seen, would have been unusual.[277] Since Philo is comparing the banquet practice of the Therapeutic society to that of the Greeks, the presence of women in such a context could also be part of his comparison; this would have been surprising to some of his readers.[278] The dedication of these women to the study of philosophy would have shocked some, as would their participation in the after-dinner singing.[279] Moreover, Philo unmistakably says that the women recline as the men do, the men by themselves on the right and the women by themselves on the left,[280] on either side of a double enclosure with a partition that does not extend all the way to the ceiling.[281] This segregation is not inexplicable given the ascetic nature of the group and the potential for sexual encounter latent in meal settings. Philo is also careful to emphasize the chastity of the women, which would also contrast with women known to frequent Greek banquets.[282] Here we have an example of a Jewish communal meal that includes women, albeit a small minority of well-educated women with a relatively high economic standing from Alexandria.[283]

From this sort of evidence it is difficult to determine the everyday meal practice of Jews in first-century Palestine and the Diaspora; nonetheless, it seems that Jewish men expected to find married women at a banquet, that women were required to recline next to their husbands at the Passover Seder, and that certain wealthy Jewish women participated in the communal meals of an ascetic Jewish community in Alexandria. Such table practices would have been notable in any Greco-Roman context and may in part explain the accusations of promiscuity leveled against Jewish women. Furthermore, excluding women from participating in the Seder liturgy is not

---

[277] Ibid., 80.

[278] Kraemer, "Monastic Jewish Women," 347ff.; D. Smith, "Table Fellowship," 616, n. 9.

[279] Kraemer, "Monastic Jewish Women," 347ff.

[280] *Vit. Cont.* 69.

[281] Kraemer, "Monastic Jewish Women," 345.

[282] *Vit. Cont.* 68; see Kraemer ("Monastic Jewish Women," 352ff.), where she suggests that these women may have been post-menopausal rather than never-married virgins; D. Smith ("Table Fellowship," 616, n. 9), also comments that the presence of women in the meals of the Therapeutic society would be a point of comparison between their meals and those of the Greeks.

[283] Kraemer, "Monastic Jewish Women," 349.

unexpected, given the opinion of many that women were to be barred from after-dinner activities, and that when their presence was allowed they were to keep quiet. The practice of the Therapeutic society, then, becomes all the more noteworthy, since the women members remained for the duration of the meal and participated fully in the worship liturgy.

The evidence for Jewish meal practice seems to correspond to that of their Greco-Roman contemporaries; consequently it is not surprising that discussions of women and women's roles in Jewish literature also reflect concern for traditional ideology governing the participation of women in banquet settings. Due to the sexual connotations of banquet settings, women present at such events would be targets for sexual advances. For instance, Sirach warns Jewish men against sitting next to women at banquets, and Philo is careful to emphasize the chastity of the *Therapeutrides*. At the Passover Seder, women are required to recline next to their husbands, rather than next to any man present.

Even for Philo, the stereotypical female who attends dinner parties with men is a whore. In the *Sacrifices of Abel and Cain* he contrasts virtue (ἀρετή) with pleasure (ἡδονή) by using the two images of the party-going prostitute and the respectable matron:

> So Pleasure comes languishing in the guise of a harlot [πόρνη] or courtesan [χαμαιτύπη]. Her gait has the looseness which her extravagant wantonness and luxury has bred; . . . her costly raiment is broidered lavishly with flowers; . . . a strumpet of the streets she takes the marketplace for her home. . . . [284]

Pleasure offers many things to those who pursue her, including:

> . . . [S]weet modulations of melodious sounds, costly kinds of food and drink, abundant varieties of delicious perfumes, amours without ceasing, frolics unregulated, chamberings unrestricted, language unrepressed, deeds uncensored, life without care, sleep soft and sweet, satiety ever filled. . . . I will join you in considering what food and drink would charm your palate, what sight would please your eyes, what sounds your ears, what perfume your nostrils.[285]

Virtue, "hidden from sight, yet within earshot," comes forward:

---

[284] Philo, *Sacr.* 21–22 (trans. F. H. Colson and G. H. Whitaker).
[285] Philo, *Sacr.* 22–24.

with all the marks of a freeborn citizen, a firm tread, a serene counte-
nance, her person and her modesty alike without false colouring . . .
her movements quiet, her clothing plain, her adornment that of good
sense and virtue. . . . And in her company came piety, holiness, truth,
justice, religion, fidelity to oaths and bonds . . . continence, meekness,
a quiet temper. . . . Ranged on each side with her in their midst, they
formed her body-guard.[286]

Like other writers in the first century, Philo contrasts the ideal
matron to the far-from-ideal courtesan. The courtesan is likened to
a slavegirl, a "public" woman who inhabits the streets, one known for
her flashy clothing and association with revelry. The ideal matron,
however, is freeborn, not a slave, hidden from sight, modest,
quiet, plainly clothed, and always escorted.[287] That Philo categorizes
women in this manner is not unexpected, given that he, like other
writers of the Greco-Roman world, held to the public/private dichotomy where women's roles were concerned.[288] Marketplaces and coun-
cil-halls were the domain of men, not respectable women, who were
better suited for the indoor life.[289] A respectable freeborn woman:

should not be a busybody, meddling with matters outside her household concerns, but should seek a life of seclusion. She should not shew
herself off like a vagrant in the streets before the eyes of other men,
except when she has to go to the temple, and even then she should
take pains to go, not when the market is full, but when most people
have gone home, and so like a freeborn lady worthy of the name, with
everything quiet around her, make her oblations. . . . [290]

Philo goes on to chasten women who argue with men in the
streets, even those who do so in order to assist in the arguments of
their husbands. Elsewhere he suggests that women were secluded in
Jewish households.[291] However, Philo's own comments here, as well
as documentary evidence to the contrary, undermine his description

---

[286] Philo, *Sacr.* 26–27.

[287] During the Roman period, well-bred women rarely went out unescorted. At
the least, they would take along a female slave. Veyne comments that the custom of
requiring this "mobile prison" was the Roman equivalent of the Greek *gynecaeum*
(Veyne, "Roman Empire," in *History of Private Life*, 1.73), and in fact had the same
result: the isolation of women.

[288] Kraemer, "Monastic Jewish Women," 355–56.

[289] Philo, *Spec. Leg.* 3.169ff.

[290] Philo, *Spec. Leg.* 3.170–71 (trans. F. H. Colson).

[291] Philo, *Flacc.* 89; Kraemer, "Monastic Jewish Women," 356.

that all the women of the Jewish community at Alexandria behaved in traditional "private" fashion.[292] Not all Jewish women in Alexandria stayed in their homes, kept quiet in public, or avoided public banquets.[293] It is not unreasonable to assume that Philo saw those Jewish matrons who overstepped their private roles and entered the public realm of men as acting like the courtesan he describes in the *Sacrifices of Abel and Cain*. Like other writers during the Roman period, Philo contrasts the ideal matron and the courtesan to influence the picture of proper behavior for Jewish women.

Josephus also shows concern for Greco-Roman propriety. As well as defending Jewish women as being proper Roman matrons who obeyed their husbands,[294] Josephus rewrites stories about women from the Septuagint that betray a similar concern. In *Antiquities*, Josephus recounts the history of the Jewish people, one which would be "respectable in content and appealing in format to his audience" (i.e., Romans and Greek-speaking Jews.)[295] In every instance, Josephus recasts ancient Jewish women like Sarah, Rebekah, and Rachel as ideal Hellenistic heroines, known for chastity, silence, and devotion to husband and hearth. Because they are virtuous women, Sarah and Rebekah are never portrayed as preparing food or serving guests a meal. Rather, the men play the hosts. During meals the women are submissive, quiet, and secluded. Amaru notes that these modest characterizations of biblical women fit "a hellenized picture."[296] Even Rahab the Harlot is not identified as such, but is rather called an "innkeeper" and is not described in seductive detail.[297] Conversely, Josephus also casts female characters from the Septuagint as villainesses. The unnamed wife of Potiphar and the Midianite women serve as antiheroines "whose vices run directly counter to his matriarchal heroines."[298] These women are neither chaste nor virtuous, but are portrayed as seductresses. The Midianite women seek to ensnare the Israelite men by coming to their camp and trying to seduce

---

[292] Kraemer, "Monastic Jewish Women," 356.

[293] Ibid., 355–56.

[294] Balch, *Let Wives Be Submissive*, 73, 83, 85, 90.

[295] Betsy Halpern Amaru, "Portraits of Biblical Women in Josephus' Antiquities," *JJS* 39 (1988): 143–70. Quote from 143.

[296] Ibid., 147, n. 14.

[297] Ibid., 160.

[298] Ibid., 153ff.

them under the guise of hospitality. The wife of Potiphar becomes a "Phaedra-like character, driven by passion and lust."[299] By editing the biblical stories in this manner, Josephus hoped to present an appealing picture of Judaism to Romans critical of the Jewish faith. Like Philo, Josephus was also attempting to influence the behavior of Greek-speaking Jewish women.[300]

The Jewish materials fit well into the context of Hellenistic sources that reflect Greco-Roman ideology governing women's participation in formal meals, and they reflect a concern for actual meal practices of Jewish women. Some of the women participating in this innovation of meal practice during the Roman period were obviously Jewish. As a target of Hellenistic writers who characterized Jewish women as promiscuous, Judaism is undoubtedly one of the religious and philosophical groups that allowed women to participate in public meals with men.[301]

Christian Women and Public Meals

One additional Hellenistic religion falls under Greco-Roman criticism for the promiscuous behavior of its women: early Christianity. Like Judaism and certain Eastern cults, early Christianities[302] were considered a threat to Greco-Roman social order.[303] Included in Greco-Roman slander against Christian groups was a criticism of their inclusive dining practices. Minucius Felix, a third-century Christian writer, lists the slanderous charges leveled against Christian groups by non-Christians:

---

[299] Ibid., 155. See also Lèonie J. Archer, "The 'Evil Woman' in Apocryphal and Pseudepigraphical Writings" in *Proceedings of the Ninth World Congress of Jewish Studies, Jerusalem, August 4–12, 1985* (Jerusalem: The World Union of Jewish Studies, 1986), 239–46.

[300] Amaru, *Portraits*, 143, n. 1.

[301] Another study carefully aligning Jewish Greco-Roman women alongside their Hellenistic counterparts, is Nathanson, "Silent Woman of Ancient Judaism," 259–79. Nathanson also mentions the Roman authors' descriptions of Jewish women as promiscuous (265), and argues that the life of Jewish women during the Roman period differed little from that of their Hellenistic peers, including Christian women.

[302] This is a term coined by Jonathan Z. Smith. See *Drudgery Divine. On the Comparison of Early Christianities and the Religions of Late Antiquity* (Chicago: Chicago University Press, 1990), vii–viii, 109–13, 135–42. Smith also endeavors to dispel the notion that early forms of Christianity were unique in their Hellenistic context.

[303] Balch, *Let Wives Be Submissive*, esp. ch. 6.

These people gather together illiterates from the very dregs of society and credulous women who easily fall prey because of the weakness of their sex. They organize a mob of wicked conspirators, who join together at nocturnal assemblies and ritual fasts and inhuman dinners. . . . Everywhere they share a kind of religion of lust, and promiscuously call one another brothers and sisters so that even ordinary sexual intercourse becomes incest by the use of a sacred name. . . . On holy days they gather for a banquet with all their children, sisters, and mothers, people of both sexes and all ages. There, after many courses of food, the party heats up and the passion of incestuous lust inflames those who are drunk. . . . In the shameless darkness they are indiscriminately wrapped in shocking embraces. . . . [304]

Such accusations undoubtedly led Greco-Roman Christians to guard the reputations of their communities. Given the pervasive Greco-Roman ideology surrounding women's proper table etiquette, it is therefore not surprising that Christian art and literature, like other Hellenistic sources, reflect concern for women's behavior and posture at meals. A telling piece of evidence is a late first-century fresco from the catacomb of St. Priscilla in Rome, the "Fractio Panis." In this fresco seven women are sharing a Eucharistic celebration. Six women are reclining at the table, with arms outstretched over the eucharistic elements. The seventh woman is sitting up, undoubtedly because she is meant to be pictured as breaking the eucharistic bread being distributed to the others. There are no men in this scene, only women; it is not a mixed group. There are other similar depictions of eucharistic meals in the catacombs in which all the participants are men. Dorothy Irvin, in her analysis of this fresco and others, comes to the following conclusion:

These eucharistic scenes show us that all-night cemetery vigils were held by small groups in which all of the members were of the same sex and that they should all be of the same sex is easy to understand in view of what we know about the early Christian concern with moral standards, and particularly the seemly conduct of their religious gatherings in the eyes of unbelievers. [305]

---

[304] Minucius Felix, *Octavius* 8.4–12.5; Translation from Jo-Ann Shelton, *As the Romans Did. A Sourcebook in Roman Social History* (Oxford: Oxford University Press, 1988), 417–18. See also Robert L. Wilken, *The Christians as the Romans Saw Them* (New Haven and London: Yale University Press, 1984), 15–47.

[305] Dorothy Irvin, "The Ministry of Women in the Early Church: The Archaeological Evidence," *Duke Divinity School Review* 45 (1980): 76–86. Quote from

Like the *Therapeutrides*, these Christian women are reclining for a ritual meal separately from men. What Irvin here infers to be a specifically Christian concern for morality is in fact a concern for meal propriety which pervaded all of Greco-Roman society during these centuries.[306]

Another helpful example of early Christian concern for Greco-Roman meal customs is found in the writings of Clement of Alexandria. Clement of Alexandria gives very conservative instruction for the attendance of women at banquets late in the second century. Again, Clement's restriction of women's activity shows a domestication of morals that is independent of Christian teaching.[307] Raised a pagan, being well versed in the Greek culture of his time, Clement understandably shows an interest in table etiquette and the impression Christians might make at a public banquet. He warns young people, both men and women, to avoid large festivals, which were known for settings in which members of both sexes might be carried away by sexual passion, particularly since it was one of the main opportunities for young people to meet. Young virgins were particularly vulnerable in such settings.[308] Clement preferred that even married women not be present for banquets in general, but if they must attend, they should be well-clothed. He warns men against reclining next to women, since the influence of wine might lead to lust:[309]

> But if any necessity arises, commanding the presence of married women (at a banquet), let them be well clothed—without by raiment, within by modesty. But as for such as are unmarried, it is the extremest scandal for them to be present at a banquet of men, especially men under the influence of wine.

Here Clement discourages unmarried women from attending under any circumstances.[310] Further in his discussion, Clement ex-

---

83–84. See also Graydon F. Snyder, *Ante Pacem. Archaeological Evidence of Church Life Before Constantine* (Atlanta: Mercer University Press, 1985), 21–26, 64–65, for descriptions of eucharistic meal scenes in early frescoes, and pp. 132–33 for the inscriptions from the catacomb of St. Priscilla.

[306] The description of the widows who are seated and served separately in Acts 6 could also be seen as an example of this type of gender-segregated seating.

[307] See Averil Cameron, "Redrawing the Map: Early Christian Territory After Foucault," *JRS* 76 (1986): 266–71; see esp. 267.

[308] Clement of Alexandria, *Paed.* 2.7; Hock, "Sexual Morality," 13–14.

[309] Clement of Alexandria, *Paed.* 2.7.54, 2. Translation from ANF, vol. 2, p. 252.

[310] See pp. 29–30 above.

horts the married women at such settings to be silent and to resist drinking too much.[311] Traditional Greco-Roman meal ideology and a concern for feminine propriety almost certainly prompted Clement to restrict the behavior of Christian women in public meals. We have seen that the impetus for Clement's teaching has its roots in a larger cultural trend rather than in a specifically Christian morality.

Conclusions on Greco-Roman Table Etiquette and Meal Ideology

From the late Republican to the early imperial period, changing social patterns affected women's participation in public formal meals or banquets. Meal customs were shifting during this period of Roman history, so that women began to attend public meals, a behavior associated with lower-class women, prostitutes, freedwomen, and slaves. Central to Greco-Roman meal ideology was the continued association of sexuality, slavery, and prostitution with banquet settings. Women who attended public meals were labeled "promiscuous" or "prostitutes." Slander connecting "liberated" behavior with "meretricious" behavior was used against those women who overstepped ideal womanly roles or who ate meals with men. Traditional meal ideology thus limited the actual participation of women in public meals. Women in Hellenistic religious and philosophical groups were subject to such accusations of sexual promiscuity against their women members. Religious groups whose women were accused of scandalous behavior include the Dionysus cult, the Egyptian Isis cult, Hellenistic Judaism, and early Christianity. Greco-Roman Cynics and Epicureans were two philosophical sects whose women members were called "prostitutes" by rival philosophical groups. This kind of slander during the Hellenistic era was often precipitated by the observation of socially innovative dining practices which included women.

This social innovation in meal practice and the concern that such innovation elicited on the part of Greco-Roman people pervaded all Hellenistic society, as can be shown from a review of art and literature from the second century BCE through the third century CE.

---

[311] *Paed.* 2.7.

Unfortunately, social ideology about women's table etiquette was not advancing at the same rate as women's actual behavior. Thus, the reaction against these women entering the "public" sphere was pervasive and harsh. However, whether they were slaves or freedwomen, freeborn or married, Jewish or Gentile, many of these women, along with other women who participated in public meals, philosophical schools, or religions of their choice, did not deserve such aspersions upon their character. Participation in public meals was merely one aspect of the new limited freedom of Greco-Roman women during the early Empire, a freedom that, as we will see, was shared by women in the Jesus movements.

Part II

Women and Meals
in the Synoptic Gospels

Women and Meals in the Gospel of Mark

Women figure prominently in the Gospel of Mark. Mark's narrative includes a series of four chreiai which feature them;[1] women are healed and receive exorcism; they are present at the cross and the tomb; and they are disciples. Moreover, the Gospel of Mark portrays women in meal gatherings. Women are present for meals, both as servants and as participants in the scene created by the slander that Jesus "eats and drinks" with "tax-collectors and sinners." Such a characterization is a typical slur upon those known for banqueting with "promiscuous" women and pimps, and Mark is fully aware that such depictions reflect these slanderous clichés. Nonetheless, of all the Synoptics, Mark seems the least concerned about the scandalous connotations of the stories involving women that he incorporates into his Gospel. He acknowledges the social conservatism of the Hellenistic world around him, particularly by keeping women primarily in private scenes; however, Mark's storytelling usually shows a concern for matters other than the seemingly scandalous behavior of the women in his account. Thus, although women are firmly embedded in his narrative, Mark is unconcerned about possible social criticism from outsiders that his narrative might produce. This chapter examines passages in Mark that connect women to meals.

---

[1]After a brief discussion of Greco-Roman rhetoric and the study of the Gospels, Mary Ann Beavis identifies four pericopes which contain chreiai about women in Mark: the stories of the woman with the hemorrhage of blood (Mark 5:24–34), the Syro-Phoenician woman (Mark 7:24–30), the poor widow (Mark 12:41–44), and the woman who anoints Jesus (Mark 14:3–9). See "Women as Models of Faith in Mark," *BTB* 18 (1988): 3–9.

The Women who "Follow" and "Serve" (Mark 15:40–41)

Most discussions of women in Mark begin with Mark 15:40–
41, a pericope not often considered as connecting women to meals.
Toward the end of his Gospel, Mark makes it clear that several
women have been part of the group following Jesus throughout the
story, indicating that women number among the disciples of Jesus.[2]

---

[2]In "Women Disciples in Mark?" *CBQ* 44 (1982): 225–41, Winsome Munro
argues that women are indeed among Jesus' disciples, but that Mark is evasive about
this. Still, she suggests that women are present to witness key kerygmatic events. In
response to Munro's somewhat negative analysis of Mark's attitude toward women,
several scholars have suggested that Mark does not hold off mentioning the women
until chapter 15 in order to "evade" them, but rather to position the women as positive
foils to the unbelieving male disciples or to emphasize that the women are part of the
larger group of fallible disciples: Beavis, "Women as Models of Faith," 3–9; Joanna
Dewey, *Disciples of the Way: Mark on Discipleship* (Women's Division, Board of Global
Ministries, UMC, 1976), 123–37; Joseph A. Grassi, "The Secret Heroine of Mark's
Drama," *BTB* 18 (1988): 10–15; Jane Kopas, "Jesus and Women in Mark's Gospel,"
Review for Religious 44 (1985): 912–20; Elizabeth Struthers Malbon, "Fallible Followers: Women and Men in the Gospel of Mark," *Semeia* 28 (1983), 29–48; see also
Malbon's *Narrative Space and Mythic Meaning in Mark* (San Francisco: Harper and
Row, 1986), 35–37; Marla J. Schierling, "Women as Leaders in the Markan Commu-
nities," *Listening* 15 (1980): 250–56; John J. Schmitt, "Women in Mark's Gospel," *BT*
19 (1981): 228–33; Marla J. Selvidge, "And Those Who Followed Feared (Mark
10:32)," *CBQ* 45 (1983): 396–400. Other scholars have concurred with this discussion, such as Charles W. Hedrick, "Narrator and Story in the Gospel of Mark:
Hermeneia and Paradosis," *PerRelSt* 14 (1987): 239–58; see esp. 253ff.; Ched Myers,
Binding the Strong Man. A Political Reading of Mark's Story of Jesus (Maryknoll, N.Y.:
Orbis Books, 1988), 280ff.; as well as various interpreters of women in the Gospels,
such as Schüssler Fiorenza, Selvidge, Witherington, Moltmann-Wendel, Stagg,
Swidler et al. Such a reading of Mark's Gospel lends support to Schüssler Fiorenza's
thesis that the early Jesus movements attracted women because they allowed for a
"discipleship of equals" (see *In Memory of Her*, 148–52). Before Winsome Munro's
article, the scholarly consensus was that the women of Mark 15:40–41 were not
disciples but were present only for menial purposes. See, for example, Howard Clark
Kee, *Community of the New Age. Studies in Mark's Gospel* (Philadelphia: Westminster
Press, 1977), 152ff. The discussion concerning women disciples falls under the larger
discussion of discipleship in general in Mark's Gospel. It has long been recognized
that the disciples in Mark are a rather hard-headed group. Wrede was the first to
notice this theme (*The Messianic Secret*), which was eventually given a polemical
function against either the Jerusalem leadership, or sometimes a "divine man"
Christology. See for example, Paul J. Achtemeier, "The Disciples in Mark," in *Mark*
(Philadelphia: Fortress Press, 1986), 105–13; Ernest Best, "The Role of the Disciples
in Mark," *NTS* 23 (1977): 377–401; idem, *Following Jesus: Discipleship in the Gospel of
Mark* (JSOT Suppl. 4; Sheffield: JSOT Press, 1981); idem, *Disciples and Discipleship:
Studies in the Gospel According to Mark* (Edinburgh: T. and T. Clark, 1986); Dewey,
Disciples of the Way; James M. Robinson, *The Problem of History in Mark and Other
Markan Studies* (Philadelphia: Fortress Press, 1985); Robert C. Tannehill, "The

Like their male counterparts, the women form a subset of Jesus' followers with a triumvirate core (Peter, James, and John/Mary Magdalene, Mary the mother of James and John, and Salome). They similarly flee the scene, show fear of epiphany, do not understand what is happening, and do not do as they are told.[3] These women, Mary, Mary, and Salome, are said to both "follow" (ἀκολουθέω) Jesus and "minister" (διακονέω) to him,[4] along with "many others" (ἄλλαι πολλαί). Thus, like the male disciples or students, women have "followed" Jesus from Galilee to Jerusalem.

Even though Mark highlights the women's discipleship by his use of ἀκολουθέω, behind his nonchalant depiction of the women as disciples is the undercurrent of scandal. This same description also portrays these women as Jesus' slaves and table servants. First of all, slaves or servant women characteristically would "follow" along behind their master, as would a female lover or sex slave.[5] A quote from Philostratus' *Life of Apollonius* makes this image clear:

> And as they fared on into Mesopotamia, the tax-gatherer [τελώνης] who presided over the Bridge (*Zeugma*) led them to the registry and asked them what they were taking out of the country with them. And Apollonius replied: "I am taking with me temperance, justice, virtue, continence, valour, discipline [σωφροσύνην, δικαιοσύνην, ἀρετήν, ἐγκράτειαν, ἀνδρείαν, ἄσκησιν]." And in this way he strung together a number of feminine nouns or names. The other, already scenting his own perquisites, said, "You must then write down in the register these female slaves [τὰς δούλας]." Apollonius answered, "Im-

---

Disciples in Mark: the Function of a Narrative Role," in *The Interpretation of Mark*, ed. W. Telford (Philadelphia: Fortress Press; London: SPCK, 1985), 134–57.

[3] Malbon, "Fallible Followers," passim. So also David Catchpole, "The Fearful Silence of the Women at the Tomb: A Study in Markan Theology," *JThSoAfrica* 18 (1977): 3–10; Grassi, "Secret Heroine," 14; Munro, "Women Disciples," 230–31; Selvidge, "And Those Who Followed Feared," passim; Tannehill, "Disciples," 152. Schmitt suggests that the women may be silent because they do not expect to be believed, due to the misogynist culture of the time (232). Jonathan Z. Smith suggests that the Markan disciples are similar to other characters in various Greco-Roman Vitae who constantly misunderstand their teacher's message and later betray him. See "Good News is No News: Aretalogy and Gospel," in *Christianity, Judaism and Other Greco-Roman Cults. Studies for Morton Smith at Sixty*, part 1, ed. Jacob Neusner (Leiden: Brill, 1975), 21–38.

[4] Dewey, *Disciples of the Way*, 123ff.; Malbon, "Fallible Followers," 40ff.; Munro, "Women Disciples," 230ff. So also Kopas, "Jesus and Women in Mark's Gospel," 912ff.; Schmitt, "Women in Mark's Gospel," 231–32; and Schierling, "Women as Leaders," 252ff.

[5] Kittel, "ἀκολουθέω, κτλ," *TDNT*, 1.210.

possible, for they are not female slaves that I am taking out with me, but ladies of quality [δεσποίνας]."[6]

The assumption of the tax-collector in this scene is that a large number of women traveling with a man in this manner would necessarily be the man's slaves. Apollonius' response further underscores for us that a man's traveling companions would typically be characterized as unvirtuous or "promiscuous" women. Apollonius' witty remark is nonsensical without this underlying connection between slave women and promiscuity. Thus, the women in Mark 15:40–41 could easily be categorized, not as the disciples Mark wishes to portray, but as sexually available slaves. It may be concern for Greco-Roman propriety that leads Mark to have the women stand "from afar" during the crucifixion proper. They are no doubt waiting to perform the tasks of burial usually assigned to women in the ancient world.[7]

Secondly, the very language of this passage calls to mind the image of women who "serve" Jesus "at table," a task often allotted to slave women in a household.[8] In Mark, it is only the women and angels that are said to "serve" Jesus himself, and even the angels no doubt are meant to "serve" Jesus by bringing him food after his long fast (Mark 1:13).[9] Thus, the connection between the service rendered by these women to Jesus and the preparation of food and meal settings is clear.[10] Mark 15:40–41 also indicates that these women disciples have been present at meals. The converging images of slavery, table service, and sexuality would not have been lost on a Hellenistic audience familiar with Greco-Roman meal protocol. Mark, however, seems unconcerned about these associations and easily incorporates this description of the women into his larger theme of discipleship.

---

[6] Philostratus, *Life of Apollonius of Tyana* 1.20 (trans. F. C. Conybeare).

[7] See p. 105 below.

[8] See pp. 48–49 above; H. W. Beyer, "διακονέω, κτλ," *TDNT*, 2.81ff. Young men sometimes fulfilled this duty as well.

[9] Beyer, "διακονέω, κτλ," 85.

[10] In a more general sense, διακονέω could indicate a more general provision of care, and it is in this wider sense that it is most often used of the work of women (Beyer, "διακονέω, κτλ," 82). See also Pomeroy, on women as food and drink servers in taverns and food counters (*Goddesses*, 201).

Peter's Mother-in-Law (Mark 1:29–31)

In one of the Gospel's first scenes, a short pericope depicts a woman serving Jesus a meal, which acts out the later activity of the women disciples in Mark 15:40–41. Here Jesus heals Peter's mother-in-law, who then proceeds to serve Jesus and his friends a meal.[11] In other places in Mark's Gospel, Jesus shows his willingness to heal women as well as men, and here the healing of a woman is paired with that of a man (Mark 1:21–28).[12]

This miracle story shows signs of Markan additions.[13] In its present form this pericope has been organized to reflect the common pattern of Greco-Roman miracle tales: (1) healing by touch; (2) immediate cure; and (3) activity on the part of the person cured which confirms the healing.[14] By saying that the fever "leaves" (ἀφίημι) her, Mark's account of the healing also reflects the ancient notion that illnesses were caused by evil spirits. This is reminiscent of the earlier exorcisms which open the Gospel.[15] Upon entering the house, Jesus' disciples inform him that Peter's mother-in-law is ill: this is designed either to bring her illness to his attention or to warn him that her usual service and hospitality might not be available.[16] Regardless, immediately following her healing, the woman gets up and "serves" (διακονέω) Jesus and his friends. When a family did not have house servants, women often performed this service for family members and close friends. Thus, her service should be limited to the physical or menial task of "table service."[17] Nonetheless, since men who are

---

[11] From 1 Cor 9:5 we know that Peter was married and was in the habit of taking his wife along on his missionary journeys, although she is not mentioned here.

[12] Witherington, *Women in the Ministry of Jesus*, 66.

[13] Gerd Theissen, *The Miracle Stories of the Early Christian Tradition* (Philadelphia: Fortress Press, 1983), 180; R. Bultmann, *History of the Synoptic Tradition*, trans. John Marsh (Oxford: Basil Blackwell, 1963), 212.

[14] Howard Clark Kee, *Miracle in the Early Christian World: A Study in Sociohistorical Method* (New Haven and London: Yale University Press, 1983), 170; Witherington, *Women in the Ministry of Jesus*, 66.

[15] Theissen, *Miracle Stories*, 86; Robert Guelich, *Mark 1—8:26. Word Biblical Commentary* (Dallas, Tex.: Word Books, 1989), 62.

[16] In any case, the comment is redundant. Witherington, *Women in the Ministry of Jesus*, 67; C. S. Mann, *Mark*. Anchor Bible (Garden City, N.Y.: Doubleday, 1986), 215; Theissen, *Miracle Stories*, 180.

[17] So Witherington, *Women in the Ministry of Jesus*, 68.

not members of her immediate family are present, the term διακονέω could carry scandalous overtones when performed by a woman in the context of a meal.[18] Mark does nothing to emphasize her activity, and the woman does not join the men for their meal. In this context, the service of Peter's mother-in-law merely verifies her healing;[19] the assertion that Mark here depicts a female diaconate is certainly incorrect.[20] Rather, the private, silent, Hellenistic role of a woman is quite naturally depicted in a domestic scene.[21]

---

[18] The scandalous nature of her service is due to Hellenistic sensibilities, not Jewish ones. It has sometimes been assumed that Jewish women were prohibited from serving men at meals, so that Jesus' allowance of the woman's service indicates his reform of Jewish society and religion (so Str. -B. 1:480; Dewey, *Disciples of the Way*, 123–25; Swidler, *Women in Judaism*, 125; Witherington, *Women in the Ministry of Jesus*, 68). Such comments are certainly incorrect, particularly since the sources used to support such allegations are from the third to fourth centuries. On the contrary, Jewish meal customs differed little from those of their Hellenistic contemporaries. In opposition to Str.–B. et al. are Guelich, *Mark 1—8:26*, 63 and Samuel Tobias Lachs, *A Rabbinic Commentary on the New Testament. The Gospels of Matthew, Mark and Luke* (Hoboken, N.J.: KTAV Publishing House; New York: Anti-Defamation League of B'nai B'rith, 1987), 62.

[19] Beyer, "διακονέω, κτλ," 85; Bultmann, *History*, 212; Guelich, *Mark 1—8:26*, 63; Kee, *Miracle*, 170; Witherington, *Women in the Ministry of Jesus*, 66.

[20] This is in opposition to Malbon ("Fallible Followers," 35) and Selvidge ("Those Who Followed," 398). Selvidge asks, "Would the Markan writer preserve a story about Jesus healing a woman just for the purpose of fixing him dinner or demonstrating her 'village hospitality'?" Kopas ("Jesus and Women in Mark's Gospel") sees the woman's service as an example of "risk taking in service," 912f. Malbon's suggestion that this is meant to be a "house-church" scene is certainly incorrect, as this is rather an example of Mark's tendency to place scenes involving women in private (Munro, "Women Disciples," 227). The exception is the scene with the woman with the hemorrhage, a person who Jesus does not seek out on his own (5:24–34). Jairus' daughter is healed in a private home (5:35–43), and Mark goes to redactional lengths to place the Syro-Phoenician woman inside a house at the time of her request. Her daughter is then healed "at home" (7:24–30). Moreover, during the feedings, which clearly have Eucharistic overtones, διακονέω is not the term used of the men's activity of serving the bread, but rather the verb παρατίθημι (6:41; 8:6). These meals are also cast as symposia, and only men are present (6:30ff.; 8:1ff.).

[21] See also Mack, *Myth of Innocence*, 240–41. Mack notes that this scene is Mark's idealistic picture of what life could have been like if the conflict within the synagogue had not occurred. The "woman in attendance" is therefore merely part of a calm, cozy scene. Thus Mark's moving of the scene to a "house" is not to highlight a contrast between "house-church" and "synagogue" (so E. Malbon, "Τῇ οἰκίᾳ αὐτοῦ: Mark 2:15 in Context," *NTS* 31 [1985]: 282–92), but rather reflects Mark's fondness for houses generally or a preference for maintaining a gender-based public/private dichotomy throughout his narrative.

Meals with "Tax-Collectors and Sinners" (Mark 2:14-17)

In Mark 2 Jesus dines at a private banquet with Levi the tax-collector and his friends. It has long been recognized that Mark's narration of the call of Levi is a Markan composition. Mack has recently suggested that here Mark expands an earlier chreia by creating a scene where Jesus actually eats with the tax-collector Levi.[22] The pun implied by the verb καλέω ("to invite") might indicate that in a pre-Markan form, the saying was meant to picture Jesus as the host of a meal, rather than as a guest as he is pictured here.[23] Thus, Jesus is shown engaging in the kind of activity the Pharisees accuse him of: "eating and drinking with tax-collectors and sinners." This swipe at Jesus' table practice also occurs in Q (7:34). In Q the connection between τελῶναι καὶ ἁμαρτωλοί and Greco-Roman banquet imagery is clear. There Jesus' table company is further linked to banquet revelry, as Jesus is accused of being a "wine-bibber" (οἰνοπότης) and a glutton (φάγος). It can be demonstrated that Mark's description of Jesus in Mark 2 recalls the slander leveled against those known for dining with promiscuous women at public banquets. Mark, however, connects Jesus' meal to his own theme of calling and discipleship.[24]

Scholars have long debated just who these "tax-collectors and sinners" might have been.[25] Tax-collectors (or perhaps "toll-collec-

---

[22] Mack, *Myth of Innocence*, 183, has established that behind Gospel narratives like this there may be detected the ancient practice of "chreia elaboration." This process was a common literary practice learned by schoolboys, whereby short, pithy, statements, called chreiai, were enlarged to create larger narratives. See Burton L. Mack and Vernon K. Robbins, *Patterns of Persuasion in the Gospels* (Sonoma, Calif.: Polebridge Press, 1989). The fact that this section was Mark's own composition was noticed long ago. See Bultmann, *History*, 47-48; Wm. O. Walker, "Jesus and the Tax-Collectors," *JBL* 97 (1978): 221-38; D. Smith, "Jesus at Table," 475-76. Mack and Robbins's study further elucidates the process of that composition.

[23] Bultmann, *History*, 47-48; D. Smith, "Jesus at Table," 476.

[24] So D. Smith, "Jesus at Table," 476.

[25] In the next paragraphs I will make reference to the following sources, which are for convenience given full citation here: I. Abrahams, "Publicans and Sinners," in *Studies in Pharisaism and the Gospels* (New York: KTAV Publishing House, 1967 (reprint of 1917 and 1924 Cambridge University Press edition), 54-61; John R. Donahue, "Tax-Collectors and Sinners: An Attempt at Identification," *CBQ* 33 (1971): 39-60; James D. G. Dunn, "Pharisees, Sinners and Jesus"; William R. Farmer, "Who Are the 'Tax-collectors and Sinners' in the Synoptic Tradition?" in *From Faith to Faith. Essays in Honor of Donald G. Miller on his 70th Birthday*, ed. D. Y. Hadidian (Pittsburgh: Pickwick Press, 1979), 167-74; J. Gibson, "Οἱ Τελῶναι καὶ αἱ Πόρναι,"

tors")[26] are usually identified as despicable folk because of their relationship with the Roman occupational forces in Palestine[27] and because of their reputation for dishonesty in collecting taxes (hence their connection with "robbers").[28] Eating with them would therefore have been considered scandalous and might also involve one in ritual impurity, since by their lifestyle and association with Romans they would be "Jews who made themselves Gentiles."[29] Or they were simply considered immoral.[30] Likewise, the term "sinners" is usually thought to designate the ritually impure, or the 'ammê hā'āreṣ, with whom the Pharisees were prohibited from eating, i.e., all non-Pharisees.[31] The group of Pharisees in the first century who would have been affected by such purity regulations, however, may have been relatively small.[32] Narrower definitions of "sinners" have also been suggested. "Sinners" might refer only to those who were habitually wicked and unwilling to repent.[33] More interesting, though, is the suggestion that "sinners" refers to those in lower-class service occupations, including former slaves of various sorts.[34]

Underlying the phrase "tax-collectors and sinners" are further associations to banquet settings. Tax-collectors were often linked in antiquity to prostitution. In ancient Greece, state revenue was collected by special tax-gatherers known as πορνοτελῶναι who kept lists

---

JTS 32 (1981): 429–33; Joachim Jeremias, *Jerusalem in the Time of Jesus* (Philadelphia: Fortress Press, 1969), ch. 14; idem, *New Testament Theology* (New York: Charles Scribner's Sons, 1971), 108–12; Delores Osborne, "Women: Sinners and Prostitutes," unpublished paper presented at the Pacific Coast Region SBL, Long Beach, Calif., April 1987; Norman Perrin, *Rediscovering the Teaching of Jesus* (New York and Evanston: Harper and Row: 1967), 102–8; E. P. Sanders, *Jesus and Judaism* (Philadelphia: Fortress Press, 1985), ch. 6. For this section I am indebted to the review of literature by D. Smith, "Jesus at Table," esp. 474–84.

[26] Donahue, "Tax-Collectors and Sinners," 59–61.

[27] Abrahams, "Publicans and Sinners"; Farmer, "Who Are the 'Tax-collectors and Sinners'?"; Gibson, "Οἱ Τελῶναι καὶ αἱ Πόρναι," 430.

[28] Abrahams, "Publicans and Sinners," 54; Donahue, "Tax-Collectors and Sinners," 52; Jeremias, *New Testament Theology*, 110–11.

[29] Farmer, "Who Are the 'Tax-collectors and Sinners'?" 168; Perrin, *Rediscovering the Teaching of Jesus*, 103.

[30] Donahue, "Tax-Collectors and Sinners."

[31] Jeremias, *New Testament Theology*, 109–13.

[32] Sanders, *Jesus and Judaism*, 182–99.

[33] Ibid., 177.

[34] Abrahams, "Publicans and Sinners," 55; Schüssler Fiorenza, *In Memory of Her*, 128; Jeremias, *Jerusalem in the Time of Jesus*, ch. 14.

of licensed harlots.[35] Prostitutes were not taxed during the Roman period until the reign of Caligula (37–41 CE), but women were still required to register as prostitutes in order to ply their trade.[36] Tax-collecting and brothel-keeping were two trades that remained linked in Hellenistic literature.[37] As a despicable set of occupations, tax-collecting and brothel-keeping were also taken up by rhetoricians to slander groups of individuals. Thus, Plutarch remarks that the Spartans slight the Athenians for collecting taxes and keeping brothels,[38] and Dio Chrysostom remarks of rulers, "Is it not plain to see that many who are called kings [βασιλεῖς] are only traders, tax-gatherers [τελῶναι], and keepers of brothels [πορνοβοσκοί]?"[39] Brothel-keepers, of course, would be expected to keep company with prostitutes.[40]

Not only was the term "tax-collector" associated with those who kept company with promiscuous women and pimps, but the term "sinner" likewise connoted sexual impropriety. Certain typical behavior identified Hellenistic persons as "sinners," especially those who participated in sexual misconduct, such as drunkards, male prostitutes, men who chased women, and adulterers.[41] In Hellenistic literature ἁμαρτωλός usually had to do with either a person's lack of education or a moral failure of some kind.[42] As such it appears in Hellenistic catalogues of virtues and vices, where it is roughly equivalent to the Latin sceleste.[43] Plutarch uses it in the first sense to slander

---

[35] See pp. 40–41 above.

[36] See pp. 40–41 and 64–65.

[37] See for example, Dio Chrysostom, where these two trades are "unseemly" and "base" (Or. 14.14); or Lucian, where tax-collectors are linked with pimps, adulterers, and other despised persons (Men. 11); and Theophrastus, whose character sketch of "Willful Disreputableness" has him seek various forms of employment, such as innkeeping, brothel-keeping and tax-collecting, as well as other lower-class jobs (Char. 6). For this association in Palestine, see Gibson, "Οἱ Τελῶναι καὶ αἱ Πόρναι," 431–33.

[38] Mor. 236C.

[39] Or. 4.98. See pp. 40–41 above.

[40] See for example, Cicero, Verr. II.1.39.101 and pp. 38–48 above.

[41] Hock, "Will of God," 35; Rengstorf, "ἁμαρτωλός, κτλ," TDNT, 1.317–18. The use of ἁμαρτωλός in inscriptions is probably not very pertinent (Rengstorf, "ἁμαρτωλός, κτλ," 318; contra Adolf Deissmann, Light from the Ancient East [London: Hodder and Stoughton, 1927], 113–15).

[42] Rengstorf, "ἁμαρτωλός, κτλ," 317. Interestingly enough, one of the few occurrences of this word is in reference to slaves (δοῦλοι ἁμαρτωλοί; Philodemeus De ira [73, Wilke] cited by Rengstorf, "ἁμαρτωλός, κτλ," 318. Text unavailable to me.).

[43] Deissmann, Light, 113–15.

his Stoic opponents. There the word carries its characteristic "ironical and disreputable flavour."[44] Luke uses the term to designate a "woman of the city" (i.e., a prostitute) who anoints Jesus at a meal. This woman "sinner" joins Jesus' followers.[45]

This background confirms the recent suggestion that "sinners" (ἁμαρτωλοί) is best understood in the context of Jewish sectarianism and philosophical debate, where it functions as rhetorical slander to denounce other Jews outside the boundaries of a particular sect.[46] Dennis Smith suggests that not only "sinners" but "tax-collectors" be viewed in this manner. Thus, the entire phrase "tax-collectors and sinners" can be categorized as a τόπος in Greco-Roman Jewish polemic.[47] The connection between these two terms and their use as slander against Jesus' or his followers' table practice is apt, since tax-collectors are connected in Greco-Roman literature to those who trafficked in prostitution and slavery, particularly to brothel-keepers and those most responsible for supplying women and servants for banquets.[48] Moreover, demeaning portraits of individuals often included a swipe at their table etiquette. For example, when Cicero wants to malign Verres,[49] he paints a rhetorical picture of his degenerate behavior at banquets with lewd women. It is therefore not surprising to find τελῶναι combined with πόρναι (Matt 21:31) or that Luke chooses a prostitute at a meal to fill in his narrative about Jesus' attitude toward "sinners" (Luke 7:36ff.).[50] Where one found tax-collectors and brothel-keepers, one would understandably expect to find prostitutes as well. Eventually, however, such language functioned as rhetorical slander, and did not identify actual tax-collectors, sinners, or prostitutes within a particular group or characterize that group's actual behavior at meals. The force of "tax-collectors and sinners" is

---

[44] *Aud. Poet.* 7 [ii, 25C]; Rengstorf, "ἁμαρτωλός, κτλ," 319.

[45] See pp. 121–30 below.

[46] Dunn, "Pharisees, Sinners and Jesus," 276–80 followed by D. Smith "Jesus at Table," 482, 484. See also Johnson, "Anti-Jewish Slander," esp. 438–39.

[47] See pp. 63–66 above.

[48] See pp. 40–41 above.

[49] See pp. 36–38; 42–53 above.

[50] See A. Plummer, "The Woman that was a Sinner," *ExpTim* 27 (1915–19): 42–43 and Luke 15: 11–32, where the Prodigal Son, another example of a "sinner" in Luke, wastes his money on "loose living" and prostitutes. Walker's suggestion that we have here an image of "sporters," "pimps," or "playboys" is not far from the truth, although one need not posit a misspelled word to make this conclusion ("Jesus and the Tax-Collectors," 237).

therefore connotative rather than denotative and merely characterizes Jesus or his followers as opponents.[51]

Thus, underlying Mark's portrait of Levi's dinner party with
Jesus is a typical slanderous remark which characterizes Jesus as one
who dines with lewd women in the context of public meals. Mark has
taken this traditional slander and expanded it into a narrative. In
Mark, however, the issue has become the later church conflict with
Pharisees over their more developed notion of ritual purity. Mark's
expansion depicts a conflict between Jesus and the Pharisees over
Jesus' practice of dining with a disreputable crowd. Those whom Jesus
"calls" are those who need to hear his message, because he has the
authority to forgive their "sins" (2:10).[52] These "sinners" are part of the
"many" for whom Jesus will give his life (10:45). He is the "physician"
who can provide the "cure" they need, i.e., forgiveness for sins.

Mark follows this account with a discussion of "feasting and
fasting" (2:18ff.) which may underscore Mark's aversion to over-
enthusiastic behavior. After Jesus is "taken away," his disciples (and
the Markan community) will "fast" like the disciples of John the
Baptist (2:20).[53] Here Mark changes the focus of the reader to the
fate which awaits Jesus later in the story—his death. Jesus and his
disciples are not characterized as behaving frivolously, but rather as
participating in a joyful time while the "bridegroom" is present. The
presence of women in the narrative is not highlighted, even though
one might expect to find them among tax-collectors and their company. The more general term ἁμαρτωλοί obscures their presence.
Thus, although Mark's narrative would call to mind Jesus' slanderous
behavior with promiscuous women, Mark does not capitalize on it.
He chooses rather to focus on other concerns, making the topic at
hand a dispute between Jesus and the Pharisees over Jesus' habit of
eating with the ritually impure.

Herod's Birthday Symposium (Mark 6:14–29)

In chapter 6, Mark narrates his version of the arrest of John the
Baptist and John's execution by Herod. Mark wants to be sure that

---

[51] See Johnson, "Anti-Jewish Slander," 441. D. Smith suggests that at the most
it might indicate Jesus was "non-ascetic" ("Jesus at Table," 486).

[52] Guelich, *Mark 1—8:26*, 99.

[53] Also connected to the "tax-collectors and sinners" material in Q. See
D. Smith, "Jesus at Table," 477ff.

the reader sees a contrast between the kind of feasting Jesus practices in chapter 2 and that of another "King of the Jews," Herod. This story serves the literary function of providing an "anti-type" of Jesus' meals in the Gospels, especially the feeding of the five thousand which immediately follows (6:30–44). Herod's guests form three groups (6:21), as do Jesus' (6:39–40), and only men attend both meals (6:21–22, 44). Both Jesus and Herod send out emissaries (6:7, 17, 27, 30), but for entirely different tasks. Furthermore, both utilize serving dishes, but again for different purposes (6:28, 43). Thus, the meals of Jesus and Herod serve as bold contrasts.[54]

The scene of Herod's banquet in Mark is undoubtedly fictitious. Here Mark portrays vividly the frivolity and banqueting behavior of a Hellenistic lord, one who gathers all the great ones (μεγιστᾶνες), military officers (χιλίαρχοι), and leading men of Galilee (οἱ πρῶτοι τῆς Γαλιλαίας) around him and lords it over them, unlike the servant-king Jesus (10:42–45).[55] When James and John request "seats" at Jesus' table, he reminds them that unlike the rule of Gentile kings, his leadership will be characterized by "service" not authority (10:37ff.). In contrast to Jesus, Herod is a tyrannical and licentious oriental monarch. He has married his brother's wife, and in this scene is depicted as decapitating a "righteous and holy man" without a trial, all because of the whim of a dancing girl. There is no attempt to obscure the presence of the girl or her role in the entertainment of the men. Herod's permitting his stepdaughter to dance in such a context is all the more shocking when compared to Philodamus' efforts to prevent his daughter from being forcibly brought into a similar banquet scene.[56]

The scene for Herod's party is stock and stereotypical for the first century: an official performs an execution in the context of a banquet at the request of a courtesan.[57] Here, the woman who makes the request (albeit through her daughter) is Herodias, even though she is offstage and plainly not present for the party (6:24, her daughter must "go out" to ask her mother what she should request).

---

[54] Robert M. Fowler, *Loaves and Fishes. The Function of the Feeding Stories in the Gospel of Mark* (SBLDS 54; Chico, Calif.: Scholars Press, 1981), 85–86, 119–27; Klosinski, "Meals in Mark," 119.

[55] Sean Freyne, *Galilee, Jesus and the Gospels: Literary Approaches and Historical Investigations* (Philadelphia: Fortress Press, 1988), 36–37.

[56] *Verr.* II.1.26.65–27.68. See pp. 36–38 above.

[57] See pp. 41–42 above.

Of all the women in Mark's Gospel, Herodias receives the most individual attention.[58] The setting of the story, its stock images, and the complete lack of decorum on the young girl's part, all help characterize both Herodias and her daughter as disreputable women—a madam and her fledgling courtesan daughter. Just as Jesus and his male disciples are to be viewed in contrast to Herod and his minions, so Herodias and her daughter are in contrast to the quiet women in Jesus' company. The women around Jesus may be present for meals, but they are not courtesans.

This narrative shows that Mark is quite capable of fully highlighting female characters in the context of a formal meal. When he does so, he also reveals his familiarity with the literary characterization of women at meals in Hellenistic literature and the social ideology which eventually contributed to the limitation of women in actual Greco-Roman meals. Even so, Herodias is not portrayed as present for this banquet. Her daughter plays a substitutionary role for her mother, the real character to make the stereotypical request. Later Mark will warn his community to "beware of the leaven" (table practice?) not only of the Pharisees, undoubtedly on account of their exclusive ritual purity, but will also warn them to "beware of the leaven" of Herod (8:17).

The Syro-Phoenician Woman (Mark 7:24–30)

Sandwiched in between Mark's feeding stories is the odd tale of the Syro-Phoenician woman who requests "crumbs." The two public feeding stories have been cast as a συμπόσιον (Mark 6:30ff.; 8:1ff.) as is the Last Supper (14:22ff.) in which only men are present and recline. The story of the Syro-Phoenician Woman which follows is one of the more hermeneutically difficult of the Markan narratives. This is due to Jesus' initial refusal to grant her request and the derogatory manner in which Jesus addresses her. Scholars have tried

---

[58] Munro, "Woman Disciples," 226. Freyne suggests that a recent discovery at Machaerus supports the accuracy of Mark 6: 22–25. The prison in which John was placed is presumed to be the fortress at this site (Lachs, *Rabbinic Commentary*, 238). This fortress contains two dining rooms side by side, one for women and one for men. See Freyne, *Galilee*, 37, n. 6; and Schwank ("Neue Funde," 434). If there were two dining rooms in use during the banquet, then Herodias' daughter would have "gone out" from the company of the men to consult her mother. See above p. 69, esp. n. 267.

to evade these difficult aspects of the story, neither of which fits neatly within modern notions of the kind, understanding, ever-helpful Savior.[59] The story is Mark's only narrative involving the healing of a Gentile and has its parallel in the healing of the centurion's servant (Matt 8:5–10/Luke 7:1–10; cf. John 4:46–54).[60] The story itself may pre-date Mark as part of a pre-Markan miracle catena which featured a series of five miracles highlighting Jesus as the *theios anēr* like Moses par excellence.[61]

Mark places this story immediately after material dealing with the issue of Jewish purity (7:1–23), in which Jesus is interpreted by Mark as having declared "all foods clean" (7:19). The account is neatly positioned in between the two miraculous feeding stories (6:33–44; 8:1–9)[62] and is connected to the two feedings by *Stichwort* associations (ἄρτος 6:38, 41; 7:27; 8:5–6 and χορτάζω 6:42; 7:27; 8:8).[63] After the narratives involving purity, Mark's story brings Jesus

---

[59] T. A. Burkill, "The Syrophoenician Woman: The Congruence of Mark 7:24–31," *ZNW* 57 (1966): 23–37; idem, "The Historical Development of the Story of the Syrophoenician Woman (Mark 7:24–31)," *NovT* 9 (1967): 161–77; A. Dermience, "La péricope de la Cananéene (Matt 15,21–28). Rédaction et théologie," *ETL* 58 (1982): 25–49; J. D. M. Derrett, "Law in the New Testament: The Syro-Phoenician Woman and the Centurion of Capernaum," *NovT* 15 (1973): 161–86; Barnabas Flammer, "Die Syro-Phoenizerin: Mark 7:24–30," *TQ* 148 (1968): 463–78; idem, "The Syro-Phoenician Woman (Mark 7:24–30)," *TD* 18 (1970): 19–24; J. Ireland Hasler, "The Incident of the Syrophoenician Woman (Matt 15:21–28; Mark 7:24–30)," *ExpTim* 45 (1933–34): 459–61; E. A. McNamara, "The Syro-Phoenician Woman," *AER* 127 (1952): 360–69; Sharon H. Ringe, "A Gentile Woman's Story," in *Feminist Interpretation of the Bible*, ed. Letty M. Russell (Philadelphia: Fortress Press, 1985), 65–72; James D. Smart, "Jesus, the Syro-Phoenician Woman-and the Disciples," *ExpTim* 50 (1939): 469–72; F. -J. Steinmetz, "Jesus bei den Heiden: Aktuelle Überlegungen zur Heilung der Syrophönizierin," *GeistLeb* 55 (1982): 177–84; W. Storch, "Zur Perikope von der Syrophönizierin (Mark 7, 28 und Ri 1, 7)," *BZ* 14 (1970): 256–57. Most articles dealing with women in Mark's Gospel also mention this passage, see Munro, "Women Disciples," 226–27; Schierling, "Women as Leaders," 253; Schmitt, "Women in Mark's Gospel," 230; Beavis, "Women as Models of Faith," 6; Grassi, "Secret Heroine," 11.

[60] Theissen, *Miracle Stories*, 254; Guelich, *Mark 1—8:26*, 382.

[61] Certain scholars acknowledge that this story predates Mark. P. J. Achtemeier ("Toward the Isolation of Pre-Markan Miracle Catenae," *JBL* 89 [1970]: 265–91 and "The Origin and Function of the Pre-markan Miracle Catenae," *JBL* 91 [1972]: 198–221) has suggested that it may have been part of an early cycle of miracle stories which were originally used in the context of Eucharist liturgy.

[62] Mark has toned down the eucharistic overtones of the traditional material he includes. See Schüssler Fiorenza, *In Memory of Her*, 138.

[63] An observation commonly made. See, e.g., Schüssler Fiorenza, *In Memory of Her*, 138; Flammer, "Die Syro-Phoenizerin," 20; Guelich, *Mark 1—8:26*, 383.

into the Gentile domain of Tyre, where Jesus is approached by a woman seeking healing for her daughter who is afflicted by an "unclean" spirit (πνεῦμα ἀκάθαρτον). In Mark's context, then, the story speaks to the mixed make-up of the Markan community (i.e., Jews and Gentiles) as well as to his community's mission to Gentiles.[64] The Syro-Phoenician woman appears merely as a representative of non-Jewish supplicants.[65] It is no doubt the mixed nature of Jesus' followers of Mark's day that leads the Pharisees to declare their meal gatherings unclean.

In verse 24 Jesus is seen traveling to the area surrounding Tyre, a coastal city north of Galilee. "And Sidon," which occurs in some manuscripts, is undoubtedly an assimilation from Matthew 15:21 and Mark 7:31.[66] The reference to Tyre was probably suggested to Mark from the designation of the woman as "Syro-Phoenician," and so Jesus is said to have traveled north to this area in this part of the narrative.[67] The possibility that she was a Greek immigrant and therefore not an unexpected inhabitant of Palestine seems to have been excluded by Mark.[68] Mark's lack of concern with feasible travel routes, given the topography of Palestine, is therefore apparent in this case.[69] Mark also goes to some lengths to locate the woman not only in the vague area of Tyre, but also in a "house," the scene of many of his narratives involving women.[70] Jesus arrives in the area and then immediately sequesters himself inside, where the woman seeks him.

---

[64] Burkill, "Historical Development," 173ff.; Derrett, "Law in the New Testament"; Schüssler Fiorenza, *In Memory of Her*, 137; Flammer, "Die Syro-Phoenizerin," 20ff.; Grassi, "Secret Heroine," 11; Guelich, *Mark 1—8:26*, 383; So also Hasler, McNamara, Mann, Munro, Steinmetz, Ringe.

[65] So Munro, "Women Disciples," 227; Theissen, *Miracle Stories*, 254.

[66] The shorter text is supported by Western and Caesarean text types. Bruce Metzger, *Textual Commentary on the Greek New Testament* (London; New York: UBS, 1971), 95.

[67] Derrett, "Law in the New Testament," 163; Guelich, *Mark 1—8:26*, 383; Theissen, *Miracle Stories*, 126. Some scholars have suggested that this story reflects the story of the widow of Zaraphath who prepares food for Elijah (1 Kgs 17:17–24) (so Derrett, "Law in the New Testament," 165ff.; Flammer, "Die Syro-Phoenizerin," 21), but the connection appears to be weak (so Burkill, "The Syrophoenician Woman," 23, n. 2; Guelich, *Mark 1—8:26*, 385).

[68] Burkill, "Historical Development," 173; McNamara, "The Syro-Phoenician Woman," 364, n. 6; Theissen, *Miracle Stories*, 126.

[69] A point often made. See for example, Howard Jackson, "The Death of Jesus in Mark and the Miracle from the Cross," *NTS* 33 (1987): 16–37, 24.

[70] See above p. 88, esp. nn. 20, 21.

The designation of a woman as a Syro-Phoenician is rare. In Jewish tradition, women from the city of Tyre or the area of Phoenicia were associated with ancient Jewish struggles with foreign religious practices of the cults involving Ba'al and 'Astarte, particularly the practice of temple prostitution. The most notable of these women is Jezebel, the Sidonian princess who became a fierce supporter of the Phoenician deities in the northern kingdom, attracting many to join her at Ba'al's "table."[71] The name of Jezebel came to evoke the image of the idolatrous and sexually available painted woman, even in Jewish and Christian literature of the first century.[72] As sources for foreign religious practices, Tyre and Sidon became objects of Yahwistic wrath in ancient Hebrew tradition.[73]

It may not be a coincidence, then, that the term "Syro-Phoenician" also describes the kind of woman whom one might meet in the seamier areas of Rome. In Juvenal's eighth satire, "Against Base Nobles," one upper-class gentleman meets a Syro-Phoenician woman on his way to a tavern:

> When he decides to go to some tavern that never closes, on his way he is met by a perfumed Syrophoenician, coming up at a run, to hail him as Lord and master.[74]

This is no doubt a perfumed prostitute who comes running up, hailing the one she calls "Lord."[75]

---

[71] 1 Kgs 16:31; 18:4, 13, passim; 2 Kgs 9:7ff. For Jezebel's "table," see 1 Kgs 18:19.

[72] See Rev 2:18–29 where a leader of an early house church is called "Jezebel" for allowing her congregants to eat meat sacrificed to idols. See also E. B. Johnston, "Jezebel," *ISBE* (Grand Rapids, Mich.: Eerdmans, 1975), 2.1057–59.

[73] See for example, Isa 23:12; Jer 25:22; 47:4; Ezek 27:8; 28:21–22; Joel 3:4.

[74] *Satire* 8:158–62, trans. Rolfe Humphries, *The Satires of Juvenal* (Bloomington and London: Indiana University Press, 1974), 107. See also Lucilius, *Lives* 15, frg. 496–97; Guelich, *Mark 1—8:26*, 385.

[75] Ringe notes that in antiquity one would only expect a prostitute to run up to a man in this manner in public, alone and unbidden ("Gentile Woman's Story," 70). The reputation of women like Jezebel was still known during the Greco-Roman period. See Josephus, *Ant.* 8.316–318; Amaru, "Portraits of Biblical Women in Josephus' Antiquities," 74–75. The area and culture of Tyre and Sidon were also well-known in Hellenistic times. See Strab. 16.23-25 and numerous references to "Tyre" and/or "Sidon" in Hellenistic literature: Achilles Tatius, 5.10; *Anth. Graec.* 7.744, 745; 16.167; Chariton, 7.4.11; Dio Cass. 54.7.6; Dio Chrys. 14.116; Diod. Sic. 16.41; 19.86; Diog. Laert. 7.29; 10.25; Eunap. *VS* 496; Herodotus, *Hist.* 2.161; 7.98; 8.67; Plut., *Demetr.* 32.7.

Mark also identifies the Syro-Phoenician woman as a "Greek." This identification may indicate that Mark intends the reader to understand that she is a wealthy woman.[76] By the time of Mark, however, "Greek" had also come to designate a member of a group distinct from Jews in the context of Gentile missionary activity.[77] To emphasize her Gentile origin, Mark describes her as Syro-Phoenician "by birth" (τῷ γένει). In Mark's story, this Gentile woman, now appropriately inside a dwelling (albeit alone), approaches Jesus, falls at his feet in obeisance, and asks for help on behalf of her daughter. His fame has obviously spread; she knows that this man is able to drive the "unclean" spirit from her daughter.

Jesus' response, "Let the children first be filled, for it is not good to take the children's bread and throw it to the dogs," seems uncharacteristically harsh. Interpreters, intent on preserving a certain image of Jesus, usually insist that the scene meant to be elicited by this comment is that of a cozy household, where even the children's little "puppies" (κυνάριον) can expect to be fed from the abundance of the messianic banquet.[78] This interpretation fails to take into account the conventional use of this diminutive in reference to women. When used of a woman it is a term of reproach for her shameless behavior or audacity; it is not a term of endearment. Moreover, it is also used of maids or other servants, particularly in the context of Greek mythology.[79]

Thus, in spite of her possible social status, Jesus is depicted as insulting the woman by calling her a "dog" (κυνάριον). As Burkill has

---

[76] This further coheres with the image of the stereotypical painted woman from Phoenicia, Jezebel, who is a princess. Guelich suggests that the appellation "Greek" may also portray this woman as an "upper-class," educated woman (*Mark 1–8:26*, 385); so also Theissen, *Miracle Stories*, 126, as well as "Lokal- und Sozialkolorit in der Geschichte von der syrophönikischen Frau (Mark 7:24–30)," *ZNW* 75 (1984): 202–25. For further discussions of this appellation," see McNamara, "The Syro-Phoenician Woman," 364, n. 6 and Ringe, "Gentile Woman's Story," 70.

[77] Guelich, *Mark 1—8:26*, 385; Theissen, *Miracle Stories*, 126.

[78] Many scholars emphasize that Jesus is really calling the woman and her child "puppies." See for example, Derrett, "Law in the New Testament," 169; Flammer, "Die Syro-Phoenizerin," 20; Hasler, "Incident," 460 (who also remarks that Jesus must have said this with a "twinkle in his eye," and suggests that the image is one of children sitting down to a meal, their "puppy playmates seated near them with expectant eyes" (461); McNamara, "The Syro-Phoenician Woman," 363, passim, who calls the woman an "alert little pet" (368); See also similar comments by Ringe, "Gentile Woman's Story," 68; Smart, "Jesus, the Syro-Phoenician Woman," 469.

[79] LSJ, 1015.

eloquently pointed out, "As in English, so in other languages, to call a woman 'a little bitch' is no less abusive than to call her 'a bitch' without qualification."[80] In the context of Jesus' image, the "little dogs" are not part of the family, as are the children, and are not at the table, but under it. Their receiving any crumbs at all (hardly "messianic abundance") is merely "an unintended consequence of the act of feeding the children."[81] It is therefore not "good" (καλός; here probably "proper") to give food meant for the family to the household animals.[82] Such images of dogs and crumbs fits well in the ethos of Hellenistic Cynicism.[83] The harshness of Jesus' retort may reveal the background of the story in an earlier chreia.[84]

Several have taken the second part of Jesus' comment, "Let the children first be filled," to be an ancillary softening of Jesus' statement by Mark[85] and a reference to the situation of the early church after Jesus' death. The "children" are the Jews, as opposed to the "dogs" which refer to Gentiles.[86] In Mark's Gospel, the Jewish rejec-

---

[80] Burkill, "Historical Development," 173; See also Mann, *Mark*, 321; Ringe ("Gentile Woman's Story," 69) notes that although the diminutive may mean "pups," it is still "offensive in the extreme."

[81] Burkill, "Historical Development," 173.

[82] In spite of their social status, Jesus' insult may also be comparing the woman and her child to servants. See Derrett, "Law in the New Testament," 171. Eating with one's slaves was considered to be highly improper, although Seneca derides those who question such a practice (Seneca, *Epist.* 47). Although admission of slaves to table was not uncommon at certain religious festivals, it may not be the case that anyone put Seneca's suggestions into practice in everyday life, even though new definitions of slavery and freedom by the Cynics, for example, seemed to encourage it (Walter C. Summers, *Select Letters of Seneca* [London: Macmillan and Co., 1926], 210); See also Wiedemann, *Greek and Roman Slavery*, 233–36. Inviting a slave to recline at table was also one means of announcing his manumission, albeit in an informal way (*per mansam*), and was always also *manumissio interamicos* since a number of fellow diners would undoubtedly be present to witness the manumission. The most popular formal manumission, however, was by will, when the slave would be freed upon the death of his or her master (Duff, *Freedmen*, 21–25).

[83] Mack, *Myth of Innocence*, 183.

[84] So Beavis, "Women as Models of Faith, " 6. See Henry A. Fischel, "Studies in Cynicism and the Ancient Near East: The Transformation of a *Chria*," in *Religions in Antiquity. Essays in Memory of Erwin Ramsdell Goodenough*, ed. J. Neusner (Leiden: Brill, 1968), 372–411, esp. 410–11.

[85] Flammer, "Die Syro-Phoenizerin," 20ff.; Schüssler Fiorenza (*In Memory of Her*, 137) notes that "first" is secondary; Guelich, *Mark 1—8:26*, 385.

[86] In Jewish and rabbinic literature, "dogs" came to be a derogatory term for Gentiles or pagans. See Derrett, "Law in the New Testament," 165ff.; Schüssler Fiorenza, *In Memory of Her*, 137; McNamara, "The Syro-Phoenician Woman," 361, 365. Storch suggests this is a reference to Judges 1:7 where a pagan king remarks that

tion of the Messiah, and Jesus' self-sacrifice for all, comes later in the story. In its present context, the story of the Syro-Phoenician woman foreshadows this development. Eventually all will "be filled" as in the stories of the miraculous feedings. Thus, Mark suggests that the admittance of Gentiles to the Christian table is prefigured in the ministry of Jesus himself. Jesus travels further in the area of the Decapolis following this story (7:31).[87] Nevertheless, the actual admittance of Gentiles into the community takes place at a later time, and thus the ministry of Jesus is portrayed as being primarily to Israel.[88] For the Markan community, of course, this later time has now come.

This eventual inclusion of Gentiles into the community and its table is confirmed by Jesus' granting of the woman's request, albeit from a distance (v. 29). What is striking is that it is the woman's wit that persuades Jesus to perform the healing.[89] It is she who gives the surprising completion to the chreia, "Lord,[90] but even the dogs under the table feed on the children's crumbs." It is because of her answer (λόγος) that Jesus agrees to cast the demon out of her daughter. Her witty retort shows her level of education and possible social class.[91] However, as we have seen, in Greco-Roman literature, courtesans were often characterized as the kind of women with the ability to construct chreiai and join in philosophical repartée.[92] Furthermore, even aristocratic women could be accused of promiscuous behavior for being too well-educated.[93] Thus, Mark's narrative could be inter-

---

his punishment of having his thumbs removed is apt since he had done this to other kings who then rummaged like dogs under his table for food ("Perikope," 256–57.

[87] Flammer, "Die Syro-Phoenizerin," 21; McNamara, "The Syro-Phoenician Woman," 368ff.

[88] Arguments to make the second feeding to "the Gentiles" are not convincing. Guelich, *Mark 1—8:26*, 386–87. See also Smart, "Jesus, the Syro-Phoenician Woman," 470.

[89] There is no indication in the text that Jesus "wavers" over the scope of his ministry, or that the refusal is "apparent," etc. (So Mann, *Mark*, 321; Smart, "Jesus, the Syro-Phoenician Woman," 469–70). Such suggestions are adequately dealt with by Burkill, "Historical Development," 171ff. On the witty intelligence of the woman, see Schüssler Fiorenza, *In Memory of Her*, 137; Guelich, *Mark 1—8:26*, 388; Mann, *Mark*, 321; McNamara, "The Syro-Phoenician Woman," 368; Ringe, "Gentile Woman's Story," 65, 69, 71; Schmitt, "Women in Mark's Gospel," 230.

[90] "Yes" (ναί) omitted in P[45].

[91] So Guelich, *Mark 1—8:26*, 385; Theissen, *Miracle Stories*, 126. Syro-Phoenicians were known for their wit and rhetorical skill generally. See Eunapius, *VS* 496.

[92] Hetaerae were known for their wit. For chreiai attributed to hetaerae, see Athenaeus, *Deipn.* 13.584c.

[93] See pp. 56–57, above.

101

preted as portraying a woman of the "public" rather than "private" Greco-Roman stereotype. Her announcement of Jesus as "Lord" (κύριε) is the only occurrence of this address in Mark and is probably merely a polite "Sir" in this instance.[94]

Again, Mark here highlights an encounter of Jesus with a woman who, according to Greco-Roman stereotypes, would be considered "public" rather than "private," promiscuous rather than chaste. Even though Mark's depiction may indicate that she is wealthy and well-educated, other aspects of his description characterize her as "promiscuous" or "improper." Mark is not interested in her "femaleness," but, by emphasizing her Gentile origin, Mark seems to downplay these overtones of scandal, her femaleness, and her relationship to men. Rather, Mark is interested in the relationship between Jews and Gentiles.[95] The Jewish/Gentile contrast of the story becomes clear within the larger context Mark gives it.[96] In Mark, Jesus objects to the woman's request, not because she may be a "promiscuous" woman, but because she is a Gentile. Mark does not seem much concerned about the scandalous nature of Jesus' encounter with this kind of woman. Setting the story as a private scene seems to suffice.[97]

The Unnamed Woman Who Anoints Jesus (Mark 14:3–9)

The story of the unnamed women who anoints Jesus is one of the few stories common to all four Gospels in which Jesus appears in the company of a woman at a meal (Mark 14:3–9; Matt 26:6–13;

---

[94] Burkill takes the address in Mark as merely polite ("The Syrophoenician Woman," 33). Flammer ("Die Syro-Phoenizerin," 22–23), who notes that the Gentiles will not be able to affirm Jesus as Messiah until after his death and resurrection, and Guelich (*Mark 1—8:26*, 388) suggests that the address here may be analogous to the Gentile centurion's declaration that Jesus is the "Son of God." See also Jackson, "The Death of Jesus," who suggests that the centurion's announcement at the cross is made in response to the miraculous tearing of the temple curtain (passim).

[95] Beavis, "Women as Models of Faith," 6; Schüssler Fiorenza, *In Memory of Her*, 137; Munro, "Women Disciples," 227.

[96] Burkill, "Historical Development," 169. Ringe notes that the Jew-Gentile reference is not clear within the story itself without the larger context which Mark gives it, and that Mark elaborates the story to bring out this theme ("Gentile Woman's Story," 69, 155, n. 8).

[97] Even the setting of the scene in a house may not have to do with the fact that the story involves a woman. Philip Sellew pointed out to me that in Mark's Gospel, Jesus often retires to homes.

Luke 7:36–50; John 12:1–8). The literature on this passage is extensive, and for many years scholars have debated over whether or not there was one anointing of Jesus in this manner or several.[98] Despite their differences, all the Gospels reflect one basic story: a woman anoints Jesus at a meal, those present object to her action, and Jesus responds by rebuking them. Scholars have identified both the version of the story in Mark and the original story behind it as a chreia.[99] Mack has suggested that the original chreia behind Mark's elaborated pronouncement story might have been as follows:

> When Jesus was at table, a disreputable woman entered and poured out a jar of perfumed oil on him. He said, "That is good."[100]

The contrived objections of those present, and the interest in the burial of Jesus as the focus of the event are later additions.[101] Mark contains no suggestion that the woman is unvirtuous.[102]

Nevertheless, as in the other Markan stories involving women and meals, in spite of Mark's own interests, the woman could be

---

[98] For articles dealing specifically with these accounts, see F. C. Burkitt, "Mary Magdalene and Mary, Sister of Martha," *ExpTim* 42 (1930–31): 157–59; J. D. M. Derrett, "The Anointing at Bethany and the Story of Zacchaeus," in *Law and the New Testament* (London: Darton, Longman and Todd, 1970), 266–85; J. K. Elliott, "The Anointing of Jesus," *ExpTim* 85 (1973–74): 105–7; Robert Holst, "The One Anointing of Jesus: Another Application of the Form-Critical Method," *JBL* 95 (1976): 435–46; André Legault, "An Application of the Form-Critique Method to the Anointings in Galilee (Luke 7, 36–50) and Bethany (Matt 26, 6–13; Mark 14, 3–9; John 12, 1–8)," *CBQ* 16 (1954): 131–45; C. J. Maunder, "A Sitz im Leben for Mark 14:9," *ExpTim* 99 (1987): 78–90; Winsome Munro, "The Anointing in Mark 14:3–9 and John 12:1–8," *SBL 1979 Seminar Papers*, vol. 1, ed. P. J. Achtemeier (Missoula, Mont.: Scholars Press, 1979), 127–30; Elizabeth E. Platt, "The Ministry of Mary of Bethany," *TToday* 34 (1977): 29–39; Plummer, "The Woman that was a Sinner," 42–43; J. N. Sanders, "Those Whom Jesus Loved," *NTS* 1 (1954): 29–41; A. R. Simpson, "Mary of Bethany; Mary of Magdala; and Anonyma," *Expositor* 8 (1909): 307–18. Other articles on Mark obviously discuss this passage, such as Grassi, "The Secret Heroine," 11ff.; Malbon, "Fallible Followers," 39ff.; Munro, "Women Disciples," 239ff. Books on the place of women in the NT also discuss these passages at length, as in for example, Schüssler Fiorenza, whose book title is derived from the Markan version (*In Memory of Her*, see esp. xiii–xxv).

[99] Mack, *Myth of Innocence*, 199–203; Burton L. Mack, "The Anointing of Jesus: An Elaboration Within a Chreia," in *Patterns of Persuasion in the Gospels*, with Vernon K. Robbins (Sonoma, Calif.: Polebridge Press, 1989), 85–106.

[100] Mack, *Myth of Innocence*, 200.

[101] Ibid.; Derrett, "The Anointing at Bethany," 267–70; Elliott, "Anointing of Jesus," 106; Holst, *One Anointing of Jesus*, 444–45.

[102] Burkitt, "Mary," 158; contra Legault, Elliott, Sanders; see also Osborne, "Women: Sinners and Prostitutes," passim. But see Holst, *One Anointing of Jesus*, 443–46.

characterized as a stereotypical promiscuous or "public" woman. First of all, as we have seen, the setting of a meal would in and of itself have indicated the possibility of frivolous behavior. There is no indication that the woman is a relation of Jesus, and yet she is present at a meal with a large group. Secondly, the very service which she performs for him carries sexual connotations. According to ancient Greek customs, anointings were regularly performed by wives for their husbands before and after sexual intercourse, and the alabastron was therefore often portrayed in private scenes with women. Hetaerae are likewise pictured with such vessels.[103] Moreover, the oil that this woman uses (μύρου νάρδου πιστικῆς—sometimes rendered "spikenard") may have been the sort that was used by women of "luxury."[104] Furthermore, anointings of men or kings at banquets by courtesans or other servants and the connection between such perfumes and sexually available women who frequented such gatherings are also ancient, both in Greco-Roman literature and in the ancient Near East.[105] Josephus, for instance, writes of Claudius, who enters the Senate after having anointed his head with perfume (χρισάμενος μύροις τὴν κεφαλὴν) as if he had just returned from a banquet.[106] Thus, given the meal setting, the action of the woman in an earlier chreia would have been viewed as improper. Mark's casting of the scene obscures its impropriety.

Mark accomplishes this in several ways. First, as in the scenes involving Peter's mother-in-law, the "tax-collectors and sinners," and the Syro-Phoenician woman, he sets the story in a private home and not in a more public place.[107] Second, as Mark describes the scene, the men object because of the cost of the ointment, not because the woman's act is improper.[108] Her gift of the expensive ointment is

---

[103] Keuls, *Reign of the Phallus*, 117–20, 170ff.

[104] I assume this is a euphemism for prostitutes. See MM, 514. See also Athenaeus, *Deipn.* 12, 553; Galen 12.604K. Πιστικός is a rare word and may also mean "liquid" or "pure." See also Legault, "Form-Critique Method,"138; Mann, *Mark*, 556; Holst, *One Anointing of Jesus*, 440.

[105] Derrett, "Anointing at Bethany," 274–75, n, 1; 277, n. 2; Legault, "Form-Critique Method,"137; W. Michaelis, "μύρον, κτλ," *TDNT*, 8.800–801, see esp. n. 3. See also Amos 6:6; Prov 27:9; Qoh 9:7–8; Wis 2:7; Philo, *Sacr.*, 21; Josephus, *Ant.* 19.238–39; 19.358; *J. W.* 4.556–565; and from the DSS, John M. Allegro, "The Wiles of the Wicked Woman" in *Discoveries in the Judean Desert* 5 (Oxford: Oxford University Press, 1968), 82–84.

[106] *Ant.* 19.238.

[107] Munro, "Women Disciples," 227.

[108] Malbon, "Fallible Followers," 39; Munro, "The Anointing in Mark 14:3–9,"

contrasted with the gift of the poor widow, which indicates her higher social position and makes the point that she too gives what she has.[109] Finally, like a virtuous Greco-Roman woman, this unnamed woman is silent, and neither reclines with Jesus nor is pictured as actually being at the table with him.

Mark's placement of this story at the beginning of his Passion narrative further shifts attention away from the impropriety of the scene.[110] The placement of the anointing here accomplishes two things. First of all, it connects the act of anointing with Jesus' death. This is Jesus' primary act of service that Mark wishes to highlight (so 10:45 and his emphasis in ch. 2).[111] Second, this connection partially relieves the problem of the respectability of the woman's act, since women were often sent to anoint a dead body for burial.[112] Thus her prophetic act becomes fully explicable in light of Jesus' fate. Moreover, it is her act of service to Jesus and her self-denial, both prefiguring his death, which will be proclaimed wherever the Gospel is preached. The point is frequently missed that this proclamation will be made in remembrance of the woman, not Jesus.[113] Mark's occasion for memorial is therefore shifted from an etiological legend of Jesus' last meal with his disciples to a meal without his disciples where he is anointed by an unnamed woman. This anointing predicts his death,

---

130; Thomas Schmidt has also suggested the intriguing possibility that Jesus himself may have been wealthier than is usually supposed, see *Hostility to Wealth in the Synoptic Gospels* (JSOT Suppl. 15; Sheffield: JSOT Press, 1987), 119ff. He cites 2 Cor 8:9: "For you know the generous act of our Lord Jesus Christ, that though he was rich, yet for your sakes he became poor, so that by his poverty you might become rich" [NRSV]. It is interesting that on a literary level, at least, Jesus is often portrayed in wealthier (although not necessarily "upper-class") settings.

[109] Grassi, "Secret Heroine," 11ff.; Malbon, "Fallible Followers," 38–39.

[110] This scene has long been considered an insertion at this point. See Mack, *Myth of Innocence*, 199ff.; Legault, "Form-Critique Method,"136; Maunder, "A Sitz im Leben," 78; Vernon K. Robbins, "Last Meal: Preparation, Betrayal and Absence," in *The Passion in Mark: Studies on Mark 14—16*, ed. W. Kelber (Philadelphia: Fortress Press, 1976), 21–40, esp. 35.

[111] Mack, *Myth of Innocence*, 311ff.; J. N. Sanders, "Those Whom Jesus Loved," 37. It is for this reason that Sanders implies that the woman who anoints Jesus is Mary Magdalene. Magdalene is the one woman who is clearly connected to the empty tomb (and therefore Jesus' death and burial) in early Christian tradition.

[112] Dewey, *Disciples of the Way*, 133; Derrett, "Anointing at Bethany," 270–71; Elliott, "Anointing of Jesus," 106; Michaelis, "μύρον, κτλ," 801, n. 13; J. N. Sanders, "Those Whom Jesus Loved," 37.

[113] So Schüssler Fiorenza, *In Memory of Her*; Beavis, "Women as Models of Faith"; Kopas, "Jesus and Women in Mark's Gospel," 918; contra Mack, *A Myth of Innocence*, 203, 311ff.; Robbins, "Last Meal," 36, who fail to mention this.

and is an event not to be reenacted or celebrated, but simply remem-bered.[114] Mack has therefore suggested that this odd interpretation of the woman's anointing of Jesus contributes to Mark's interest of countering an enthusiastic Christ-cult by an increased focus on Jesus' service of death.[115] As for Jesus, he is the one who is anointed like a king at a banquet, but ironically he is really the one who has come to serve others by means of his death (Mark 10:45). The woman, like the women who "serve" Jesus in 15:40–41, is following Jesus' example of service by her deed. Accordingly, she becomes an excellent ex-ample of Markan discipleship.[116] As in other scenes, Mark does not emphasize the moral character of the woman but is occupied with other theological concerns.

Mark, Women, and Meals: Some Conclusions

Women figure prominently in the Gospel of Mark. They follow Jesus, receive healing, and are the only followers of Jesus in Mark's narrative depicted as acting out Mark's ideal of discipleship, taking on the humble stance of a slave, or "table servant."[117] Women also

---

[114] Mack, *Myth of Innocence*, 311ff. The Last Supper in Mark is also not an event to be re-enacted but remembered (Klosinski, "Meals in Mark," 199–202).

[115] Mack, *Myth of Innocence*, 311ff.; Robbins also connects the Last Supper and the anointing in Mark ("Last Meal," 35–36). Note also that Judas immediately exits stage left to work on the betrayal following both meals.

[116] Lee Klosinski sees this as a new assessment of social hierarchy. "Service at table," the lowly work of a slave, becomes the major example of Christian discipleship. This new social ethic would have undermined the Greco-Roman ideal of rank ("Meals in Mark," 206).

[117] Ibid. Except for the angels, who serve Jesus after the Temptation (Mark 1:13). Marvin W. Meyer has suggested another model disciple may have been present in an earlier version of Mark, that being the young man (νεανίσκος) present in the garden and the tomb (Mark 14:51–52; 16:5–6). Meyer has suggested that should the fragments of the *Secret Gospel of Mark* which feature this young man be considered as part of the original Markan narrative, then Mark would be depicting an ideal disciple throughout his story similar to the "Beloved Disciple" in the Gospel of John ("The Youth in the Secret Gospel of Mark," *Semeia* 49 (1990): 129–53; see also "The Youth in Secret Mark and the Beloved Disciple in John," in *Gospel Origins and Christian Beginnings: In Honor of James M. Robinson*, ed. James E. Goehring et al. (Sonoma, Calif.: Polebridge Press, 1990), 94–105). Meyer notes in reference to recent discus-sions concerning the women, that in comparison to the νεανίσκος, even the disciple-ship of the women falls short, as they too flee the scene, and tell no one about the resurrection ("The Youth in the Secret Gospel," 147). This observation was made to me by Winsome Munro. In personal correspondence she was gracious enough to share

appear in Markan meal scenes; however, Mark's tendency to use these scenes to underscore other theological points about discipleship, Jewish/Gentile relations, or the crucifixion shows his general lack of concern for the scandalous nature of his stories about women. Women disciples follow Jesus, but these female companions merit little comment from Mark. The woman's anointing of Jesus is not objectionable because of its impropriety, but on account of its cost. Likewise, the request of the Syro-Phoenician woman is rejected by Jesus not because she might be considered overeducated or "promiscuous," but rather because she is a Gentile. The Pharisees object to Jesus' dining with "tax-collectors and sinners," not because the group includes women, but because it includes Gentiles and therefore makes him ritually unclean.

Mark's use of these scenes to further his theological ends does serve a secondary purpose. Mark's redirection of his audience to other theological concerns obscures their undercurrent of scandal. Thus, the social conservatism of the Hellenistic world is not completely absent from Mark's Gospel. His encouragement to those who would be leaders to take on a subservient role does not set a tone for full egalitarianism. Women are never explicitly depicted as eating or reclining with men, and they rarely speak in public. On the contrary, the women around Jesus are set in contrast to the daughter of Herodias. These women may be wealthy, "liberated" ladies or "table-servants," but Mark does not call them πόρναι. Mark merely embraces the undertones of scandal by incorporating these depictions of women into his Gospel and skillfully uses them to further his other theological ends.

with me an unpublished copy of "Women Disciples: Light from Secret Mark," now in *JFSR* 8 (1992), 47–64. As young men were also commonly used for serving meals at banquets (See pp. 48–49.), the νεανίσκος could also be likened to the ideal διάκονος who "serves" at table (Mark 10:43–45).

Women and Meals in the 4
Gospel of Luke

Of all the Synoptic Gospels, the Gospel of Luke has always been considered a Gospel for women. Luke acknowledges the ample presence of women in the early stages of the Jesus movement and in the Hellenistic mission. Moreover, Luke arranges his materials in complementary fashion, so that stories about a man are followed by or paralleled with a story about a woman.[1] In light of these observa-

---

[1]These observations are often made. See for example, Margaret G. Adams, "The Hidden Disciples. Luke's Stories About Women in His Gospel and in Acts" (D.Min. diss., San Francisco Theological Seminary, 1980), 10ff.; Mary Rose D'Angelo, "Images of Jesus and the Christian Call in the Gospels of Luke and John," *Spirituality Today* 37 (1985): 196–212; Neal M. Flanagan, "The Position of Women in the Writings of St. Luke," *Marianum* 40 (1978): 288–304; Joseph A. Grassi, *The Hidden Heroes of the Gospels. Female Counterparts of Jesus* (Collegeville, Minn.: Liturgical Press, 1989), 83ff.; Jane Kopas, "Jesus and Women: Luke's Gospel," *TToday* 43 (1986): 192–202; Eugene H. Maly, "Women and the Gospel of Luke," *BTB* 10 (1980): 99–104; Constance F. Parvey, "The Theology and Leadership of Women in the New Testament," in *Religion and Sexism*, ed. Rosemary Radford Ruether, 139–46 (New York: Simon and Schuster, 1974); Charles H. Talbert, *Reading Luke. A Literary and Theological Commentary on the Third Gospel* (New York: Crossroad, 1982), 90ff.; E. Jane Via, "Women in the Gospel of Luke," in *Women in the World's Religions, Past and Present*, ed. Ursula King (New York: Paragon House, 1987), 38–55. On the complementary pairing of stories, see for example Zacharias and Mary (Luke 1:11–20/1:26–38; 1:46–55/1:67–79), Simeon and Anna (2:25–38), the centurion of Capernaum and the widow of Nain (Luke 7:1–17), the man with the mustard seed and the woman with the leaven (13:18–21), the man who looks for his sheep and the woman who searches for the lost coin (15:4–10), the men on the couch and the women at their mills (17:34ff.). Helmut Flender (*St. Luke. Theologian of Redemptive History* [Philadelphia: Fortress Press, 1967], 9ff.) sees this complementary pairing as an aspect of Luke's fondness for dialectical structure in his overall composition, a characteristic feature of Lukan style in general.

tions, an early feminist discussion cast Luke as a radical revisionist of Jewish women's roles.[2] Following this lead, scholars have argued that Luke portrays women as disciples,[3] apostles,[4] prophets, and deacons.[5] An analysis of Luke's portrayal of women in meal settings, however, reveals that of all the Synoptics, Luke is the most concerned to maintain a traditional, Greco-Roman, private role for women. Luke maintains a traditional Greco-Roman public/private gender dichotomy throughout his narrative. Thus, Luke's meal scenes with women remain private, and women do not recline with men for meals. Rather, women in meal settings take on a submissive, traditional stance. Women, even repentant prostitutes, join Jesus' followers, but women around Jesus are usually respectable patronesses. Their activity is not connected to "table service" or public meals as it is in Mark. This discussion will further buttress recent conservative assessments of women in Luke–Acts.[6]

---

[2] Parvey, "Theology and Leadership of Women."

[3] Adams, "The Hidden Disciples," 104ff.; Kopas, "Jesus and Women: Luke's Gospel," 198; Maly, "Women and the Gospel of Luke," 103; Rosalie Ryan, "The Women of Galilee and Discipleship in Luke," *BTB* 15 (1985): 56; E. Jane Via, "Women, the Discipleship of Service, and the Early Christian Ritual Meal in the Gospel of Luke," *StLukeJ* 29 (1985): 39. See also E. Earle Ellis, *The Gospel of Luke* (London and Edinburgh: Thomas Nelson, 1966), 160–61; Joseph A. Fitzmyer, *The Gospel According to Luke* (Garden City, N. Y.: Doubleday, 1981–85), 2.891ff.; Alfred Plummer, *The Gospel According to Luke* (New York: Charles Scribner's Sons, 1925), 291; Eduard Schweizer, *The Good News According to Luke* (Atlanta, Ga.: John Knox Press,1984), 142ff.; Talbert, *Reading Luke*, 125.

[4] Sr. Philsy, "Diakonia of Women in the New Testament," *IndJTh* 32 (1983): 110–18; Quentin Quesnell, "The Women at Luke's Supper," in *Political Issues in Luke–Acts*, ed. R. J. Cassidy and J. Scharper (New York: Orbis Books, 1983), 59–79; Ryan, "Women of Galilee," 56–59; Via, "Women, the Discipleship of Service," 37–60; Ben Witherington, "On the Road with Mary Magdalene, Joanna, Susanna, and Other Disciples—Luke 8:1–3," *ZNW* 70 (1979): 243–44; more recently, F. Beydon, "A temps nouveau, nouvelles questions. Luc 10,38–42," *FoiVie* 88 (1989): 25–32, who has argued that Luke 10:38–42 legitimizes Mary's role as a "minister of the word." See also D'Angelo, "Images of Jesus," 197; Flanagan; Talbert, *Reading Luke*, 90ff.; Via, "Women in the Gospel of Luke," passim.

[5] D'Angelo, "Images of Jesus," 203; Maly, "Women and the Gospel of Luke," 102–3; Philsy, "Diakonia of Women," 111; Ryan, "Women of Galilee," 56ff.; Quesnell, "The Women at Luke's Supper," 60; Witherington, "On the Road," 243–44; Via, "Women, the Discipleship of Service," passim; idem, "Women in the Gospel of Luke," 42, 46–48.

[6] More recently, it has been argued that Luke in fact does not revise women's roles in a radical direction. For example, it has been noticed that Luke seems to limit the mission of the 72 to men, and his emphasis on Peter and the Twelve obscures the place of women among the disciples. The most recent scholar to call into question earlier assessments of Luke in this area is Mary Rose D'Angelo, "Women in Luke–

The "Ministering Women" of Luke 8:1–3

The Gospel of Mark describes women as "followers" and "table servants" in Mark 15:40–41, connecting the women around Jesus to community meal settings and identifying them as disciples. This is not the case in Luke. Luke 8:1–3 describes the women who follow Jesus. Along with the Twelve, "some women who had been healed of evil spirits and sickness" accompany Jesus, among them Mary Magdalene, Joanna the wife of King Herod's steward, Susanna, and "many others" (ἕτεραι πολλαί). Luke further comments that these women "served them" (διηκόνουν αὐτοῖς)[7] "from" or "out of" their own "possessions" or "resources" (ἐκ τῶν ὑπαρχόντων αὐταῖς). This passage has been identified as Lukan composition.[8] Furthermore, it reflects Luke's interest in parallel structures, as the list of the women and the Twelve introduces the following parables discourse as the first listing of the Twelve introduces the Sermon on the Plain (6:12–19).[9] As in Mark, women as well as men make up the number of those Galileans who witness Jesus' entire ministry (Luke 23:49; Acts 10:37–39) and travel with him as he preaches and teaches "from town to town."[10]

Luke, however, makes notable changes in the material he inherits from Mark. First of all, he separates this description from that of

---

Acts: A Redactional View," *JBL* 109 (1990): 441–61. D'Angelo connects Luke's portrayal of women to an apologetic agenda which contrasts Christian women to women in eastern cults and Judaism. One major contribution of D'Angelo's more recent study is her correction of earlier descriptions of Hellenistic Judaism. See also J. A. Grassi, *Hidden Heroes*, 85ff.; Schüssler Fiorenza, *In Memory of Her*, 145; idem, "Theological Criteria and Historical Reconstruction: Martha and Mary, Luke 10:38–42," *Colloquy* 53 (Berkeley, Calif.: Center for Hermeneutical Studies in Hellenistic and Modern Culture, 1987); Stuart L. Love, "Women's Roles in Certain Second Testament Passages: A Macrosocial View," *BTB* 17 (1987): 50–59; Elizabeth M. Tetlow, *Women and Ministry in the New Testament* (New York: Paulist Press, 1980), 101; Elisabeth Moltmann-Wendel, *The Women Around Jesus* (New York: Crossroad, 1982), 27.

[7] The plural is well-supported by the Alexandrian, Western, and Caesarean text types. The singular (αὐτῷ) may reflect the influence of Matt 13:4 and Mark 4:4 and a Christocentric correction by Marcion. The editors of both the UBS and NA editions prefer the plural reading, and the editors of the UBS rate their decision with a {B}. Metzger, *Textual Commentary*, 144.

[8] Fitzmyer, *Luke*, 1.695; Schweizer, *Luke*, 141; Witherington, *Women in the Ministry of Jesus*, 116.

[9] D'Angelo, "Images of Jesus," 203.

[10] Fitzmyer, *Luke*, 1.696; Ellis, *Luke*, 127; Witherington, "On the Road," 244.

the women who "follow" Jesus to the crucifixion (Luke 23:49). In Luke's version, not only women witness the crucifixion, but many of Jesus' male acquaintances or friends as well (οἱ γνωστοί). Given his familiarity with literary banquet themes, Luke probably intends his readers to understand these men to be Jesus' dining companions.[11] According to Luke's editing of this section, the key correspondence between Mark 1:17 and Mark 15:41 that allows for the women's discipleship has all but disappeared.[12] Thus, the women, now unnamed in this instance, follow to watch the crucifixion, accompanied by a masculine counterpart. They are part of a larger group that includes men and women, but they are no longer set apart as a special group of women "disciples."

Earlier in chapter 8, Luke also reworked the description of the women's "service" to become an act of charity. The women are no longer "table servants," which indicates in Mark that they were present for meals. In Luke these women are cast instead as Greco-Roman "patronesses." At least one among this feminine retinue, Joanna, is respectably married. The connection of Joanna with the court of Herod and the description of the women's philanthropic efforts on behalf of the entire troupe reveal Luke's overall interest in portraying a more highly placed movement.[13] The service of the women is not limited to mere table preparations, as Mark 15:41 suggests, but seems to be a more general reference to overall financial support.[14]

On the basis of Luke 8:1–3 and other passages, Quentin Quesnell has suggested that the "service" of the women should be interpreted to include ministerial duties. His arguments deserve attention here. He suggests that women, as disciples and perhaps as apostles,

---

[11] The theme of friendship is a literary banquet theme. See D. Smith, "Jesus at Table," 477ff.; 480ff.; idem, "Table Fellowship," 634. Jesus is a "friend" of tax-collectors and sinners. He may therefore be assumed to eat with them. See pp. 92–93 above and 114, esp. n. 27, below.

[12] Grassi, *Hidden Heroes*, 85ff.

[13] Highly placed, but by no means "upper-class." Even a steward or manager of an estate would still be a slave or freedman, but would certainly have more actual funds at his disposal. Such a person would still be deprived of real status. Pervo argues quite convincingly that it would be precisely this kind of individual that the author of Luke–Acts is addressing (*Profit with Delight: The Literary Genre of the Acts of the Apostles* [Philadelphia: Fortress Press, 1987], 40, 77ff., 106). See also Fitzmyer, *Luke*, 1.698; Witherington, "On the Road," 246.

[14] Fitzmyer, *Luke*, 1.696; Schweizer, *Luke*, 142; Witherington, "On the Road," 244.

were present at the Last Supper, where Jesus tells his followers that the greatest should be as one who serves (ὁ διακονῶν), just as he will serve them at the eschatological banquet (22:26–27; 12:37).[15] Of all those thought to be present, he suggests that it is the women who would best identify with this eschatological role reversal.[16] Women, then, as the only ones actually described as "serving at table" (διακονέω) would best exemplify a Lukan discipleship of service (διακονία).[17]

Luke's strategy at this point is subtle. It is true that these women follow Jesus from Galilee, and no doubt they are the same women who witness the crucifixion (Luke 23:49) and visit the empty tomb (24:10). These same women appear later in association with Mary the mother of Jesus, the Twelve, and the brothers of the Lord (Acts 1:14). It is doubtful, however, that in Luke 8:2–3 a more technical metaphor for leadership is meant. Although it is also true that Jesus puts forward the model of a "servant" (ὁ διακονῶν) as the true leadership role that the apostles should imitate (Luke 12:37; 22:26–27), Jesus makes this pronouncement at the Last Supper, where the attendance is limited to the male apostles. Quesnell's arguments for the women's presence at this point of the narrative are simply not convincing.[18]

Quesnell bases his conclusion on several points. First, he suggests that the narrative of the Last Supper presupposes a group larger than the Twelve living and acting together before and after the Last Supper proper. In 22:11, therefore, Jesus requests that Peter and John find a place for him to eat the Passover meal with his "disciples" (μαθηταί). A Passover feast would by definition include women, since women and children took part in the Passover ritual.[19] Second,

---

[15] Quesnell, "Women at Luke's Supper," passim; Ryan, "Women of Galilee," 58; Via, "Women, the Discipleship of Service," 40

[16] Quesnell, "Women at Luke's Supper," 71; Via, "Women, the Discipleship of Service," 40.

[17] Beydon, "A temps nouveau"; Quesnell, "Women at Luke's Supper," 71; Via, "Women, the Discipleship of Service," 40; idem, "Women in the Gospel of Luke," 47–48; Ryan, "Women of Galilee," 58.

[18] Quesnell, "Women at Luke's Supper." He is followed by Ryan, "Women of Galilee," 58; Via, "Women, the Discipleship of Service," 42–43; idem, "Women in the Gospel of Luke," 47–48.

[19] So Eduard Schweizer, who argues on this basis that the Markan Supper is not a Passover meal since the women are absent (*Good News According to St. Mark* (Richmond, Va.: John Knox Press, 1970), 295; J. Jeremias (*The Eucharistic Words of Jesus* [New York: Charles Scribner's Sons, 1966], 46ff.) suggests on this basis that the women should not be assumed absent from Mark's version of the Supper; Quesnell, "Women at Luke's Supper," 62.

Quesnell argues that Jesus addresses those present by referring to the sending out of the Seventy-two, not the Twelve (22:35–38; 10:1–4), which further indicates that the group addressed is not limited to the Twelve apostles.[20] Moreover, the women in the entourage are the ones who best identify with Jesus' comments about becoming like servants, since it is only the women who actually carry out the activity of "serving" (διακονέω) Jesus and the rest of the group (4:39; 8:3; 10:40).[21] Likewise, it is the women who persevere throughout Jesus' ministry (22:28) and remain faithful from Galilee to the tomb.[22] Because of the weight of the evidence suggesting that the women are indeed present for the proceedings, Quesnell concludes that the text limiting the group to "apostles" (22:14) must be the result of a tendency in the textual tradition to narrow the guest list of the Last Supper to the Twelve.[23] In fact, 22:14 might, in Quesnell's view, have originally read "disciples" (μαθηταί) not "apostles" (ἀπόστολοι).[24]

Quesnell's argument that the group following Jesus from Galilee, observing the events of the Passion week and receiving the Holy Spirit in the Upper Room includes women is correct. This is clear from 8:1–3; 24:6 (see 9:18ff.); 23:49, 55; 24:1ff. and Acts 1:14. From the beginning of Jesus' earthly ministry, Luke portrays women as being part of the larger community of the faithful. Nonetheless, Quesnell's other arguments break down at several points. First, although it is true that in Luke the verb διακονέω refers exclusively to the activity of women (see Luke 4:39), this is not Luke's term for the kind of service which denotes authority or leadership. The "service" of the women in Luke 8:1–3 is their financial support of the group. It is the noun διακονία which is reserved for the ministry and apostleship of men in the later mission of the church.[25]

As an activity of a woman, διακονία occurs only once in Luke–Acts, in Luke 10:40 where Martha is criticized for being distracted with "much service."[26] As for the women being the only ones who

---

[20] Quesnell, "Women at Luke's Supper," 65.

[21] Ibid., 71.

[22] Ibid.

[23] Ibid., 66.

[24] Ibid.

[25] Luke T. Johnson, *The Literary Function of Possessions in Luke–Acts* (SBLDS 39; Chico, Calif.: Scholars Press, 1977), 120. Via, "Women, the Discipleship of Service," 38. Note Acts 1:17, 25; 6:1, 4; 11:29–30; 12:25; 20:24; 21:19. Ὁ διακονῶν is his model for discipleship (Luke 22:26–27), διακονία his term for actual ministry.

[26] See pp. 133–44 below.

really persevere, it is precisely this aspect of Mark's portrayal of the Twelve which Luke goes to such efforts to correct. In spite of the betrayals of Peter and Judas, there are male dining companions of Jesus present to witness the crucifixion (οἱ γνωστοί;[27] Luke 23:49), and Luke highlights Peter, not Mary Magdalene, as the recipient of the first resurrection appearance (Luke 24:34).[28] The role of the

---

[27] Οἱ γνωστοί: "acquaintances," but also "friends" (LSJ, 355). Table companions were those who gathered together in friendship, not enmity, hence friendship is a major category of ancient table ethics. See D. Smith, "Table Fellowship," 634ff.; Grassi, *Hidden Heroes*, 86ff. on friendship as a table theme.

[28] The conflict between these two figures as representatives of apostolic tradition is well-known. Mary Magdalene, the woman who is always listed first among the women followers of Jesus, was also known in some communities as the one who first witnessed the risen Lord (John 20:1–18; Mark 16:9). Many scholars have noted that she comes close to meeting the requirements of an apostle, particularly the Pauline requirements, and apart from her gender, the Lukan as well (Raymond Brown, "The Role of Women in the Fourth Gospel," *TS* 36 [1975]: 688–99; Tetlow, *Women and Ministry*, 118). Her ninth-century biographer therefore called her "the apostle to the apostles" (Rabanus Maurus, PL 112, 1474b). Mary Magdalene appears with frequency in those documents labeled "gnostic" where she is often portrayed in conflict with Peter (*Gospel of Philip*, CG II, 63:30–36; *Dialogue of the Savior*, CG III, 139:12; *Gospel of Mary*, BG 8502, I, passim; *Pistis Sophia*, passim; *Gospel of Thomas*, CG II, 51:19–25 (Saying 114). See also the *Questions of Mary*, mentioned by Epiphanius (*Pan.* 26:81), and the *Apostolic Church Order*, where Mary is present for the Last Supper, but excluded from the priesthood because she "laughs" (a gnostic theme) (*The Apocryphal New Testament*, ed. M. James [Oxford: Clarendon Press, 1963], 36). Mary Magdalene and other women, Salome among them, also appear in the Coptic Manichaean Psalms, where they are sent out preaching in a passage reminiscent of Q 9. See *Manichaean Psalmbook*, ed. C. R. C. Allberry (Stuttgart: W. Kohlhammer, 1938), II.192; 194; 222; Kathleen E. Corley, "Salome," *ISBE* (Grand Rapids, Mich.: Eerdmans, 1988), 4.286, idem, "Salome Traditions in the Early Church" (unpublished manuscript). In spite of the predominance of Mary Magdalene in this literature, the other literature from the same period now labeled "orthodox" seems to avoid her, rarely citing texts like John 20:1–18. This is apparently due to Jesus' untouchability in this passage, which left open the possibility of a spiritual resurrection. Other church writers preferred to highlight the appearance to Thomas in John 20:24–25, where Jesus invites Thomas to touch his wounds, thereby affirming the bodily nature of the resurrection. It is interesting that the Lukan accounts of the resurrection run exactly counter to the Johannine accounts, in that Luke focuses on Peter, who loses the foot race in John 20:4. Luke also has an interest in affirming the bodily nature of the resurrection (esp. Luke 24:39ff.). For more on the Peter-Mary conflict in these traditions, see Kathleen E. Corley, "*Noli Me Tangere*: Mary Magdalene in the Patristic Literature," paper presented at the SBL Pacific Coast Regional Meeting, Claremont, Calif., March 16–18, 1989; Karen King, "The Figure of Mary in Gnosticism," paper presented at the SBL Pacific Coast Regional Meeting, Claremont, Calif., March 16–18, 1989; Marvin Meyer, "Making Mary Male: The Categories 'Male' and 'Female' in the Gospel of Thomas," *NTS* 31 (1985): 554–570.

women is now to "remember the words" of Jesus, not be the first witnesses to the resurrection (24:6–8). That role is reserved for Peter.[29]

In Luke, the entire company of disciples, but particularly representatives of the Twelve, hold firm until the end. Moreover, although Luke does seem to allude to the comments made to the Seventy-two rather than to the Twelve in 22:35 (see 10:4), this may be more due to the inexactitude of his language at this point than to any attempt to enlarge the group addressed at the Last Supper.[30] In any case, Luke's addition of "wives" to the family and property left behind by Jesus' followers indicates that the group sent out to preach is limited to men.[31] This may also refllect Luke's preference for asceticism.[32] Finally, Quesnell's suggestion that 22:14 originally read μαθηταί in the virtual absence of any manuscript support is tenuous at best. On the contrary, the tendency of the manuscript tradition to narrow the term "apostles" to "the Twelve" indicates not that the term was to be more broadly understood, but the opposite.[33] Even though one could argue that the ranks of the "apostles" might be widened to include the likes of Paul and Barnabas (Acts 14:14), given that Luke limits the Twelve to men in Acts 1:21ff.[34] and given that the only other persons called "apostles" are Paul and Barnabas, it is more likely that the ranks of both the Twelve and the apostles are meant to be closed to women in Luke–Acts. It should be noted that Luke also places Paul and Barnabas and the entire Gentile mission under the authority of the Twelve.[35]

---

[29] Grassi, *Hidden Heroes*, 86ff.; 91ff.

[30] Johnson, *Literary Function of Possessions*, 114, n. 1.

[31] Schüssler Fiorenza, *In Memory of Her*, 145. Moreover, the authority of the Twelve is also shown in their ability to work signs and wonders as did Jesus. As the 72 also do this, Luke undoubtedly sees them in the same trajectory of those commissioned by Jesus and the Twelve to preach and teach. See Johnson, *Literary Function of Possessions*, passim.

[32] Luke 14:26; 17:22ff.; 18:28; 20:27ff.; Pervo, *Profit with Delight*, 181, n. 79.

[33] Quesnell, "Women at Luke's Supper," 66ff.

[34] Fitzmyer, *Luke* 1.697; cf. 613ff.; Via, "Women, the Discipleship of Service," 42–43, n. 18. Via concludes that women are most certainly excluded from the ranks of the Twelve, but that it is not clear that they are excluded from the ranks of the "apostles" which is not limited to the Twelve. In Via's opinion, the problem with Quesnell's thesis is Acts 6, where seven men are appointed by the Twelve. I would also add that the only other two persons called "apostles" in Luke–Acts are men, Paul and Barnabas (Acts 14:14).

[35] It is also interesting that Luke drops the term διάκονος altogether. In Luke

Luke's vision of the community under the new servant leadership of the Twelve may be gleaned from Luke 12:37ff. Jesus likens the coming of the eschaton to a lord (κύριος) who puts a "steward" (οἰκονόμος; always a man, and usually a slave or freedman)[36] in charge of his estate, and who will hold him accountable for his treatment of the other slaves in his care—both men and women (τοὺς παῖδας καὶ τὰς παιδίσκας; 12:45). Preceding this pericope Peter (always the figurehead of the all-male Twelve) queries, "Lord, are you addressing this parable to us, or to everyone else as well?" (12:41). Clearly the audience is meant to be limited to the Twelve. Thus, the community which comes under the authority of a male leadership symbolized by Peter and the Twelve includes both men and women.[37]

The entire discussion of Luke 8:1–3 is therefore best seen in the context of Luke's interest in highlighting the authority of the Twelve, who take the place of Jesus in the early Christian community and are responsible for distributing goods to the rest of the community.[38] The authority of the Twelve is defined as διακονία, which is shown on the literary level by their distribution of food to the community, after members of the community have shown their submission to that authority by laying all their personal possessions at the apostles' feet.[39] Likewise the women in Luke 8:1–3 give up their "possessions" to Jesus and the Twelve. This coheres nicely with Luke's general literary strategy involving possessions and the authority of the Twelve.[40] This restriction of the community's leadership to men is continued in the limitation of the servers of the feeding to the Twelve (Luke 9),[41] the probable limitation of the itinerant preachers to

---

22:26–27, Luke changes διάκονος to ὁ διακονῶν and omits all other passages which contain it (Via, "Women, the Discipleship of Service," 37). Διάκονος does not occur in Acts. In Luke 12:37, it the role of the δοῦλος which is reversed with that of the κύριος (Johnson, *Literary Function of Possessions*, 203ff.).

[36] See pp. 48–49 above.

[37] Johnson, *Literary Function of Possessions*, 165–66.

[38] Ibid., 120, 165ff.

[39] Paul and Barnabas also show their submission to the Twelve in this manner (Johnson, *Literary Function of Possessions*, 165ff., 203ff., 211).

[40] Johnson also comments that Mary's posture in Luke 10 indicates her submission to Jesus. Just as the members of the community lay all their possessions at the feet of the Twelve to show their submission to their authority, so also Mary here submits to Jesus (*Literary Function of Possessions*, 202). One might also add that as the Twelve take the place of Jesus in Acts, Mary would also be shown in submission to them here (see pp. 133–44 below.).

[41] Johnson, *Literary Function of Possessions*, 113–14.

men,[42] and the choice of the seven male "deacons" in Acts 6. Both the feeding and the Last Supper, being stylized accounts which reflect the literary theme of the symposium, might also exclude women for literary reasons. This limitation also contributes to Luke's focus on the Twelve. The women in Luke–Acts therefore become part of the community that is "served" by the representatives of Jesus in their midst, the all-male Twelve, and the Seven, who subsequently receive the Twelve's authority.[43] The issue of gender is secondary to Luke's larger literary strategy of giving prominence to the Twelve.

Thus, the role reversal inherent in Luke's paradigm for leadership in no way negates the larger social structures present in Greco-Roman society. This role reversal is played out by the men "serving" the women (as in Acts 6). The "service" (διακονία) done by the men is in reality the activity of the male leadership in preaching and teaching and is no longer simple table service. After being selected to wait tables, the Seven are thereafter pictured in missionary roles.[44] Portraying a community that acted in a way contrary to the mores of the larger Greco-Roman society would pose a barrier to Luke's oft-mentioned interest in winning the known Hellenistic world. Up until the time of the eschaton, certain social roles therefore remain constant. Servants do what is expected of them at mealtime—and so do women.[45]

Luke's traditional stance is even reflected in many of the parallel passages concerning men and women. Men tend sheep outside whereas women search for coins inside the house (15:4–10). A more striking example of this is an often misinterpreted image of the unexpected nature of the coming judgment:

> I tell you, on that night there will be two men on one couch [κλίνη]; one will be taken, and the other left. There will be two women grinding at the same place; one will be taken, the other left (Luke 17:34–35).

---

[42] Schüssler Fiorenza, *In Memory of Her*, 145.

[43] Johnson, *Literary Function of Possessions*, 211ff.; Grassi, *Hidden Heroes*, 88ff. Note also that the Seven, once ordained to "serve" the widows, are never pictured as actually serving at table, but rather go out to preach and teach. The distribution of goods by the Seven therefore serves a literary function to identify the Seven as having been chosen by the Twelve and having been given their authority.

[44] Johnson, *Literary Function of Possessions*, 211ff.; Via, "Women, the Discipleship of Service," 42–43, n. 18.

[45] Luke 17:7ff.; 19:12ff.

Two men will be (as expected) reclining for a meal together, two women will be preparing a meal. The interpretation of this parallel as an example of the traditional roles of men and women in the context of ancient meal customs avoids certain interpretive problems.[46] Even Acts 6 reflects community meal practices sensitive to Greco-Roman meal propriety. The "widows" seem to be seated off by themselves.[47]

In his description of the women's "serving" as charity, Luke apparently does not question Greco-Roman social hierarchy. Women during the Roman period regularly gave religious groups financial backing; however, although it was not uncommon for women to support groups out of their own finances,[48] this scene creates a scandalous image. The scandal of such wealthy women actually traveling around the countryside without their husbands has not been lost on many commentators.[49] As we have seen, the scandalous nature of such a retinue, though, is due less to the background of Judaism as it is to the Hellenistic ideology which sought to limit the public movements of so-called respectable women.[50] Luke is aware that this scene evokes the cliché of scandal. Unlike Mark, who seems unconcerned about such a misinterpretation, Luke is careful to ex-

---

[46] RSV with emmendations. Ellis (*Luke*, 272) suggests that they may be angels; see also Fitzmyer, *Luke*, 2.1172; Flanagan, "Position of Women," 291; Plummer, *Luke*, 409–10. The Q saying also maintains both the parallel of male and female and the gender role distinction between their activities (plowing/grinding). See Matt 24:40–41. For another image of the time immediately preceding the impending judgment being like a time when people gather for a meal, see the section on the "days of Noah" (Luke 17:22ff.).

[47] A gender-based segregation for formal meals may have been common during the Hellenistic era, particularly at weddings and religious gatherings. The seating of the Jewish Therapeutrides in Egypt and the Christian women depicted in the catacomb of St. Priscilla in Rome are cases in point (see pp. 70–72; 76–77 above). Schüssler Fiorenza also suggested that Acts 6 reflects a concern for women's presence at communal meals (*In Memory of Her*, 166).

[48] Talbert, *Reading Luke*, 92; Witherington, "On the Road," 244.

[49] Fitzmyer, *Luke*, 1.696; Schweizer, *Luke*, 142; Talbert, *Reading Luke*, 92ff.; Via, "Women in the Gospel of Luke," 46. Burkitt argues that the "sinner" of Luke 7 cannot be identified with Mary Magdalene in 8:1–3 as "it is not very likely that Johana (*sic*) the wife of Chuza would be traveling about Galilee with a notorious courtesan. There is nothing whatever in Luke 8:1–3 to suggest that the Mary Magdalene there mentioned was anything but a respectable invalid" (Burkitt, "Mary Magdalene and Mary the Sister of Martha," 158). This is, of course, precisely the impression Luke is trying to create in 8:1–3.

[50] See ch. 2. Here many commentators again fall into the habit of criticizing Judaism in order to elevate Christianity (see previous note).

plain their presence among the men as gratitude for the healings Jesus wrought[51] and to describe their role as financial backers. The connection of the women's "service" to meal settings found in Mark is thus negated by Luke, and the "women who serve" become respectable Greco-Roman patronesses.

Peter's Mother-in-Law (Luke 4:38–39)

Luke's first meal scene including a woman follows the healing of Simon's mother-in-law. Here, as in Mark, the healing of the woman follows the exorcism of the demoniac. This particular parallel grouping of miracles does not originate with Luke, but rather reflects the content and order of Mark 1:21–31.[52] As we have seen this sort of pairing permeates Luke's Gospel.[53] As in Mark, the setting for the healing of the woman shifts from the public synagogue to the private space of a house, which is also a social dichotomy that predominates in Luke.[54] The passage shows signs of Lukan redaction, but reflects the basic pattern of Greco-Roman miracle tales, particularly the immediacy of the cure and the activity of the healed person as evidence for the cure.[55] Since he has not yet introduced the disciples into the narrative, Luke omits references to Peter's brother, Andrew, and to James and John.[56] Simon (Peter), however, seems well enough known not to need an introduction, and Jesus is here depicted as healing the relative of the future leader of the disciples.[57] Jesus appears to enter the house of Simon alone. Thus, due to the omission of the names of the other disciples, the identity of the group that reports the woman's condition to Jesus remains ambiguous (v. 39; Mark 1:31).[58] Luke alters the method of healing to the verbal command of Jesus, and it is not necessary for Jesus to touch the woman's hand as in Mark (v. 39; Mark 1:30), even though the

---

[51] Fitzmyer, *Luke*, 2.698; Witherington, "On the Road," 245, n. 13.

[52] Fitzmyer, *Luke*, 1.548; Flanagan, "Position of Women," 288–89; Kopas, "Jesus and Women: Luke's Gospel," 195; Witherington, *Women in the Ministry of Jesus*, 66.

[53] See p. 108 above.

[54] Love, "Women's Roles."

[55] Kee, *Miracle*, 170; Witherington, *Women in the Ministry of Jesus*, 66.

[56] Fitzmyer, *Luke*, 1.548–49; Schweizer, *Luke*, 99.

[57] Fitzmyer, *Luke*, 1.549.

[58] Ibid.

fever here is more serious (v. 38; Mark 1:30).[59] Jesus "rebukes" (ἐπιτιμάω) the fever, which casts the account as an exorcism, further heightening the parallel with the previous exorcism. This emphasizes the supernatural power of Jesus to perform the deed.[60] Moreover, Luke adds emphasis to Jesus' miraculous power by stressing the immediacy of the woman's cure.[61] It is this power to command demons that causes many to follow him (4:37, 42; 5:1–3).[62] The calling of the disciples therefore occurs in short order (5:1–11). Luke intends to show that the witness of miracles may serve as a basis for discipleship.[63]

As in the Markan narrative, Peter's mother-in-law rises immediately after she is healed and "serves" the men (διηκόνει αὐτοῖς; v. 39). Without the mention of the others in v. 38, one is left with the impression that only Jesus and Peter are served. Here the meaning of the verb διακονέω surely carries the regular meaning "serve at table."[64] Again, the question arises as to the significance of her service, apart from its indication of her recovery. As in the case of the Markan version, it is highly doubtful that Peter's mother-in-law performs a function usually prohibited in Jewish families.[65] Via, Quesnell, and others maintain that Peter's mother-in-law is here depicted as performing a diaconal function, since the scene recalls the early Christian ritual meal.[66] Quesnell suggests that it is only here and in 8:3 that any in Luke's narrative are actually said to "serve" (διακονέω) Jesus and his company, and these are the women.[67] As we have seen, however, Luke's language for leadership and "service" is limited to the terms ὁ διακονῶν and διακονία, whose application is

[59] Ellis, *Luke*, 100; Fitzmyer, *Luke*, 1.548; Plummer, *Luke*, 137; Schweizer, *Luke*, 99.

[60] Fitzmyer, *Luke*, 1.549–50; Kee, *Miracle*, 204; Schweizer, *Luke*, 99; Talbert, *Reading Luke*, 58; Theissen, *Miracle Stories*, 86.

[61] Fitzmyer, *Luke*, 1.548, 550; Witherington, *Women in the Ministry of Jesus*, 67.

[62] Talbert, *Reading Luke*, 58.

[63] Ibid. Signs and wonders also play a key role in conversions in Acts.

[64] Adams, "The Hidden Disciples," 105–6; Quesnell, "Women at Luke's Supper," 71; Via, "Women, the Discipleship of Service," 38; Witherington, *Women in the Ministry of Jesus*, 67; 172, n. 123. Fitzmyer maintains that the kind of service here may be more general, although he acknowledges that "waiting at table" may also be meant (*Luke*, 1.550). See earlier discussion of Mark 1:29–31 in pp. 87–88.

[65] See p. 88, n. 18 above.

[66] Philsy, "Diakonia of Women," 112; Quesnell, "Women at Luke's Supper," 71; Via, "Women in the Gospel of Luke," 42, 47.

[67] Quesnell, "Women in Luke's Supper," 71.

restricted to Jesus, the Twelve, and other male leaders. This is especially notable in that Martha is discouraged from concerning herself
with διακονία in Luke 10.[68] The women in Luke 8 "serve" Jesus and
the others through their financial support. Eucharistic overtones do
not appear to be present, as they are, for example, in Luke 9:14ff.
(Feeding of the 5,000), 22:14ff. (Last Supper), or 24:30ff. (Road to
Emmaus). In this instance we have an example of one such woman
who is healed by Jesus and who therefore "serves" him and his
company out of gratitude,[69] as do the women in Luke 8:1–3. In this
regard, 4:38–39 serves as a corollary to 8:1–3 just as Mark 1:29–31
serves as such to Mark 15: 40–41.[70] It seems doubtful that the scene
is meant to be anything other than a private, mealtime scene.[71] This
is underscored by the fact that the choice of only men in Acts 6 seems
to restrict the diaconate to men. When this woman "serves" she
actually waits at table. When men "serve" or distribute goods to the
community it symbolizes a leadership role.[72]

Luke's rendition of the story also betrays a concern for Greco-
Roman meal propriety. The other disciples have disappeared in Luke.
Thus, the "service" of Peter's mother-in-law is for Jesus and Peter
alone, underscoring the private nature of the scene; had Peter's
mother-in-law "served" several men in her home, it might have had
scandalous overtones. Rather, the scene becomes a private cameo
which focuses attention on a close early relationship between Jesus
and Peter, the eventual Lukan leader of the Twelve.

The "Sinner" Who Anoints Jesus at a Meal (Luke 7:36–50)

In chapter 7 Luke presents a story which involves Jesus in a
meal scene with a woman. Here Luke introduces a second category
of women who number among the followers of Jesus—repentant
sinners. Luke's story of this repentant woman has been seen as an
excellent example of Lukan concern for women.[73] In this story Jesus'

---

[68] See pp. 133–44 below.

[69] Fitzmyer, *Luke*, 1.549; Kopas, "Jesus and Women: Luke's Gospel," 195.

[70] This makes it likely that in 8:1–3 and 23:49 Luke has reworked Mark
15:40–41, rather than relying completely on special material to construct 8:1–3.

[71] As it is in Mark. See pp. 87–88 above.

[72] See pp. 133–44 below.

[73] The literature on this passage is therefore abundant. Thomas L. Brodie,

interest is widened to include even those women who inhabit the back alleys, marketplaces, and streets of a Hellenistic city, namely, slave women and prostitutes. As such, this unnamed woman serves as an example of one of the "tax-collectors and sinners" that Jesus is portrayed as befriending (Luke 7: 29, 39). She also is an example of one of the "servants" waiting in the marketplace who now "call out" to those who refuse to respond (7:32).

In spite of the various attempts to distinguish two or more separate anointing stories, historical or otherwise, it is more than likely that behind this and other accounts in the Gospels (Matt 26:6–13; Mark 14:3–9; Luke 7:36–50; John 12:1–8) lies one original chreia, which has been variously elaborated or expanded by the individual writers.[74] Although many have suggested that here Luke utilizes a separate source,[75] it is not unlikely he is also reworking some aspects of the Markan narrative according to his own theological interests.[76] As we have seen, although Mark does not address it, the moral reputation of the woman highlighted by Luke still underlies Mark's story.[77] Nor is a connection to the death of Jesus entirely absent here.[78] In any case, the basic story seems to have been gener-

---

"Luke 7, 35–50 as an Internalization of 2 Kings 4, 1–37: A Study in Luke's Use of Rhetorical Imitation," *Bib* 64 (1983): 457–85; David Daube, "The Anointing at Bethany and Jesus' Burial," *ATR* 32 (1950): 186–99; J. Delobel, "L'onction par la pécheresse: La composition littéraire de Lc. VII, 36–50" *ETL* 42 (1966): 415–75; J. Duncan Derrett, "The Anointing at Bethany," esp. 275–85; J. K. Elliott, "Anointing of Jesus," 105–6; Holst, "One Anointing of Jesus," 435–46; John J. Kilgallen, "John the Baptist, the Sinful Woman, and the Pharisee," *JBL* 104 (1985): 675–79; Legault, "Form-Critique Method," 131–45; Mack, "Anointing of Jesus," 85–106; Osborne, "Women: Sinners and Prostitutes," 1–35; Plummer, "The Woman that was a Sinner," 42–43; L. Ramaroson, "Le premier, c'est l'amour (Lc 7, 47a)," *ScEs* 39 (1987): 319–29; D. A. S. Ravens, "The Setting of Luke's Account of the Anointing: Luke 7,2–8,3" *NTS* 34 (1988): 282–92; Simpson, "Mary of Bethany," 307–18. See also Adams, "The Hidden Disciples," 63ff.; D'Angelo, "Images of Jesus," 203ff.; Schüssler Fiorenza, *In Memory of Her*, 128ff.; Flanagan, "Position of Women," 289; Grassi, *Hidden Heroes*, 100ff.; Kopas, "Jesus and Women: Luke's Gospel," 196; Maly, "Women and the Gospel of Luke," 99; Via, "Women, the Discipleship of Service," 49ff.; idem, "Women in the Gospel of Luke," 42ff.; Witherington, *Women in the Ministry of Jesus*, 53–57.

[74] Mack, *Myth of Innocence*, 200. See also Fitzmyer, *Luke* 1.686;

[75] Brodie, "Luke 7, 35–50," 458; Ellis, *Luke*, 123; Fitzmyer, *Luke*, 1.685; Holst, "One Anointing of Jesus," 436; Legault, "Form-Critique Method," 140;

[76] Fitzmyer, *Luke* 1.685; Mack, "Anointing of Jesus," 84; Witherington, *Women in the Ministry of Jesus*, 54.

[77] See pp. 102–6 above.

[78] Against Daube, "Anointing at Bethany," 196; See D'Angelo, "Images of Jesus," 205; Derrett, "Anointing at Bethany," 278; Grassi, *Hidden Heroes*, 100–101.

ally known in the early church, as evidenced by its inclusion in all four canonical Gospels. Thus, some reliance on oral or other tradition by Luke should not be ruled out.[79] The basic outline of the story remains constant: in the context of a meal Jesus is anointed by a woman, others present object to her action, and Jesus defends her.

As in many of Luke's scenes, Jesus is portrayed as teaching in the context of a meal.[80] In this instance, however, the connection of this event to a meal setting undoubtedly pre-dates Luke.[81] As in his other meal scenes, Luke's version of this story reflects symposium imagery.[82] That the setting of the meal involves a Pharisee is Lukan; Luke typically portrays this kind of friendship and interaction between Jesus and certain Pharisees. Later in Acts, Luke records continued interaction between the early Christians and Pharisees.[83] In spite of the conviviality inherent in the scene, Simon the Pharisee, as the host, is eventually criticized by Jesus for not extending the usual banquet niceties to his guest.[84] In Luke, as in Mark, the elaboration of Jesus' defense of the woman functions to portray Jesus as a master of rhetoric.[85] Inserted in Luke's elaboration

---

[79] Legault, "Form-Critique Method," 144; Mack, "Anointing of Jesus," 85; Witherington, *Women in the Ministry of Jesus*, 54.

[80] D. Smith, "Table Fellowship."

[81] Delobel suggests that it is Luke who gives the story its mealtime setting, but this is probably incorrect ("L'Onction," 460). Fitzmyer, *Luke*, 1.685; Holst, "One Anointing of Jesus," 439; Legault, "Form-Critique Method," 144; Mack, "Anointing of Jesus," 85.

[82] Delobel, "L'onction," 459; D. Smith, "Table Fellowship," 614; E. Springs Steele, "Luke 11:37–54—A Modified Hellenistic Symposium?" *JBL* 103 (1984): 379–94, esp. 380.

[83] Derrett, "Anointing at Bethany," 275; Holst, "One Anointing of Jesus," 438, n. 20; Talbert, (*Reading Luke*, 84ff.) emphasizes the contrast Luke sets up between the woman (as an example of a "sinner") and Simon (as an example of a Pharisee). On Luke's interest in Pharisees, see Robert L. Brawley, *Luke–Acts and the Jews. Conflict, Apology and Conciliation* (SBLMS 33; Atlanta, Ga.: Scholars Press, 1987), 84–106; X. de Meeûs, "Composition de Lc., XIV et genre symposiaque," *ETL* 37 (1961): 847–70, esp. 859; D. Smith, "Table Fellowship," 622, n. 28; 633ff.; J. A. Ziesler, "Luke and the Pharisees," *NTS* 25 (1978–79): 146–57. Fitzmyer agrees that the identification of Simon as a Pharisee is secondary to the tradition, but not that it is Lukan (*Luke* 1.688), as does Schweizer (*Luke*, 138). See also Plummer, *Luke*, 210.

[84] Derrett, "Anointing at Bethany," 277; Elliott, "Anointing of Jesus," 105; Fitzmyer, *Luke*, 1.691; Legault, "Form-Critique Method," 104; Schweizer, *Luke*, 140; D. Smith, "Table Fellowship," 632; Witherington, *Women in the Ministry of Jesus*, 55.

[85] Mack, "Anointing of Jesus," passim. See also Ellis, *Luke*, 124; Talbert, *Reading Luke*, 86. Brodie further suggests that in this story Luke utilizes the Greek literary convention of *imitatio* ("Luke 7,36–50"), passim.

as the analogy is the "Parable of the Two Debtors,"[86] which some have suggested Luke may have composed himself for inclusion here.[87]

The scene is a formal banquet. Jesus and his friend the Pharisee are depicted as "reclining" (κατακλίνω) at table together. An unnamed woman enters the room and approaches Jesus from behind. Plummer, interestingly enough, suggests that the woman may have entered the room with the disciples and then approaches the men as the meal proceeds.[88] Luke describes her as a "woman who was a sinner in the city" (γυνὴ ἥτις ἦν ἐν τῇ πόλει ἁμαρτωλός), i.e., a woman with a bad reputation (v. 37). The combination of the term "sinner" with her identification as a woman known in the city makes it more than likely that Luke intends for his readers to identify her as a prostitute, or more colloquially, a "streetwalker" or "public woman."[89] She is known for her sexual promiscuity. But as we have seen, this identification might also indicate that she is a lower-class working woman or freedwoman who may have earned her freedom by prostituting herself. She may now support herself by one of the few avenues open to her.[90] That she has been successful at whatever her trade may be is shown by the kind of costly ointment she uses to anoint Jesus (v. 37).[91] Luke has artfully omitted any discussion of the cost of the ointment; his overall interest in the care for the poor would make a story about financial waste (even on Jesus) awkward to say the least.[92] The objection here is not that the woman has wasted

---

[86] Mack, "Anointing of Jesus," 101; Bultmann maintained that the opposite was the case, i.e., that the parable was the original nucleus to which the rest was added (*History*, 20–21).

[87] Fitzmyer, *Luke* 1.687, 690; D. Smith, "Table Fellowship," 622–23.

[88] On the basis of ἀφ᾽ ἧς εἰσῆλθον "since the time I came in." Plummer, *Luke*, 213.

[89] See pp. 38–39 above. Some commentators hesitate to draw this conclusion, but those who do are correct. See Adams, "The Hidden Disciples," 68; Delobel, "L'onction," 425–26; Derrett, "Anointing at Bethany," 278; Ellis, *Luke*, 123; Schüssler Fiorenza, *In Memory of Her*, 129–30; Mack, "Anointing of Jesus," 88; Osborne shows how such a designation would identify a woman as a prostitute in Jewish literature ("Women: Sinners and Prostitutes," passim); Plummer, *Luke*, 210 and in "The Woman that was a Sinner," 42–43; Schweizer, *Luke*, 139; Simpson, "Mary of Bethany," 316; Witherington, *Women in the Ministry of Jesus*, 54; Legault suggests that her sin was only known to a few friends and family members (a private affair perhaps?) ("Form-Critique Method," 141). Fitzmyer doubts she is a harlot (*Luke*, 1.689).

[90] See p. 52 above.

[91] See pp. 104–5 above; Holst, "One Anointing of Jesus," 440.

[92] Holst, "One Anointing of Jesus," 440.

money, but that her act is immoral, given the identity of Jesus and the formal nature of the proceedings. This is surely the tension underlying the basic story behind Luke's narrative, and it may be why some commentators suspect that Luke somehow preserves an earlier version of the story.[93] After she reaches the dining couch of the men, the woman first washes Jesus' feet with her tears (v. 38). After drying them with her unbound hair, she kisses them and anoints them with the costly perfume. In Luke, given the setting, the description of the woman, and the fact that she anoints and fondles Jesus' feet, the erotic overtones of the story are obvious. Only slaves or prostitutes would perform such a function in the context of a meal.[94] Simon's private thoughts in this instance are therefore not unfounded, and Luke may intend for the reader to assume that Simon's concern includes a regard for ritual purity as well as morality.[95] If Jesus were really a prophet, so Simon reasons, he would not allow a woman such as this to touch him.

However, John J. Kilgallen has suggested that the previous pericope indicates that the woman is here depicted expressing her gratitude because she is in fact no longer a "sinner." Although many commentators have suggested that it is Jesus who is responsible for the woman's forgiveness of sins,[96] Kilgallen suggests that the woman's sins "have been forgiven" (ἀφέωνται, perfect tense) sometime in the past.[97] For this reason, Kilgallen suggests that the woman is probably among the "tax-collectors" and others who underwent the baptism of John earlier in the chapter (7:29–30).[98] Her act here

---

[93] So Adams; Daube; Holst; Mack, "Anointing of Jesus."

[94] Richard I. Pervo, "Wisdom and Power: Petronius' Satyricon and the Social World of Early Christianity," *Anglican Theological Review* 67 (1985): 314; D. Smith, "Table Fellowship," 632; Witherington, *Women in the Ministry of Jesus*, 56;

[95] Schweizer, *Luke*, 139; Via, "Women in the Gospel of Luke," 42ff.; Witherington, *Women in the Ministry of Jesus*, 55.

[96] Ramaroson suggests that Jesus forgives the woman on account of her great love, rather than on account of her faith, taking the ὅτι of v. 47a as causal ("Le premier"). Others emphasize her faith in Jesus. See Fitzmyer, *Luke*, 1.692; Plummer, *Luke*, 214; Schweizer, *Luke*, 138; Witherington, *Women in the Ministry of Jesus*, 57.

[97] Many commentators acknowledge that the tense indicates that her forgiveness took place some time in the past, but as to when Jesus accomplished this is usually not clarified. See Ellis, *Luke*, 125; Derrett, "Anointing at Bethany," 276, esp. n. 1; 278; Fitzmyer, *Luke* 1.692; Kopas, "Jesus and Women: Luke's Gospel," 196; Mack, "Anointing of Jesus," 102; note discussion of Kilgallen by Ravens, "Luke's Account of the Anointing," 284; Witherington, *Women in the Ministry of Jesus*, 57.

[98] Kilgallen, "John the Baptist."

should therefore be seen as one of gratitude for something previously achieved, with the verb "to love" (ἀγαπάω) here meaning "to thank."[99] Her tears might therefore be a sign not of nascent penitence,[100] or even joy over her new found forgiveness,[101] but of something else (to which we will return).[102] Her gratitude mitigates the erotic overtones of the story, just as the mention of the healings and exorcisms done on behalf of the women in 8:1–3 explains their presence among the company of Jesus and the other men. The parable in vv. 40ff. supports Kilgallen's interpretation, because the argument of the parable leads to the conclusion that a presupposed forgiveness (here release from debt) is that which leads to gratitude.[103] That the woman's "debt" was great may be derived from the lavish nature of her act of gratitude. Nonetheless, her very presence at the meal makes her sexually suspect, and so Simon objects to her actions. However, in light of her genuine response to him, Jesus accepts her in spite of her reputation and her presence at the meal.

The contrast between the repentant prostitute and the Pharisee in 7:36–50 is therefore clarified by the previous contrast between "the people and the tax-collectors" (who did accept the baptism of John) and the Pharisees (who did not; 7:29–30).[104] In view of the continued connection between tax-collectors and those who trafficked in pros-

---

[99] H. G. Wood, "The Use of Ἀγαπάω in Luke Viii (sic), 42, 47," ExpTim 66 (1954–55): 319–20; Fitzmyer, Luke 1.687.

[100] So for example, D'Angelo, "Images of Jesus," passim; Elliott, "Anointing of Jesus," 107; Fitzmyer, Luke 1.687; Simpson, "Mary of Bethany," 316; Witherington, "Women in the Ministry of Jesus," 55.

[101] Fitzmyer, Luke 1.689; Holst, "One Anointing of Jesus," 440ff.

[102] Only Via expresses doubt over exactly what the motivation is for the woman's tears. "A worthwhile question, which commentators often do not reach, is why was the woman crying? Was she crying in sorrow, repentance, shame? Or was she crying because she was a woman whose ultimate self-worth had never been acknowledged by any other man than Jesus?" ("Women in the Gospel of Luke," 53, n. 21). I suggest that her tears are a sign that she, like other women and slaves, responds to Jesus with tears. These tears also literally connect this pericope both with the preceding discussion of the "tax-collectors and others" who respond both to Jesus and John, and with the pericope concerning the upcoming death of Jesus. See below, pp. 127–30.

[103] Kilgallen, "John the Baptist."

[104] So Kilgallen, "John the Baptist." This is one aspect of his argument which is convincing. Tax collectors are also mentioned earlier in the narrative as being open to John's message (Luke 3:12). See also Talbert (Reading Luke, 84ff.), who interprets this entire story as a contrast between the woman sinner (who does accept Jesus) and a Pharisee (who does not), which plays out the comparison of the previous pericope.

titution and slavery as well as with "sinners,"[105] it is not unreasonable to assume that the phrase ὁ λαὸς ἀκούσας καὶ οἱ τελῶναι (7:29) would encompass the likes of the woman "sinner" in 7:36ff. As a "sinner" (ἁμαρτωλός), she represents one of the "tax-collectors and sinners" that Jesus is accused of befriending. It thus seems likely that the narrative of 7:36ff. dramatizes the preceding pericope.[106] Significantly, in the passage in Matthew which corresponds to Luke 7:29ff., Jesus remarks that both "tax-collectors and prostitutes" (οἱ τελῶναι καὶ αἱ πόρναι) believed (πιστεύω) John, and therefore will enter the kingdom of God before the Pharisees who did not believe him (Matt 21:31–32).[107] Just why the woman thanks Jesus for a forgiveness wrought by a baptism done by John is not clear. Immediately following this story, Luke describes other women who also respond to Jesus out of gratitude; this may not be a coincidence.[108]

The woman's tears, mentioned only in Luke,[109] further contrast her with the Pharisee Simon. Her tearful response shows her acceptance of Jesus, and John before him, and it foreshadows the tears of other women who will accept Jesus and "mourn" his death.[110] This

---

[105] See pp. 40–41; 90–92 above.

[106] Johnson, *Literary Function of Possessions*, 101–3. Talbert, *Reading Luke*, 84ff.

[107] See pp. 154–57 below. It is hard to believe that Q did not contain some form of this particular comparison between John the Baptist and the Pharisees, and that John was also accused of having tax-collectors and prostitutes among his followers. A clear reference to "prostitutes" among the followers of John who subsequently join the Jesus movement would further explain Luke's connection of this woman "sinner" with the "servant/children" flute players who respond to John and Jesus. If Q did include "tax-collectors and prostitutes" at this point, this would indicate that the same kind of sectarian/philosophical slander was directed at John as well as Jesus. This would push the characterization of Jesus as philosopher back into the time of John's movement. See David Seeley, "Was Jesus Like a Philosopher?" I hope my colleague Sterling Bjorndahl's dissertation on the relation between Jesus and John in Q will shed some light on this interesting correspondence. The close connection between John and Jesus is striking, even in Luke, who is interested in elevating Jesus over John.

[108] Some suggest that Luke intends particularly to highlight the female following of Jesus, and thus has grouped together stories about healings of women, the anointing story, and the narrative about the "ministering women." Notably, Johnson suggests that the description of the women in 8:1–3 follows the story of the anointing precisely because these women would also be included under the definition of ἁμαρτωλοί from 7:34 (*Literary Function of Possessions*, 102). See also Ravens, "Luke's Account of the Anointing," 286. Moreover, Luke tends to combine the images of meals and women. See Via, "Women, the Discipleship of Service," 49.

[109] Delobel ("L'onction," 430) considers κλαίω a term favored by Luke. See Luke 6:21, 25; 7:13, 32; 8:52; 19:41; 23:28, and Holst, "One Anointing of Jesus," 441.

[110] Holst ("One Anointing of Jesus," 440) notes this individuality of the Lukan narrative, but sees the woman's tears as a sign of joy, not contrition.

acceptance of Jesus is revealed in that she "weeps" (κλαίω) over his feet (7:38). This is not surprising; several scholars have suggested that this story is indeed connected thematically to the death of Jesus, just as it is in Mark. For example, the repentant criminal on the cross, after expressing faith in Jesus, is promised salvation (23:41–42).[111] A more striking correspondence to the crucifixion scene is the account of the large group of people, most notably the "daughters of Jerusalem," who "mourn" (κόπτω) and "lament" (θρηνέω) Jesus' fate as they follow after him while he carries the cross (23:27). Jesus tells these "daughters of Jerusalem" to "weep" (κλαίω) for their "children" (τέκνα) since a worse fate awaits them in the future (23:28–31). This undoubtedly refers to the destruction of Jerusalem (see 21:20–24). Moreover, it is women who first "remember" Jesus' words concerning his impending suffering (Luke 24:8, 24). The woman's tears therefore serve to connect this pericope with the death of Jesus later in the narrative.

Besides anticipating the crucifixion and to the subsequent fate of Jerusalem, the "weeping" of the woman in Luke 7 may also hark back to another aspect of the preceding comparison between those who reject John and Jesus (the Pharisees) and those who accept them (tax-collectors and sinners/others). This is found in the passage Luke derives from Q:

> To what then shall I compare the people of this generation, and what are they like? They are like children sitting in the marketplace [παιδίοις τοῖς ἐν ἀγορᾷ καθημένοις] and calling to one another, "We played the flute for you and you did not dance; we wailed [θρηνέω] and you did not weep [κλαίω]" (Luke 7:31–32, NRSV).

Again, the question of acceptance or rejection of Jesus and John is the general context. John came fasting, and the Pharisees did not accept him; Jesus came "eating and drinking" and the Pharisees did not accept him either (7:33–35). The "children" have been variously interpreted to be John and Jesus, who continue to call out to an unresponsive "this generation" or the unresponsive "this generation" who accuse John and Jesus, Wisdom's children. Conversely, it has been suggested that an unresponsive John and Jesus refuse to respond to "this generation."[112] Because Jesus and John are characterized as

---

[111] Grassi makes this connection clear in *Hidden Heroes*, 100–101, but see also D'Angelo, "Images of Jesus," 205; Derrett, "Anointing at Bethany," 278; Witherington, *Women in the Ministry of Jesus*, 56.

[112] Wendy J. Cotter, "The Parable of the Children in the Marketplace, Q

"children" (τέκνα) of Wisdom (v. 35), however, identifying the "children" of the marketplace who do the calling with John and Jesus and identifying those who refuse to respond with "this generation" seems the preferable interpretation.[113] Likewise, the followers of Jesus and John can also be seen by extension to be "children" of Wisdom, who likewise "call" out to those who refuse to respond.[114] This becomes particularly apt in the cases of the sinful woman in chapter 7 and the women who mourn Jesus' crucifixion in chapter 23. True respondents to the call of John and Jesus "weep" (κλαίω), as does the woman in Luke 7:38.

This response can be further supported in several ways. First, it may not be that the image of Luke 7:32 is meant to call to mind petulant children sitting in the ἀγορά.[115] Cotter suggests that in spite of the use of the term "children," the activity of these "children" is really that of adults, and, as she argues, adults in the sphere of the courts.[116] Their activity of "piping" and "mourning," though, suggests that these "children" may be other than small children. On the one hand, though it is true that one might expect to find small unattended orphans running around the marketplace, why such children would be playing pipes and wailing is not clear. On the other hand, one would expect to find slaves waiting in the marketplace to be hired, especially since slave owners often sent their idle slaves to the marketplace to look for extra work.[117] We noted earlier that slave women/prostitutes and young boys were often hired for banquets. Slaves could also be among those hired to play instruments and mourn at funerals.[118] These may indeed have been young slaves, particularly the boys, but it is not necessarily their age that is meant to be the central focus of this image. The focus is rather on their servile class. A better translation for παῖδες in this context is not "children" but "slaves" or "servants."[119] For this meaning see also

---

(Luke) 7:31–35; An Examination of the Parable's Image and Significance," *NovT* 29 (1987): 289–304, esp. 293ff.; John S. Kloppenborg, *The Formation of Q: Trajectories in Ancient Wisdom Collections* (SAC; Philadelphia: Fortress Press, 1987), 111.

[113] Kloppenborg, *Formation of Q*, 111.

[114] Cotter, "Parable of the Children," 303; Johnson, *Literary Function of Possessions*, 102.

[115] So Cotter, "Parable of the Children," 296–98; Kloppenborg, *Formation of Q*, 111.

[116] Cotter, "Parable of the Children."

[117] See pp. 48–49 above.

[118] Ibid., and p. 153, n. 26, below.

[119] Klosinski, "Meals in Mark," 129; LSJ, 1289. This might also indicate that

Luke 12:45, where a steward (usually a male slave) is put in charge over other slaves, both male and female ones (τοὺς παῖδας καὶ τὰς παιδίσκας). The woman who was a sinner/prostitute, like many tax-collectors and others who responded to John the Baptist and to Jesus, therefore "weeps" in response to Jesus. Others present for the meal, Simon the Pharisee in particular, do not respond either to Jesus or to her. Future generations of Jews will also not respond, even when the "daughters of Jerusalem" likewise "wail" (θρηνέω) over the death of Jesus (23:27), mimicking the παῖδες who "wail" (θρηνέω) in the marketplace (7:31–32).[120] Furthermore, the woman's position at Jesus' feet in Luke 7 underscores her servile posture and her submission to him.[121] She does not join him at the table but becomes an image of the many παῖδες (servants) who respond to John and Jesus. The response of this kind of woman juxtaposed to the lack of response on the part of the Pharisees contributes to Luke's literary irony.[122] In Luke, repentant women, including at least one repentant prostitute, number among those "sinners" who have left the followers of John the Baptist to join the followers of Jesus. That such a woman remains at Jesus' feet, not joining him at the table, suggests Luke's concern for Greco-Roman propriety.

Meals with "Tax-Collectors and Sinners"[123]

In light of the more extensive discussion above, additional comments on Luke's use of the motif of "tax-collectors and sinners" are in order. As Mark does before him, Luke takes over the accusation leveled against Jesus, which we have seen has its roots in earlier sectarian philosophical slander, and enlarges this image to create narratives. Luke repeats the story of the call of Levi with the subsequent narrative of a banquet where Jesus and his disciples are the guests of Levi.[124]

---

the τέκνα of 7:35 is a secondary.

[120] So also the beatitude concerning the "poor" connects the rejection of the "poor" (other outcasts among Jesus' followers) with the rejection of Jesus (Luke 6:21–22). The "poor" now "weep" (κλαίω) but later will not. See Johnson, *Literary Function of Possessions*, 133–34.

[121] See pp. 26, 29, 105, 142.

[122] Delobel, "L'onction," 425–26; Holst, "One Anointing of Jesus," 438.

[123] This discussion presupposes that of pp. 89–93.

[124] D. Smith, "Jesus at Table," 474ff.; idem, "Table Fellowship," 636ff.

Luke makes a few important changes in the narrative he receives from Mark. Although he keeps the phrase "tax-collectors and sinners" (τελῶναι καὶ ἁμαρτωλοί) in the accusation against Jesus (Luke 5:30), it is "tax-collectors and others" (τελῶναι καὶ ἄλλοι) who are actually described as reclining (κατάκειμαι) with him. Luke also omits the information that many such characters were "following" Jesus as in Mark (cf. Luke 5:29 and Mark 2:15). Luke also omits the reference to the presence of other "disciples" (μαθηταί) for the meal.

With Q before him, Luke also includes a second version of this accusation against Jesus, namely, that Jesus is a "wine-bibber and a glutton, a friend of tax-collectors and sinners." The idea of "friendship" would include conviviality. He therefore may be assumed to "eat" with them.[125] (7:34). Here, as in Luke 5, this remains an accusation. Likewise, in Luke 15:1ff., when the phrase "tax-collectors and sinners" occurs, the "tax-collectors and sinners" are listening (ἀκούω) to Jesus. The reference to Jesus eating (συνεσθίω) with "sinners" (ἁμαρτωλοί) again remains in the Pharisee's accusation (15:2). In a later scene, Jesus appears as the guest of another tax-collector, Zacchaeus (Luke 19:1–10) who is also called a "sinner" (ἁμαρτωλός) by Jesus' opponents (19:7). Although one would expect a meal to occur during such a visit, Luke does not describe one in this instance. Rather, Luke downplays the possibility that a meal has occurred, in that Jesus is merely "passing through" (διέρχομαι) the town (19:1). Luke does not say whether any other disciples stayed with Zacchaeus.

Several observations may be made on the basis of these texts. First, Jesus is actually pictured as eating with only one tax-collector (Levi) and residing with a tax-collector who is also a "sinner" (Zacchaeus). He is never described as eating with both tax-collectors *and* sinners as he is in Mark. The term "others" (ἄλλοι) in Luke 5:29 is ambiguous here and in Luke 7:29.[126] Furthermore, the prostitute identified as a "sinner" in chapter 7 does not join Jesus at the table. Thus, Jesus does not recline with either women, prostitutes, or

---

[125] D. Smith, "Jesus at Table," 477ff., 480ff.; idem, "Table Fellowship," 634.

[126] The ambiguity of this term makes me suspect that Q did include the term "prostitutes," but that Luke avoids it. As part of a larger omission, Luke also does not include the odd story of the Syro-Phoenician woman or the account of Herod's birthday symposium with a courtesan. Furthermore, if Q did not include this section, why does Matthew use the term "kingdom of God" (which is not characteristic of him) in Matt 21:31–32?

"sinners" in Luke's Gospel. This is in spite of the fact that the parable of the Lost Son indicates that one young "sinner" at least might be known to keep company with prostitutes (πόρναι, Luke 15:30), and in spite of the fact that Luke clearly understands that the adjective ἁμαρτωλός may refer to a woman. This suggests that Luke is avoiding picturing Jesus actually reclining with "sinners." His hesitance to do this further suggests that the phrase "tax-collectors and sinners" is interpreted by Luke to include women.[127]

Second, many of these "tax-collectors and sinners" seem to have been followers of John the Baptist, having received the "baptism of John" before joining the company of Jesus (3:12ff.; 7:29ff.). This may be particularly true in the case of the woman sinner. If certain of these "sinners" remain in their sin, Jesus has come to call these social outcasts to repentance, as John did before him.[128] Still, although Jesus is accused of consorting with "sinners," Luke's editing leads the reader to believe that Jesus does not readily eat with them. It is interesting that these lower-class characters are not the focus in Acts; rather, Acts emphasizes a more highly placed group.[129] Leading men and "not a few" of the leading Greek women are the kind of converts we meet in the pages of Acts, along with slaves and other women.[130] This development is foreshadowed in the Gospel, in that some wealthier women, probably freedwomen, a few of the wealthier, well-educated Pharisees, and a Roman centurion number among Jesus' followers.[131]

The portrayal of Jesus as one who knew and welcomed "tax-collectors and sinners" creates an extremely negative image of one with particularly degenerate dining habits and lower-class table company. Dennis Smith suggests that in Luke such imagery becomes "idealized" and functions as a literary motif.[132] Jesus the hero figure is accused of presiding over various Hellenistic symposia, even attending banquets with the scum of the Hellenistic city. It has been shown,

---

[127] Which may have significance for the Gospel of Mark. Are the women servants who follow Jesus meant to be identified with the "sinners" of Mark 2?

[128] Luke 5:32.

[129] Although "tax-collectors" and "prostitutes" do not occur in Acts, slaves and women are still converted (Pervo, *Profit with Delight*, 19). Wealthier folk also undergo conversion and thus status is a major concern of the book, which portrays the early community as respectable (Pervo, *Profit with Delight*, 40, 77ff., 106).

[130] Acts 13:12; see Pervo, *Profit with Delight*, 77ff.

[131] Luke 7:1–10; 8:1–3; etc.

[132] D. Smith, "Jesus at Table" and "Table Fellowship."

however, that while Luke keeps the accusation against Jesus, he portrays him as dining only once with a tax-collector. Luke's motivation behind keeping even the accusation, much less an "idealized" scene, though, is seldom clarified. Just how such an image can be construed as "heroic" is difficult to determine. Consorting with lower-class tax-collectors and their women is decidedly unheroic behavior.[133] It may well be that this tradition, present as it is in both Mark and Q, is too early for Luke to deny. In any case, although Luke is reticent to clarify this aspect of Christian beginnings, he does acknowledge it. By his redaction, however, Luke betrays his discomfort with these traditions. Thus, Jesus dines neither with women nor with "sinners" in the Gospel of Luke.

Martha and Mary (Luke 10:38–42)

In Luke 10 we find another scene which includes women in a meal setting with Jesus. The story of Jesus' visit with Martha and Mary contains the only pericope dealing with these sisters in the Synoptic Gospels.[134] This pericope appears to be a unitary construction; most scholars affirm that the pronouncement of Jesus at the end of the scene could not have existed on its own.[135] As such it is variously categorized as a biographical apophthegm or a pronouncement story.[136] The legendary or "ideal" character of the passage is usually affirmed[137] and it may be entirely a Lukan construction.

---

[133] Recent studies categorizing Luke–Acts within the boundaries of ancient romances, however, may provide a possible context within which such an "idealization" may be understood. Pervo has suggested that "ideal" is really a euphemism for "fictional." Ancient novels and historical fictions in fact capitalized on depictions of every exciting aspect of ancient life, even the seedier side. Bandits, pirates and hookers adorn the pages of this kind of literature. Moreover, this genre of literature was meant to appeal to the class of people that were on their way up and out of these lower-class rungs of ancient society, such as former slaves and wealthy freedmen and women. See Pervo, *Profit with Delight*, 18, 40, 45, 77ff., 106.

[134] Mary and her sister Martha are elsewhere found only in the Gospel of John, particularly in chs. 11 and 12.

[135] Bultmann, *History*, 33; Witherington, *Women in the Ministry of Jesus*, 100.

[136] Bultmann, *History*, 33; Schüssler Fiorenza, "Theological Criteria," 4; Fitzmyer, *Luke* 2.891; Witherington, *Women in the Ministry of Jesus*, 100.

[137] Bultmann, *History*, 33; Fitzmyer, *Luke* 2.891–92; Schüssler Fiorenza, "Theological Criteria," 4. As Pervo has suggested, "ideal" is a euphemism for "fictional" (*Profit with Delight*, 45).

This section is heavily laden with Luke's own language and style.[138] Although this story is sandwiched in between the parable of the Good Samaritan and the Lord's Prayer, it may be unconnected with this surrounding material.[139] Some scholars have suggested from this context that this passage is meant to dramatize "love of God" following the example of "love of neighbor" in the previous pericope.[140] As we shall see, this story about Mary and Martha has more links with the sending out of the Seventy-two (10:1ff.) than with the parable of the Good Samaritan.

The story is well-known.[141] Martha, apparently the mistress of the house, receives Jesus (ὑπεδέξατο αὐτόν) into her house (v. 38).[142]

---

[138] Still, Schweizer believes verses 38–41 contain some "un-Lukan elements" (*Luke*, 188ff.); Witherington, *Women in the Ministry of Jesus*, 100, acknowledges the Lukan style of the section, yet affirms the story as historical.

[139] Fitzmyer, *Luke* 2.892.

[140] Schüssler Fiorenza, "Theological Criteria," 3; Flanagan, "Position of Women," 290; Talbert, *Reading Luke*, 120–26; Witherington, *Women in the Ministry of Jesus*, 100.

[141] M. Augsten, "Lukanische Miszelle," *NTS* 14 (1968): 581–83; Aelred Baker, "One Thing Necessary," *CBQ* 27 (1965): 127–37; F. Beydon, "A temps nouveau, nouvelles questions. Luc 10, 38–42," *FoiVie* 88 (1989): 25–32; C. M. De Melo, "Mary of Bethany—the Silent Contemplative," *Review for Religious* 48 (1989): 690–97; Gordon D. Fee, " 'One Thing Needful'? Luke 10:42," in *New Testament Textual Criticism. Its Significance for Exegesis. Essays in Honour of Bruce M. Metzger*, ed. Eldon Jay Epp and Gordon D. Fee (Oxford: Clarendon Press, 1981), 61–75; Schüssler Fiorenza, "Theological Criteria," passim; A. Knockaert, "Structural Analysis of the Biblical Text," *LV* 33 (1978): 471–81; E. Laland, "Marthe et Marie. Quel message l'église primitive lisait-elle dans ce récit? Luc 10, 38–42," *BVC* 76 (1967): 29–43; A. O'Rahilly, "The Two Sisters," *Scripture* 4 (1949): 68–76; F. Puzo, "Marta y María. Nota exégetica a Luc 10, 38–42 y 1 Cor 7, 29–35," *EstEcles* 34 (1960): 851–57; J. Sudbrack, " 'Nur eines ist notwendig' (Luke 10,42)," *GeistLeb* 37 (1964): 161–64. See also Adams, "The Hidden Disciples," 100–12; D'Angelo, "Images of Jesus," 204; Flanagan, "Position of Women," 290; Kopas, "Jesus and Women: Luke's Gospel," 196–97; Maly, "Women and the Gospel of Luke," 103; Philsy, "Diakonia of Women," 8; Quesnell, "Women at Luke's Supper," 71; Ryan, "Women of Galilee," 56; Via, "Women, the Discipleship of Service," 45; Via, "Women in the Gospel of Luke," 46; Witherington, *Women in the Ministry of Jesus*, 100–16.

[142] As we shall see, this entire passage is beset with textual problems. The shorter reading, ending verse 38 at αὐτόν, is attested by the earliest witnesses (P⁴⁵·⁷⁵ B et al.). Other readings include the added words [αὐτὸν] εἰς τήν οἰκίαν attested by P³ᵛⁱᵈ ℵ C (ℵ¹ C² add αὐτῆς); [αὐτόν] εἰς τὸν οἶκον αὐτῆς is attested by A D W Θ and other witnesses. Metzger notes that there is no apparent reason that the phrase "into her house" would have been deleted, whereas the shorter reading might have called for further explanation. The editors rate their decision with only a {C} (Metzger, *Textual Commentary*, 153). Since the external evidence is somewhat inconclusive, and since the attestation to the inclusion of "into [her] house" in some form is weighty, one of the longer readings should be favored in this instance. The omission

Jesus seems to go into the house alone, though earlier in the narrative he is accompanied by many others, including, presumably, women (8:1–3; 10:38). That Luke drops the others from the narrative at this point may be less an indicator of Jesus' superior acceptance of women over against that of Judaism[143] as it is a literary technique to highlight the conversation between Jesus and Martha. Mary seats herself (παρακαθεσθεῖσα) at the feet of "the Lord" (πρὸς τοὺς πόδας τοῦ κυρίου)[144] "listening to his word" (ἤκουεν τὸν λόγον αὐτοῦ; v. 39). Martha is described as being preoccupied with "serving" (διακονία) and implores Jesus to instruct her sister to "leave" (καταλείπω) her place at his feet and help her "serve" (διακονέω; v. 40). Jesus rebukes Martha for being concerned about "many things" (πολλά v. 41) and elevates Mary for having chosen "the better part" or "portion" (τὴν ἀγαθὴν μερίδα; v. 42).

This passage has been variously interpreted. Many consider this to be a story about discipleship or the elevation of devotion to the word of God over other worldly concerns—even ministry.[145] Likewise, the vast majority of interpreters concerned with feminist issues suggest that here, as in no other passage, Luke's positive concern for women as members of the Christian community can be discerned. Mary, seated as a disciple at the feet of Jesus the teacher, embodies the new, unique image of a woman who is allowed to learn from Jesus as a rabbinical student, a role denied to women within Judaism.[146]

---

of "into [her] house" might be explained by a hesitance to attribute leadership of house churches to women, and would therefore coincide with the tendency to shorten Jesus' response to Martha in vv. 41–42, thereby negating any possibility of Martha's right to practice διακονία. Such a reading supports the contention that the social context of the passage is that of early itinerant preaching and house churches in the early Christian mission. See Adams, "The Hidden Disciples," 102–3; Laland, "Marthe et Marie"; Schüssler Fiorenza, "Theological Criteria," 7ff.; Gerd Theissen, *Sociology of Early Palestinian Christianity* (Philadelphia: Westminster Press, 1976), 8–16.

[143] Adams, "The Hidden Disciples," 104; Schweizer, *Luke*, 188; Witherington, *Women in the Ministry of Jesus*, 101.

[144] Some MSS read "Jesus" ('Ιησοῦς) (P[45.75] A B* C[2] W etc.). On the other hand, P[3] ℵ B[2] D L etc. read "Lord" (κύριος). Fitzmyer suggests that the reading of "Lord" reflects the influence of v. 41 (*Luke*, 2.893).

[145] Adams, "The Hidden Disciples," 108; Ellis, *Luke*, 160; Laland, "Marthe et Marie," passim; Plummer, *Luke*, 290; Puzo, "Marta y María," passim; Schweizer, *Luke*, 189–90; Sudbrack, " 'Nur eines ist notwendig," 161–64; Talbert, *Reading Luke*, 125–26; Witherington, "On the Road," 247, n. 18; Witherington, *Women in the Ministry of Jesus*, 103.

[146] Adams, "The Hidden Disciples," 104; D'Angelo, "Images of Jesus," 204; Ellis, *Luke*, 160–61; Fitzmyer, *Luke*, 2.892–93; Robert J. Karris, *Luke: Artist and*

Following this line of reasoning, Martha's role is seen as the traditional role of the hospitable housewife, which she is being encouraged to leave behind, and become a full disciple like Mary, who is seeking the nontraditional role of a religious student. Nevertheless, many scholars hasten to add that Martha's traditional role is not completely ruled out by Jesus' remarks, nor is this meant to be taken as an absolute denial of the validity of traditional women's roles. Martha is simply being instructed to keep her household concerns in proper perspective.[147] Women, like men, should not allow everyday tasks to impede their relationship with God. Further, this passage has historically been interpreted to support those women who choose a life of religious contemplation, without denying the validity of the more traditional woman's life as wife and mother.[148] For many years, then, this passage has been central to an affirmation of women's participation in the life of the Christian community.

In recent years this positive assessment has been called into question. Elisabeth Schüssler Fiorenza suggests that this traditional interpretation denigrates the active role of Martha, while elevating the passive role of Mary, who sits silently throughout the entire proceeding.[149] Schüssler Fiorenza suggests that this passage is best understood in conjunction with Acts 6. There the apostles (all men) do not wish to "leave" (καταλείπω) the "ministry of the word" (διακονία τοῦ λόγου) in order to wait on tables (διακονέω). Subsequently, seven are chosen for this task (again all men), who then proceed, not to wait on tables, but to teach and preach. Here Martha, who should be seen not as a mere hostess, but as a leader of an early Christian house church, "receives" (ὑποδέχομαι)[150] Jesus but is subsequently

---

Theologian. Luke's Passion Account as Literature (New York/Mahwah/Toronto: Paulist Press, 1985), 50; Maly, "Women and the Gospel of Luke," 103; Plummer, *Luke,* 291; Ryan, "Women of Galilee," 56; Schweizer, *Luke,* 189; Talbert, *Reading Luke,* 125; Via, "Women in the Gospel of Luke," 46; Witherington, *Women in the Ministry of Jesus,* 101.

[147] Laland, "Marthe et Marie," passim; O' Rahilly, "The Two Sisters," pp. 70–71; Philsy, "Diakonia of Women," 8; Plummer, *Luke,* 292; Puzo, "Marta y María," passim; Witherington, "On the Road," 247, n. 18; idem, *Women in the Ministry of Jesus,* 101–2.

[148] Now all but abandoned as too allegorical. Schüssler Fiorenza, "Theological Criteria," 5; Fitzmyer, *Luke,* 2.892–93; Plummer, *Luke,* 293; Schweizer, *Luke,* 189–90. But see O' Rahilly, "The Two Sisters"; De Melo, "Mary of Bethany."

[149] Schüssler Fiorenza, "Theological Criteria," 6–7.

[150] As others "receive" ministers in the Pauline letters. See for example, Rom 16:1 (Phoebe is to be "received" [προσδέχομαι]) and Phil 2:25–29 (Epaphroditus is

criticized for her concern for διακονία. Mary, who is passive and silent, sits "listening to his word" (ἤκουεν τὸν λόγον αὐτοῦ). Martha requests that Jesus instruct Mary to "leave" (κατλείπω) her position at his feet in order to help her "serve" (διακονέω). Mary's role, unlike that of the men in the book of Acts, does not seem to include preaching or leadership (τῇ διακονίᾳ τοῦ λόγου; Acts 6:4), but only "listening to the word" (ἤκουεν τὸν λόγον; Luke 10:39). Mary's attention to the "word" is therefore one of reception, not proclamation, signaling the true Lukan agenda behind this text, which becomes prescriptive, not descriptive.[151] Schüssler Fiorenza's interpretation coincides somewhat with that of other scholars who have interpreted this passage, not in the context of the earthly life of Jesus, but rather in the context of an early Christian community expanding through the efforts of itinerant missionary groups. Such missionaries would stay and preach in early house churches as they traveled from town to town.[152] Schüssler Fiorenza's observations have been followed by various scholars, and as a result the notion that Luke gives an essentially "positive" portrayal of women has been undermined.[153] There is no doubt that Schüssler Fiorenza's reassessment of this pericope turns the traditional interpretation on its head. The topic at hand is not hospitality put in proper perspective, but a struggle in the Lukan community over women's leadership.

Schüssler Fiorenza's position has much to commend it. In support of her interpretation of Mary's "portion" is that, in the context of the meal customs of the Hellenistic world, Mary's stance is that of a traditional, silent wife, who sits at the feet of her husband at the table.[154] Her place at Jesus' feet, therefore, undoubtedly stems more from the fact that this is a meal setting than from an attempt to portray Mary as a rabbinical student. The setting is clearly that of a meal: food is being prepared; table service seems imminent; the passage includes several puns on meal terminology, in that Mary

---

to be "received" [προσδέχομαι]).

[151] Adams, "The Hidden Disciples," 106; Schüssler Fiorenza, "Theological Criteria," 7; Tetlow, *Women and Ministry*, 104. Kopas fudges a bit on this text when she remarks, "Though we do not see them (Martha and Mary) preaching in word, we do see it in action" ("Jesus and Women: Luke's Gospel," 197). Philsy suggests that "listening to the word" is a dimension of diakonia ("Diakonia of Women," 113).

[152] Theissen, *Sociology of Early Palestinian Christianity*, 8–16; 33; and see below, pp. 142–43, and above, n. 142.

[153] D'Angelo's article, "Women in Luke–Acts," shows this general direction.

[154] See pp. 26, 29, 105, 142.

chooses a "portion" (μέρος), a word often used to describe a dish at a meal, and Martha is told that only a "few things (i.e., dishes)" are really necessary for Jesus' meal.[155] Because teaching scenes are often set in the context of a meal,[156] the underlying point of the passage is still that Mary is included for a time of instruction. But like the two women in Plutarch, she remains silent. Furthermore, Mary is quietly seated at the feet of Jesus and is not portrayed as reclining as his equal on the dinner couch. It is therefore not necessary to denigrate Judaism in order to make the point that Mary is here receiving instruction, particularly since there is ample evidence that certain rabbis did encourage the education of daughters, even in Torah.[157] Furthermore, the removal of the others from the narrative at this point underscores the private nature of the scene. Although it is true that such a scene of Jesus alone with two women might cause a scandal, to include a large host of other men and women in the scene would be worse. In the context of Greco-Roman social ideology governing women's behavior at meals, this text unmistakably extols the traditional, private role of a Hellenistic woman.

There are several other reasons, however, for accepting Schüssler Fiorenza's contention that the topic of the pericope has less to do with traditional household chores than it has to do with ministry roles in the Lukan community. This passage, like many others in the Gospels, is beset with textual problems, a clue that scribes often found aspects of the narrative difficult to understand. Unfortunately, it is the punchline of the pronouncement itself which contains the most difficult of textual problems. There are no less than six textual variants extant for vv. 41–42, and scholars may never be certain as to whether Luke wrote that only "one thing" is necessary for Martha and Mary, or "a few things are necessary" or "a few things are necessary, but really only one."[158] In spite of the editorial decision

---

[155] Epictetus, *Ench.* 34; Dion. Hal., 8.30; Lucian, *Cyn.* 7; Ellis, *Luke*, 161; Fitzmyer, *Luke*, 2.894; O' Rahilly, "Two Sisters," 69, n. 42; Plummer, *Luke*, 292; Witherington, *Women in the Ministry of Jesus*, 103.

[156] D. Smith, "Table Fellowship."

[157] See p. 67. Moreover, even in Acts 16 a group of Jewish women gather on the sabbath at a synagogue. D'Angelo also mentions Acts 16, commenting on the reality of Jewish women's experience, which was undoubtedly better than Christian interpreters have suggested ("Women in Luke–Acts," 459).

[158] Fee argues that of four possible readings, that witnessed by P³ ℵ B C² L 1. 33. 579. 2193 is preferred: Μάρθα, Μάρθα, μεριμνᾷς καὶ θορυβάζῃ περὶ πολλά, ὀλίγων δέ ἐστιν χρεία ἢ ἑνός· Μαριὰ(μ) γάρ . . . See his discussion, "One Thing

of major critical texts[159] and the affirmation of the majority of modern interpreters,[160] Gordon Fee has argued persuasively that the longer reading is to be preferred in this instance.[161] Though the external evidence is inconclusive, and in spite of the witness of P[75],[162] Fee concludes on the grounds of transcriptional probability that the longer reading, ὀλίγων δέ ἐστιν χρεία ἢ ἑνός, is the more difficult and hence preferred reading. Fee rules out the possibility that the longer reading arose as a result of conflation and subsequently refutes the argument that the longer reading was the result of a nonsensical conflation.[163] Indeed, Fee argues, the sense of the longer reading is not intolerable, but subtle. Such subtlety may have led scribes, as perplexed by the sense as many modern interpreters, to rewrite the text into the more manageable ἑνὸς δέ ἐστιν χρεία.[164]

Given the inconclusiveness of the external evidence, Fee's decision may still be accorded no more than the {C} rating suggested by the editors who prefer the shorter one,[165] but additional reasons that might support Fee's reading also buttress Schüssler Fiorenza's contention that this text concerns ecclesiastical struggles over women's roles, even though she uses the shorter reading to support her position.[166] The shorter reading makes the contrast between Mary and Martha clear, and effectively rules out the more active role of Martha. The longer reading, while still elevating the role of Mary, leaves open the possibility that Martha's role might still be practiced—"a few things" still being necessary, "one" simply being preferred.[167] In the longer reading, Jesus' comments to Martha gently

---

is Needful," 63–65.

[159] UBS, Nestle-Aland; Metzger, *Textual Commentary*, 153–54.

[160] Aelred Baker is the most recent proponent of the shorter reading ("One Thing Necessary"). See also Ellis, *Luke*, 160–61; Schüssler Fiorenza, "Theological Criteria," 3; Fitzmyer, *Luke*, 2.894; Schweizer, *Luke*, 188; Witherington, *Women in the Ministry of Jesus*, 102–3. Talbert refuses to decide: *Reading Luke*, 125–26. Only Augsten favors the reading ὀλίγων δέ ἐστιν χρεία ("Lukanische Miszelle"), which Fee dismisses once and for all as being an unviable option ("One Thing is Needful?").

[161] Fee, "One Thing is Needful?" See also O'Rahilly, "Two Sisters," 69, n. 42; 71; Plummer, *Luke*, 292.

[162] The deciding factor for many, see for example, Fitzmyer, *Luke* 2.894; See discussion by Fee, "One Thing is Needful?" 73.

[163] Fee, "One Thing is Needful?" 71.

[164] Ibid., 71–72.

[165] Ibid., 75; Metzger, *Textual Commentary*, 153–54.

[166] Schüssler Fiorenza, "Theological Criteria," 3.

[167] Perhaps D. Smith presupposes the longer reading when he remarks,

rebuke her, rather than sharply criticize her.[168] It is interesting that both early witnesses to the shorter reading, P[75] and P[45], omit the reference to Martha's "house" in v. 38, which further limits Martha's role in the passage. One could argue that this omission further deemphasizes her position and obscures the image of Martha as a leader of a house church. Furthermore, another aspect of the confused textual tradition in vv. 41–42 indicates that the "trouble" Martha causes concerns a community, not just an individual, and that is the substitution of the rare word θορυβάζω with the more common τυρβάζω in the textual tradition. Θορυβάζω is rarely used of individuals and usually refers to groups and assemblies that are in a state of uproar or riot. Therefore it occurs with words like ἐκκλησία.[169] Editors are therefore more certain that scribes changed θορυβάζω to τυρβάζω, since the former did not seem to fit the context of Luke 10. Θορυβάζω is the more difficult reading in this instance. Although θορυβάζω does not occur elsewhere in Luke–Acts, cognates of it (θορυβέω and θόρυβος) do. In each of these passages, a rioting crowd, an assembly, or the potential uproar of mourning by a large group is in view (Acts 17:5; 19:40—20:1; 21:34; 24:18 [see v. 12]). Luke's usage of these cognates indicates that he was fully aware of the communal connotation of θορυβάζω in Luke 10:41. Thus the tendencies of the textual tradition to portray Martha's reaction as simple personal agitation, to omit the reference to the scene being "in her house," and to rule out completely her role in διακονία contribute to the choice of the longer reading as a case of *lectio difficilior potior*.

These textual considerations further support Schüssler Fiorenza's contention that the original Lukan intent was to discourage women from taking on Martha's role and that the real issue at hand was the leadership of women in the Lukan community. The longer reading, while not ruling out Martha's role, still makes the same point: Mary's quiet, submissive role is preferable.[170] Moreover, we have seen that, except for Luke 10:38–42, διακονία occurs nowhere else in the Gospel, and where it does occur in Acts it refers to the διακονία and apostleship of either the Twelve or Paul and Barnabas.

"Though the story functions to legitimate Mary's role as listener rather than a servant at the table, yet it by implication assumes the legitimacy of the role of Martha to serve" ("Table Fellowship," 633).

[168] Fee, "One Thing is Needful?" 75.

[169] LSJ, 803.

[170] Fee, "One Thing is Needful?" 71.

All are men.[171] Luke also omits the term διάκονος (which could be used of a woman),[172] and Jesus' pronouncements about becoming like "one who serves" (ὁ διακονῶν)[173] are made to the men.[174] Furthermore, those who accompany Paul to "serve" him (διακονέω) on his missionary journeys are not women, but Timothy and Erastus (Acts 19:22) or perhaps John Mark (Acts 13:5; 15:37–39). This is in spite of the numerous references in the authentic Pauline epistles that women "served" with Paul in the Hellenistic mission as "fellow-workers."[175] Thus, part of Luke's intent in this meal scene is to discourage, although not prohibit, Martha's active role in διακονία.[176]

The "good part" (τὴν ἀγαθὴν μερίδα, v. 42) chosen by Mary further underscores her submissive role in that she "listens to the word" (ἤκουεν τὸν λόγον αὐτοῦ) of Jesus (v. 39). Throughout the Gospel, large groups of people listen to Jesus, whose words are often identified as the "word of God" (λόγος τοῦ θεοῦ) or the word of the Lord (τοῦ κυρίου).[177] Those who are really part of the community (Jesus' true "mother and brothers" [μήτηρ καὶ ἀδελφοί]) are those who "hear the word of God and do it" (οἱ τὸν λόγον τοῦ θεοῦ

---

[171] See p. 115 above.

[172] Rom 16:1; Luke's avoidance of the term διάκονος may also reflect an intent to deemphasize the Seven, who may in fact have been rivals of the Twelve, as well as omit the possibility that such a role might be taken on by women (implied in Mark 9:35 and 10:43). See Pervo, *Profit with Delight*, 40. Via ("Women, the Discipleship of Service," 37ff.) discusses the omission of διάκονος in Luke–Acts, but does not suggest any significance of this omission in so far as women's leadership is concerned. On the contrary, as women are the only ones who "wait tables," they best exemplify Lukan discipleship of service (45) (following Quesnell, "Women at Luke's Supper," 71).

[173] Although I agree with Via ("Women, the Discipleship of Service") that Lukan discipleship involves "the adoption by the male disciples of this feminine role model for their relationships to the sacred and to one another. As the women serve, so shall they serve" (p. 45), I do not agree that it therefore follows that women are thereby encouraged to take on the leadership role of the men.

[174] See pp. 112–15 above.

[175] In Acts 18:18 both Priscilla and Aquila are "with" Paul, but the verb διακονέω does not occur. The various women to whom Paul refers with missionary terminology are: Phoebe, also called "deacon" and "patron" (Rom 16:1); Priscilla (Rom 16:3; 1 Cor 16:19); Mary (Rom 16:6); Junia, also called "apostle" (Rom 16:7); Tryphaena, Tryphosa, and Persis (Rom 16:12); Euodia and Syntyche (Phil 4:2–3). See Schüssler Fiorenza, *In Memory of Her*, 169ff.

[176] D'Angelo also makes this point ("Women in Luke–Acts," 455).

[177] For example Luke 5:1; 6:18; 7:29; ch. 8, passim; 10:8; 11:28; 15:1. Via ("Women, the Discipleship of Service") comments that in Luke, "The word, the word of God, and the word of Jesus are the same in Luke's gospel" (p. 56).

ἀκούοντες καὶ ποιοῦντες; Luke 8:21), having heard the "word" with a "good heart" (ἐν καρδίᾳ καλῇ καὶ ἀγαθῇ ἀκούσαντες τὸν λόγον; Luke 8:15). Jesus then gives this authority to those he sends out to preach from town to town (Luke 10:1–16). Jesus tells the Seventy-two that "the one who listens (ἀκούω) to you listens to me, and the one who rejects you rejects me; and he who rejects me rejects the one who sent me" (Luke 10:16). The preachers are instructed to stay in one house (οἰκία) in each town that they visit, "eating and drinking" (ἐσθίοντες καὶ πίνοντες) whatever is set before them (10:7), and healing whoever might be ill in the house (Luke 10:9). Thus, it is not surprising to find in Acts that crowds "listen" (ἀκούω) to the "word" (λόγος) of the various male preachers such as Peter, Stephen, Philip, Paul, and Barnabas.[178] As these preachers—the Twelve in particular—continue to convey the words of Jesus, disobedience to their commands is met with unusually heavy-handed punishment.[179] Paul and Barnabas are portrayed as continuing to follow the directives of Luke 10 in that they "shake the dust from their feet" (ἐκτιναξάμενοι τὸν κονιορτὸν τῶν ποδῶν) when they leave a town that has rejected their message (Acts 13:51; cf. Luke 10:11).

Luke 10:38–42 should therefore be regarded as thematically connected to the first part of chapter 10, the sending out of the Seventy-two, and not to the pericope immediately preceding it. The role of women in the context of early itinerant missionary practice is to host the itinerant preachers. They are discouraged from concerning themselves with the διακονία—that is the activity of the men. The story of the healing of Peter's mother-in-law also fits nicely into this context, although a simple meal and not actual διακονία seems to be in view.[180] Women, although hosts of house churches, no doubt due to their financial position, continue to have a secondary role to the leadership of the men. The wealthy women in Luke 8:1–3 show their submission to Jesus and the Twelve by giving them their possessions;[181] likewise Mary's position at Jesus' "feet" shows her submission to Jesus, and therefore her submission to the Lukan leadership.[182]

---

[178] Acts 1:15; 4:4; 6:2, 12; 8:14; 10:44; 13:7, 44–49; 15:6; 16:14ff.; 19:10; Johnson, *Literary Function of Possessions*, passim.

[179] Acts 4:32–5:11; Johnson, *Literary Function of Possessions*, 191ff.

[180] See pp. 119–21 above.

[181] See pp. 26, 29, 105, 116–19 above.

[182] Johnson, *Literary Function of Possessions*, 202.

In light of the correspondence between Luke 10:38–42, 10:1–16, and Acts 6, there is yet another passage in Acts which corresponds to Luke 10:38–42 that should not be overlooked, Acts 16. In Acts 16, Paul comes to the city of Philippi, where he and his company look for a "place of prayer" (προσευχή) on the Sabbath. Undoubtedly they are seeking a synagogue.[183] When they find one, lo and behold they discover a group of women assembled there, and they begin to preach to them (Acts 16:13). Among this group of Jewish women is a Greek convert to Judaism named Lydia. She is here identified as a "God-fearer" (σεβομένη τὸν θεόν; 16:14) and a "seller of purple" (πορφυρόπωλις), that is, a dealer in a costly purple dye used in the textile industry. This was a common luxury item sold by freed-women.[184] As a seller of such an expensive commodity, she undoubtedly was rather wealthy by ancient standards, although hardly a member of the aristocracy. As Paul speaks, the Lord (κύριος) opens her "heart" (καρδία) as she was listening (ἀκούω) to the things being spoken by Paul (16:14). Like those who respond with a "good heart" (Luke 8:15), she converts, and she and her household are baptized (16:15). That she has a household (οἶκος) underscores that she is a successful businesswoman. Following the baptisms she invites Paul and the other missionaries to stay in her house (οἶκος; 16:15, 40). In light of this scene, Lydia is often considered the first leader of a house church in Philippi,[185] but this scene has much in common with Luke 10:38–42, given the overall context of early itinerant missionary practice. A wealthy woman serves the community by hosting visiting preachers whose message she has heard and obeyed. In the subsequent narrative, she does not reappear in a missionary role, but as a host (16:40). As in the case of Martha, Lydia's role should not involve διακονία, an activity reserved for men.

In spite of the foregoing observations the positive ramifications of the scene in Luke 10:38–42 ought not to be forgotten. Mary is portrayed as joining Jesus for a meal, even though her posture reflects a more traditional, matronly role and she remains silent while seated

---

[183] Although Luke prefers the term συναγωγή, προσευχή also may be translated "synagogue." See LSJ, 1511 and discussion by Kraemer, "Monastic Jewish Women," 367ff.

[184] See p. 52, and Horsley, "The Purple Trade," 25–32. Also note Schüssler Fiorenza's remarks, *In Memory of Her*, 178.

[185] Schüssler Fiorenza, *In Memory of Her*, 175ff., esp. 178.

beside the table.[186] Although not recumbent, she is not excluded. Even a seated woman in the context of a meal scene with such paedagological overtones is a rarity in Hellenistic literature. That others are not included in the narrative surely reflects Luke's interest in maintaining a Hellenistic public/private dichotomy as he does elsewhere.[187] Although the point of the text discourages Martha, it also encourages Mary, and as such it has encouraged Christian women throughout the centuries. As a prescriptive, rather than descriptive text, it also supports the view that there were indeed women leaders in communities like Luke's, but for social and theological reasons their active role was discouraged by developing ecclesiastical hierarchies.[188]

Luke, Women, and Meals: Some Conclusions

In his scenes involving women and meals, Luke upholds the traditional, submissive role for Greco-Roman women. Women do appear in large numbers in his Gospel, and women followers of Jesus support his work out of their personal wealth. Even former slave women and prostitutes, such as the woman who anoints Jesus, and other "sinners" respond to Jesus' message. Nonetheless, although Luke encourages the presence of women of varying social classes in his community, he uses meal terminology to encourage subtly the more traditional Greco-Roman role for women. For example, he discourages women from taking on active leadership roles in the early Christian mission in preaching and teaching. Although the role of a table servant (enacted by Peter's mother-in-law) is put forward as the primary role for early Christian leaders, Luke's vocabulary limits women to actual "table service" (διακονέω), or charitable giving, while reserving his terms for "ministry" (διακονία) and apostleship for the men. Luke's literary strategy involving "possessions" also brings the women, along with the rest of the community, under the leadership of Peter and the Twelve or under those the Twelve appoint

---

[186] A few commentators, unfamiliar with Mary's traditional posture here, suggest that she is not at the table, but seated away from it. See Plummer, *Luke*, 291; Ellis, *Luke*, 161.

[187] Love, "Women's Roles."

[188] So Schüssler Fiorenza, *In Memory of Her*, Part 3; idem, "Theological Criteria," 8ff.

to preach and teach the "word." Although it is likely that Luke knew of women leaders of house churches, his portrayal of the conflict between Martha and Mary discourages women from seeing their role in the community as equal to that of men. Luke does mention women prophets, but even these women never say anything in public.[189] Thus, Luke's depictions of women in meal situations uphold the ideal, silent, submissive role of a Greco-Roman matron.

Luke's traditional depiction of women may be connected to his knowledge of Greco-Roman literature. He seems to have been well-read and aware of the literary structures and motifs of Greco-Roman literature.[190] His two-volume work is compared to ancient histories or biographies,[191] and more recently to the Apocryphal Acts.[192] As an author, then, Luke consciously uses various literary structures, forms, and motifs in an attempt to imitate the more serious literary works of his day and to cast his characters as respectable literary figures.[193] One of the literary conventions that Luke employs is the meal setting.[194] Of all the evangelists, then, Luke is indeed familiar with the literary images of women in symposia settings and the social criticisms of women's behavior at meals which these literary themes influenced. Luke's portrayal of women in the context of meals demonstrates his sensitivity to literary traditions which connected women to public meals or banquets. Hence, women and "sinners" do not join

---

[189] Although the author of Luke–Acts characterizes the new age of the Spirit by quoting from Joel 2:28–32 (Acts 2:17ff.), which promises both male slaves and female slaves will prophesy (δοῦλος/δούλη), the issue of public social protocol dictates the role of women. For example, the prophetess/widow Anna does not give one of the major speeches of Luke 1—2 (Mary and Elizabeth presumably speak out in the private home of Elizabeth). Likewise, even though Luke mentions the daughters of Philip, it is Agabus who warns Paul not to go to Jerusalem (Acts 21:9–14). This undoubtedly reflects Luke's interest in maintaining a public/private dichotomy with respect to women's proper behavior (so Love, "Women's Roles").

[190] Karris, *Luke: Artist and Theologian*; D. Smith, "Table Fellowship," 613ff.; Talbert, *Reading Luke*; Fitzmyer, *Luke*, 1.91ff.

[191] David E. Aune, "Greco-Roman Biography," in *Greco-Roman Literature and the New Testament*, ed. David E. Aune (Atlanta, Ga.: Scholars Press, 1988), 107–26; I. Howard Marshall, *Luke: Historian and Theologian* (Exeter: Pasternoster, 1970); Pervo, *Profit with Delight*, 3ff.; D. Smith, "Table Fellowship," 613, n. 2.

[192] Pervo, *Profit with Delight*; D. Smith, "Table Fellowship," 613, n. 2. See Ronald F. Hock, "The Greek Novel," in *Greco-Roman Literature and the New Testament*, 127–46.

[193] Pervo, *Profit with Delight*, 40, 77ff., 106.

[194] Karris, *Luke: Artist and Theologian*, 47–78; Delobel, "L'onction," 458–64; de Meeûs, "Composition"; D. Smith, "Table Fellowship"; Steele, "Luke 11:37–54."

Jesus at table. Secondarily, the traditional depiction of women in Luke–Acts may also betray an intention to counteract more active heroic depictions of women in the Apocryphal Acts.[195] Unlike untraditional heroines like Thecla who don men's clothes, speak in public, and refuse to marry, the women in Luke's meal scenes are traditional Greco-Roman women: silent, submissive, and ready to learn at Jesus' feet.

---

[195] Women are often noted as the primary audience of both Hellenistic romances (Pervo, *Profit with Delight*, 84–85) and the Apocryphal Acts. For recent discussions on women in the Apocryphal Acts, see Virginia Burrus, *Chastity as Autonomy. Women in the Stories of the Apocryphal Acts* (Lewiston: E. Mellen Press, 1987); S. L. Davies, *The Revolt of the Widows. The Social World of the Apocryphal Acts* (Carbondale and Edwardsville: So. Illinois Univ. Press; London and Amsterdam: Feffer and Simons, 1980); Dennis R. MacDonald, *The Legend and the Apostle. The Battle for Paul in Story and Canon* (Philadelphia: Westminster, 1983); Pervo, *Profit with Delight*, 127ff.; Bonnie B. Thurston, *The Widows. A Women's Ministry in the Early Church* (Minneapolis: Fortress, 1989). Unlike the canonical Acts, in the Apocryphal Acts women figure as the primary heroines of stories, even in those which focus on male characters. The chastity stories in particular could have been popular among women in the early churches who found literary figures like Thecla an inspiration (Schüssler Fiorenza, *In Memory of Her*, 173ff.). In the *Acts of Paul and Thecla*, Thecla dons men's clothes, leaves her betrothed behind, and joins men like Paul on the mission field. For many women in the ancient church, such a single, ascetic lifestyle may have proven to be a relief from the burdensome roles of childbearer and mother. As in Luke–Acts, widows figure prominently in the Apocryphal Acts, as does the interest in asceticism (cf. Luke 20:34, Mark 12:25 and Luke 18:29). Pervo comments, "Luke 11:27–28 does not support the notion that a woman's role was the production of babies." Moreover, only Luke gives recent marriage as one reason some refuse to attend the eschatological banquet (14:20). Pervo also notes that the women extolled in Luke–Acts are celibate, such as the Virgin Mary, Anna, and Philip's daughters (*Profit with Delight*, 181, n. 79; 24–25; 127ff.). Given this interest in asceticism in Luke, it might be wise not to so easily dismiss the possibility that Luke 10:38–42 may have "contemplative" overtones. Puzo, for example, suggests that there is a relationship between Luke 10:38–42 and 1 Cor 7 which discusses virginity and celibacy ("Marta y María"). Luke may be promoting a celibate lifestyle for women, just not one that negates the traditional or ideal Greco-Roman womanly role. If Luke–Acts is to be placed alongside the Apocryphal Acts as Pervo and others have suggested, it may have served as a corrective to other Acts in which women are portrayed as overstepping ideal roles (so now D'Angelo, "Women in Luke–Acts"). There are no heroines in Luke–Acts, and widows, prophetesses, and ascetic women keep their place. Luke drops the term διάκονος completely, which we know was used equally for women deacons (Rom 16:1). Pervo also suggests that Luke's limitation of women serves as a contrast of Acts with the Apocryphal Acts. According to Pervo, the author of Luke–Acts did not wish to portray Christianity as a destabilizing factor in Roman social life (*Profit with Delight*, 128). Additionally, it has been suggested that conservative letters like the Pastorals were also written in reaction against earlier oral forms of these apocryphal traditions about Paul and women (MacDonald, *The Legend and the Apostle*).

Women and Meals in the Gospel of Matthew

5

The Gospel of Matthew has received little attention by New Testament scholars interested in the place of women in early Christian groups. Few articles focus on Matthew as a whole[1] or even on isolated pericopes involving women,[2] unless it is in conjunction with a larger discussion of popular narratives found in other Gospels.[3] As a Gospel often characterized as "Jewish-Christian," it is no doubt regarded as overly patriarchal and therefore infertile ground for feminist exegesis.[4] However, in the context of this discussion, which sees clues to attitudes about women from depictions of women in meal settings, the Gospel of Matthew stands out as the only Gospel to portray women reclining with men at meals; it is the only Gospel to dare to identify explicitly women in its community with the slanderous term πόρναι.

"Prostitutes" and the Matthean Genealogy (Matt 1:1–17)

The first hint of Matthew's interest in women can be found in the first chapter. Matthew begins with a family register of Jesus'

---

[1]Janice Capel Anderson, "Matthew: Gender and Reading," *Semeia* 28 (1983): 3–27.

[2]Ringe, "Gentile Woman's Story," 65–72.

[3]For example, scholars comparatively discuss narratives such as the woman who anoints Jesus (Mark 14 par.) and the story of the Syro-Phoenician woman (Mark 7 par.). Except for Ringe, however, few of the scholars who discuss these passages in Matthew are interested in the topic of women or feminist hermeneutical methods.

[4]See comments by Anderson, "Gender and Reading," 7.

ancestry, in which the names of five women unexpectedly occur. The stereotypical pattern for a biblical genealogy does not include women in the line of descent.[5] Not even Luke, usually thought to want to "liberate" women,[6] includes women in his genealogy. Luke's family register for Jesus does not even mention Mary, even though she is the focus of much of his birth narrative. Thus, it is significant that Matthew 1's pattern of male ancestor δὲ ἐγέννησεν τὸν male ancestor(s), which is repeated thirty-nine times, is broken by the inclusion of the names of five women:

ἐκ τῆς Θαμάρ (1:3)

ἐκ τῆς 'Ραχάβ (1:5a)

ἐκ τῆς 'Ρούθ (1:5b)

ἐκ τῆς τοῦ Οὐρίου (Bathsheba, 1:6)

Μαρίας ἐξ ἧς ἐγεννήθη 'Ιησοῦς (1:16)[7]

Why does Matthew include women at this point, and why these women? Scholars have pondered the significance of the inclusion of these women in the family register of Jesus. Raymond Brown discusses the common interpretations in his book, *The Birth*

---

[5] Names of women are rare in Jewish genealogies. Exceptions occur when there is an irregularity in the line of descent, or when there is something exceptional about a woman's name. Marshall D. Johnson, *The Purpose of the Biblical Genealogies with Special Reference to the Setting of the Genealogies of Jesus* (Cambridge: Cambridge University Press, 1969), 153. See also Anderson, "Gender and Reading," 8.

[6] A generalization that is misplaced (see ch. 4).

[7] There exist three main readings for Matt 1:16: (1) "and Jacob begot Joseph *the husband of Mary, of whom Jesus was born, who is called Christ*," which is supported by a wide range of early Greek textual families and other versions, including P[1] ℵ B C L W Maj vg sy[p.h]; (2) "and Jacob begot Joseph, *to whom being betrothed the virgin Mary bore Jesus, who is called Christ*," which is supported by Caesarean and some Old Latin text types (Θ f[13] it[a (b) c d (k)] q); (3) "Jacob begot Joseph; *Joseph, to whom was betrothed Mary the virgin, begot Jesus who is called the Christ*," which is attested by the Sinaitic Syriac MS. External evidence supports (1) since it is the reading of all known Greek uncial MSS except Θ, and is attested by all other MSS and versions except those which support (2) and (3). If (2) were thought to be original it would be difficult to imagine why scribes would have omitted a clear reference to the virginity of Mary. There is no evidence that (3) ever existed in a Greek version. The editors of the UBS therefore choose (1) to be the best reading, and rate their decision with a {B}. See Metzger, *Textual Commentary*, 2–7, and concurring discussion by Raymond E. Brown, *The Birth of the Messiah. A Commentary on the Infancy Narratives in Matthew and Luke* (New York: Doubleday, 1977), 62–64.

of the Messiah. His overview is neatly summarized by Janice Capel Anderson:[8]

> (1) " . . . the four Old Testament women were regarded as sinners and their inclusion for Matthew's readers foreshadowed the role of Jesus as the savior of all sinful men" (*sic*).

> (2) " . . . the women were regarded as foreigners and were included by Matthew to show that Jesus, the Jewish Messiah, was related by ancestry to the Gentiles." (This would not apply to Mary.)

> (3) The women have two qualities in common with Mary: "(a) there is something extraordinary or irregular in their union with their partners—a union which, though it may have been scandalous to outsiders, continued the blessed lineage of the Messiah; (b) the women showed initiative or played an important role in God's plan and so came to be considered the instrument of God's providence or of His Holy Spirit."

Proposal (1) is usually ruled out on the grounds that Jewish Christian readers of Matthew's time no longer saw these women as "sinners" but as heroines who had done marvelous things for the Jewish people.[9] The second proposal, popularized by Martin Luther,

---

[8] Brown, *The Birth of the Messiah*, 71–74. Brown titles this section "Why Bring on the Ladies?"; I am following Anderson for this convenient outline of Brown's discussion (see "Gender and Reading," 8–9).

[9] This was first argued by Friedrich Spitta, "Die Frauen in der Genealogie des Matt." *ZWT* 54 (1912): 1–8. See also Brown, *Birth of the Messiah*, 71–72; Edwin D. Freed, "Women in Matthew's Genealogy," *JSNT* 29 (1987): 3–19, esp. 3–4; Andrew D. Heffern, "The Four Women in St. Matthew's Genealogy of Christ," *JBL* 31 (1912): 68–81. Heffern also emphasizes the Gentile origins of the four women; Johnson, *Purpose*, 154–55; 176. Ulrich Luz also dismisses the view that these women are included as "sinners" (*Matthew 1—7. A Commentary*, trans. Wilhelm C. Linss [Minneapolis, Minn.: Augsburg Press, 1989], 109–10). For further discussion of Jewish harlots as heroines in Jewish tradition, see Phyllis A. Bird, "The Harlot as Heroine: Narrative Art and Social Presupposition in Three Old Testament Texts," *Semeia* 46 (1989): 119–39 and Amaru, "Portraits of Biblical Women," 143–70, in which Amaru discusses Josephus' description of Rahab as an "innkeeper" (*Ant.* 5.9). See discussion of Josephus' interest in portraying Jewish heroines like Rahab as chaste in pp. 74–75 above. Freed also has a further discussion of the attempt in post-biblical Jewish literature to portray Rahab the Harlot, Ruth, and Bathsheba as chaste heroines. Freed suggests that their behavior is not denied, but rather excused. Thus, according to Freed, Matthew's genealogy prepares the reader for the illegitimacy of Jesus, who is known by the name of his mother and not his father (Mark 6:3; Matt 13:55; Luke 4:22; compare John 6:42 ["The Women in Matthew's Genealogy"]). The suggestion that Matthew selects these women to address a growing controversy over the illegitimacy of Jesus is not new. See Heffern, "Four Women," 76ff. For a compilation of

is often questioned in that the women listed were also known in post-biblical Jewish literature as proselytes, and therefore Jewish converts.[10] Brown's third proposal relies on later Jewish opinion that the irregular behavior of all of these women was in actuality guided by the Holy Spirit.[11] Most scholars find some truth in each theory, but commonly focus on the place of these women in Matthew's notion of God's messianic plan.[12]

Given early Hellenistic slander of meretriciousness against early Christian women as an indication of its social libertarianism, it is significant that none of the women leading up to Mary were known for chaste or moral behavior. Tamar, a Canaanite woman, disguised herself as a prostitute in order to seduce her father-in-law Judah, so that she could have children (Gen 38). Rahab, known as Rahab the Harlot,[13] was the Canaanite professional prostitute in

---

rabbinic references questioning the legitimacy of Jesus' birth, see Str.-B. 1.36–42 and Lachs, *Rabbinic Commentary*, 2. Lachs also relates the reputation of the women to a Matthean interest in countering a charge that Jesus was the illegitimate son of Mary. Johnson (*Purpose*) also discusses the tendency of Jewish tradition to exonerate Tamar, Rahab, Ruth, and Bathsheba in order to portray them as examples of faith in spite of their questionable behavior. Johnson attributes this concern to a polemic within Judaism itself, a controversy over the ancestry of the Davidic Messiah (177ff.). However, Greco-Roman concern over women's behavior, and the apologetic function of defending Jewish women's character generally by defending the moral character of Jewish heroines has already been demonstrated (pp. 74–75).

[10] Brown, *Birth of the Messiah*, 72–73; Freed, "Women in Matthew's Genealogy," 4; Johnson, *Purpose*, 154–55. Luz sees the non-Jewishness of the women to show Matthew's universality, although he notes that this has little to do with Mary (*Matthew 1—7*, 110).

[11] Brown, *Birth of the Messiah*, 73–74; Freed, "Women in Matthew's Genealogy," 4; Johnson, *Purpose*, 155–58; Herman C. Waetjen, "The Genealogy as the Key to the Gospel of Matthew," *JBL* 95 (1976): 205–30.

[12] Raymond E. Brown et al., *Mary in the New Testament* (Philadelphia: Fortress Press; New York: Paulist Press, 1978), 82–83; Freed, "Women in Matthew's Genealogy," 4–5; A.T. Hanson, "Rahab the Harlot in Early Christian Tradition," *JSNT* 1 (1978): 53; Waetjen, "Genealogy as the Key," 229–30.

[13] Due to the odd spelling of her name, and given the fact that Rahab's name occurs late in the line of descent (too late for someone connected to the period of the Conquest), Jerome Quinn questions the identification of Ῥαχάβ as Rahab of Jericho ("Is Ῥαχάβ in Matt 1,5 Rahab of Jericho?" *Bib* 62 [1981]: 225–28). Brown comments, "Despite the difference of spelling, it is virtually certain that Matthew means the Rahab of the conquest" (*Birth of the Messiah*, 60). It is Rahab the Harlot who became a popular heroine of faith in both rabbinic and Christian sources. See James 2:25 where Ῥαάβ ἡ πόρνη is mentioned along with Abraham as one justified by her works, as well as Heb 11:31, where she is mentioned along with other male examples of faith. 1 Clem 12 also extols Rahab for her faith and hospitality. See Hanson, "Rahab the Harlot," 53–60; Johnson, *Purpose*, 162–65; Freed, "The Women in Matthew's Gene-

ancient Jericho who aided the returning Israelites (Josh 2:6). Ruth, a Moabitess, although virtuous in her loyalty to her mother-in-law, demoralized herself by sneaking into bed with Boaz during a grain festival known for its illicit sexual activity (Ruth 3). Bathsheba the wife of Uriah the Hittite, had an adulterous affair with King David after conveniently bathing in a location where David could see her. After Bathsheba became pregnant, David had her husband killed in battle so they could be wed (2 Sam 11—12).[14] The final woman in the list, Mary, given the unique nature of her pregnancy, is also suspected of illicit sexual relations.

In the context of general Hellenistic concern for the behavior of women, Matthew's inclusion of these five morally suspect women in a genealogy—which would not usually include women—is significant. The one feature that all five women share is a bad reputation. Matthew does not deny that the circumstances surrounding Jesus' birth give Mary a morally suspect reputation. Rather, Matthew admits the stain upon Mary's reputation and emphasizes the presence of Jewish heroines with morally suspect reputations in Jesus' legal ancestry.[15] That the first four women are Gentiles should not be discounted, but rather considered as secondary.[16] It is significant that the prevailing opinion of early church writers was that the inclusion

---

alogy," 8. The traditional use of women accused of harlotry as examples of Christian faith is noteworthy. Mary Magdalene has also traditionally been considered a prostitute in Christian tradition.

[14] Freed, "Women in Matthew's Genealogy," 3–4. See also Lachs, *Rabbinic Commentary*, 2.

[15] So Jane Schaberg, *The Illegitimacy of Jesus: A Feminist Theological Interpretation of the Infancy Narratives* (San Francisco: Harper & Row, 1987), 20–32. She also emphasizes the bad reputations of these women. In light of Mary's reputation, Waetjen's suggestion that Matthew is not identifying Mary as a literal virgin seems inviting ("Genealogy as the Key," 228–29). Παρθένος may also merely indicate the age and marriageability of a young woman. Hence a widowed woman, if still young, might also be designated "virgin." See J. Massingberd Ford, "The Meaning of 'Virgin' " *NTS* 12 (1966): 293–99. James Lagrand challenges Waetjen's position by suggesting that the virginity of Mary is to credit her with transcending natural maternity, and to show her to be the "logical first candidate for entry into the new kingdom 'like a man' " ("How was the Virgin Mary 'Like a Man'? A Note on Matt 1:18 b and Related Syriac Christian Texts," *NovT* 22 (1980): 97–107). I would suggest that if Mary is the "first candidate for entry into the kingdom" as Lagrand contends, it is rather because of her similarity to other women who enter the kingdom in Matt 21:31–32.

[16] That Mary is by implication also Gentile has been rejected. See Brown, *Birth of the Messiah*, 73, n. 29 and Luz, *Matthew 1—7*, 110, n. 43. Brown notes that this "implausible thesis" has been proposed, and that it was popular during the Third Reich among German scholars.

of these women foreshadowed the concern of Jesus in Matthew's Gospel for sinners and Gentiles.[17] Repentant "sinners" numbered among Jesus' followers.[18] It is my contention that it is on account of their reputation for promiscuity as "sinners" that leads Matthew to mention these five women in the first chapter of his Gospel.

"Tax-Collectors, Sinners, and Courtesans" (Matt 9:9–13; 11:18–19; 21:31–32)

Like Luke, Matthew inherits narratives showing Jesus dining with "tax-collectors and sinners" (Mark 2:14–17/Matt 9:9–13). Matthew also includes a similar accusation from Q (Matt 11:18–19). Unlike Luke, Matthew describes Jesus and his disciples as reclining at table with both "tax-collectors and sinners" (τελῶναι καὶ ἁμαρτωλοί; Matt 9:10–11). Moreover, Matthew is the only Synoptic Gospel that states that "prostitutes" (πόρναι), along with "tax-collectors," will enter the "kingdom of God" (Matt 21:31–32). Thus, Jesus' group includes various and sundry folk, among them women who have previously responded to the message of John the Baptist.

Given the connection between "tax-collectors," "prostitutes" or "courtesans," and bad behavior generally, especially at dinner parties where women are present,[19] Matthew 9:9–13, 11:18–19, and 21:31–32 should be read as closely connected. They contribute to Matthew's larger portrayal of a segment of Jesus' own followers. In light of this, in Matthew the "sinners" mentioned in 9:9–13 (ἁμαρτωλοί), which would include women, should be viewed as synonymous with the group of "courtesans" (πόρναι) in 21:31–32 who enter the kingdom of God along with tax-collectors.[20] In Matthew, the accusations made by Jesus' opponents include the charge that he dined in public

---

[17] Among these writers are Origen, Chrysostom, Jerome, and Ambrose. See Heffern, "Four Women," 69–70. Heffern himself still sees more significance to the women being Gentiles, i.e., that in the genealogy Matthew here foreshadows not the scandal of Jesus' birth, but rather the scandal of the admission of pagan Gentiles to the church; Johnson, *Purpose*, 154.

[18] Hanson suggests that a woman like Rahab was known also for her remarkable repentance from her immoral life ("Rahab the Harlot," p. 54).

[19] See pp. 39–43, 90–93, 130–33.

[20] The relationship of the "prostitutes" in Matthew 21:28–32 to the "sinner" in Luke 7 was noticed by S. Légasse, "Jésus et les prostituées," *RTL* (1976): 137–54.

with women, i.e., women "sinners." Moreover, identifying this group as "foreign" or "Gentiles" coheres with the scandalous portrayal of pagan, promiscuous women.[21] The accusation that Jesus dines with women "sinners" therefore includes the notion that they were also "Gentiles." Jesus is portrayed as overstepping social boundaries by eating with those considered immoral according to traditional Greco-Roman standards.[22] Matthew's incorporation of such sectarian slander terminology reflects the situation of the Matthean community, that of a Jewish-Christian sect in controversy with other Jews.[23]

The identification of the "sinners" Jesus dines with in Matthew 9:9–13 with the image of "courtesans" from 21:31–32 can be further substantiated by Matthew's use of the so-called children of the marketplace pericope from Q (Matt 11:16–19). In this passage, "this generation" is likened to παῖδες who sit in the ἀγορά bemoaning the lack of response to their flute playing and mourning. As previously discussed, this image does not reflect a judicial stance being played out by children,[24] but rather the image of hired slaves or servants who were often sent to the marketplace by their masters to seek additional employment.[25] Matthew even includes female flute players in the mourning scene in 9:23.[26]

Matthew has previously contrasted Jesus' behavior with regard to food with that of John the Baptist. Jesus "feasts" whereas John "fasts" (9:14–15). This contrast in behavior is continued in Matthew 11:13–19. The behavior of John the Baptist is likened to that of a slave who mourns at a funeral, while the behavior of Jesus is compared to a slave hired to play a flute at a dinner party. However, in

---

[21] See pp. 1–98, ch. 2 passim.

[22] According to certain Jewish standards, these people would also be considered "impure." See pp. 90–93. W. F. Albright and C. S. Mann interpret "sinners" here in Matthew to be "non-observant Jews." See, *Matthew* (Anchor Bible; Garden City, N.Y.: Doubleday, 1971), 105–6. Robert H. Gundry points to the inclusion of Gentiles in the meal (*Matthew. A Commentary on His Literary and Theological Art* [Grand Rapids, Mich.: Eerdmans, 1982], 167).

[23] See J. Andrew Overman, *Matthew's Gospel and Formative Judaism. The Social World of the Matthean Community* (Minneapolis, Minn.: Fortress Press, 1990); Dunn, "Pharisees, Sinners and Jesus," 274–80; Johnson, "Anti-Jewish Slander," passim; and in discussion on pp. 64–65 above.

[24] So Cotter, "Children in the Marketplace." See pp. 128–30 above.

[25] See pp. 48–49.

[26] Even poor families hired at least two flute players and one woman mourner for funerals. See *b. Ketub.* 46b; Gundry, *Matthew*, 175; Lachs, *Rabbinic Commentary*, 172. See also the connection of "flute girls" with the term πόρνη in BAGD, 700.

both instances the response of those who hear their message is the same. Both Jesus and John are rejected: "For John came neither eating nor drinking, and they say, 'He has a demon'; the Son of Man came eating and drinking, and they say, 'Look, a glutton and a drunkard, a friend (dining companion)[27] of tax-collectors and sinners'" (11:18–19). The behavior of both John and Jesus is here likened to that of servants, and they are accused of having women in their company; John in the context of a funeral, Jesus in the context of a dinner.

The combination of female courtesans and tax-collectors described as leaving John to follow Jesus (Matt 21:31–32) coheres with the image in Matthew 11:13–19, which Matthew derives from Q. Matthew 21:31–32 reads:[28]

> Jesus said to them, "Truly I tell you, the tax-collectors and the courtesans are going into the Kingdom of God ahead of you. For John came to you in the way of righteousness and you did not believe him, but the tax-collectors and the courtesans believed him; and even after you saw it, you did not change your minds and believe him."

This pericope is attached to the parable of the two sons, a parable long considered to be a Matthean composition (21:28–30).[29] Here Jesus contrasts Jewish disobedience with Gentile repentance. Matthew 21:31–32 further demonstrates this contrast by juxtaposing "tax-collectors and courtesans" (who do believe) to the Pharisees (who do not).[30] Thus in Matthew, in similar fashion to Luke 7:36–50, Pharisees are likened to those invited to a dinner party but do not attend, even though some "tax-collectors and courtesans" do (Matt 22:1–14). In 11:25, Matthew also compares those who do hear and understand Jesus and John to "infants" (νήπιοι). This probably reflects the influence of the original reading of Q 7:35, in which the secondary ending to the children of the marketplace pericope read: "Wisdom is justified by her children" (τῶν τέκνων αὐτῆς), not "Wis-

---

[27] See pp. 92–93; 111, n. 11; 114, esp. n. 27 and D. Smith, "Jesus at Table," 477ff., 480ff.; idem, "Table Fellowship," 634.

[28] NRSV with emendations.

[29] Bultmann, *History*, 177; Gundry, *Matthew*, 421–22.

[30] This parallelism rests on favoring the reading in 21:29–31 supported by a C* K W and others, and the inclusion of οὐδέ in 21:32. The textual transmission of the parable is very confused, and this confusion seems to have affected the final clause of v. 32. Even the UBS editors mark their decision with a {C}. For a more lengthy discussion, see Metzger, *Textual Commentary*, 55–57, and additional comments by Gundry, *Matthew*, 421–22.

dom is justified by her deeds" (τῶν ἔργων αὐτῆς).[31] Accordingly, "tax-collectors and courtesans" should be viewed as part of Matthew's church of "little ones" who await the coming messianic banquet which the Pharisees refuse to attend (Matt 22:1–14).[32] In fact, here the "faith" (πιστεύω) of the "tax-collectors and courtesans" is highlighted for the Matthean community, many of whom might better identify with "those of little faith" (ὀλιγόπιστος) in other portions of the narrative.[33] Hence, along with "tax-collectors," "courtesans" enter the "kingdom" (βασιλεία). Accepting Jesus' teaching concerning the "kingdom" is a qualification of Matthean discipleship.[34] Matthew similarly highlights the "great faith" of the Canaanite woman in chapter 15.

However, Matthew 21:31–32 not only coheres with the so-called children in the marketplace pericope found in Q, but given the inexact parallel found in Luke 7:29–30, there is reason to suspect that some form of this pericope may have occurred in Q. Immediately preceding the children in the marketplace pericope in Luke, we find an enticing parallel to Matthew 21:31–32:

> "I tell you, among those born of women no one is greater than John; yet the least in the kingdom of God is greater than he." (And all the people who heard this, including the tax-collectors, acknowledged the justice of God, because they had been baptized with John's baptism. But by refusing to be baptized by him, the Pharisees and the lawyers rejected God's purposes for themselves) (Luke 7:28–30, NRSV).

There are several reasons for suggesting that some form of this pericope might have been present in Q. Despite the fact that most agree that Q did not contain some form of this saying,[35] some commentators still infer that here Luke and Matthew are drawing on

---

[31] Ron Cameron, " 'What Have You Come Out to See?' Characterizations of John and Jesus in the Gospels," *Semeia* 49 (1990): 35–69, esp. 40–41; Cotter, "Children in the Marketplace," 292–94; Kloppenborg, *Formation of Q*, 111.

[32] See pp. 174–77 below.

[33] See discussion of Matthean understanding of "faith" in Ulrich Luz, "The Disciples in the Gospel According to Matthew," in *The Interpretation of Matthew*, ed. Graham Stanton (Philadelphia: Fortress Press, London: SPCK, 1983), 98–128, esp. 107 on Matt 21:32. This article was originally published in German, in *ZNW* 62 (1971): 141–71. I cite Robert Morgan's translation.

[34] Luz, "Disciples in the Gospel According to Matthew," 109.

[35] Cameron, "Characterizations" 36–38; Gundry, *Matthew*, 422–23; Kloppenborg does not include this pericope in Q 7 (*Formation of Q*). But see remarks by Bultmann, *History*, 177.

source material.[36] The most likely source material Luke and Matthew would have drawn on at this point is Q.

A reading of Luke's version of this pericope presents several arguments that favor Luke's having a source that included πόρναι as in Matthew 21. First of all, the presence of πόρναι in Q would explain the portrayal of the woman in Luke 7 as a prostitute (πόρνη).[37] Second, a reference to πόρναι in Q 7 would explain Luke's connection of the "servants/children" in the marketplace in Q 7:32 to the female "sinner" in Luke 7:36ff.[38] An occurrence of πόρναι in Q 7 would explain Luke's inclusion of the anointing story at this point. Moreover, a Q passage contrasting the response of "prostitutes" or "courtesans" to Jesus and John with the lack of response of the Pharisees would also explain Luke's setting of the anointing story in the house of "Simon the Pharisee." Furthermore, a Lukan shift from οἱ τελῶναι καὶ αἱ πόρναι to πᾶς ὁ λαὸς καὶ οἱ τελῶναι is likely, given Luke's tendency to avoid depicting Jesus joining women for meals and his tendency to cast the women around Jesus as respectable.[39]

Luke also shows a tendency to redact passages in such a way as to keep Jesus from dining with "sinners" (5:29; 7:34; 15:1ff.; 19:1–10). This is probably because Luke interpreted the "sinners" found in Mark 2 to be women or to include women. He identifies the one woman "sinner" with the adjective ἁμαρτωλός. Luke also tries to identify Jesus' "dining companions" as men, by adding "male friends" (and therefore "dining companions"; οἱ γνωστοί) to the crowd that watches the crucifixion.[40] Thus, a clear reference to female "courtesans" in connection with "tax-collectors" in Q 7 would readily explain Luke's identification of the "sinners" in Mark 2 with women.

Furthermore, if a reference to "tax-collectors and courtesans" were present in Q 7, Luke's redaction of Mark 2 in chapter 5 is easily explained. Luke has Jesus eat with the ambiguous "tax-collectors and others" (ἄλλοι), not "tax-collectors and sinners" (ἁμαρτωλοί).[41] I would suggest that again Luke avoids portraying Jesus as dining with

---

[36] Gundry, *Matthew*, 211; Eduard Schweizer, *The Good News According to Matthew*, trans. David E. Green (Atlanta, Ga.: John Knox Press, 1975), 410.

[37] See pp. 121–33.

[38] Ibid.

[39] Ibid.

[40] See comments on connection of the theme of "friendship" to banquets, pp. 92–93; 111, n. 11; 114, esp. n. 27; 154.

[41] See pp. 131–32.

women. Luke's shift from Mark's ἁμαρτωλοί to ἄλλοι in Luke 5:29 corresponds neatly to a shift from πόρναι (in Q) to πᾶς ὁ λαός in Luke 7:29. Thus, Luke's interpretation of the children in the market-place pericope, his use of the story about the woman who anoints Jesus, and his redactional activity all suggest that Luke's version of Q might have contained a reference to "tax-collectors and courtesans" (πόρναι) in Q 7.

Indications in Matthew's Gospel also suggest that some form of Matthew 21:31–32 might have been present in Q. First, the occurrence of the non-Matthean phrase "kingdom of God" in v. 31 has puzzled commentators.[42] Moreover, Matthew's children of the marketplace pericope reflects the connection between Jesus' and John's followers to female servants or slaves (prostitutes).[43] Further-more, recent scholarship on Q and Matthew suggests that Matthew continues an egalitarian tradition which may predate him, a tradition that may be traced back to his own community's roots in the Q community.[44] If Q scholars determine that Q 7 included "courtesans," then the egalitarian tradition Matthew inherits might have allowed for the inclusion of women in meals as well as the rejection of an overly hierarchical leadership structure.

The proposal that Q 7 linked Jesus and John to "courtesans" would further buttress Ron Cameron's affirmation that Q charac-terizes both John and Jesus as two types of Cynics: one "ascetic," the other "hedonistic."[45] Cynics were one of the philosophical sects that were well-known for their inclusion of women. Women connected to Greco-Roman Cynicism were characterized as prostitutes or courte-sans.[46] If this kind of slander leveled against the followers of Jesus and John were present in Q, it would enhance the connection be-tween Jesus and John at the level of Greco-Roman philosophical sectarianism, particularly the argument that they both might be characterized as Cynics of some kind. Matthew's possible retention of πόρναι from Q could be one aspect of that connection.[47] Lest

---

[42] Albright and Mann, *Matthew*, 263; Gundry, *Matthew*, 423–24; Schweizer, *Matthew*, 410.

[43] See pp. 154–55.

[44] See p. 179.

[45] Cameron, "Characterizations," 60.

[46] See pp. 63–65, esp. 63, n. 230.

[47] At this juncture we must await the further work of the International Q Project, particularly the dissertation of Sterling Bjorndahl which will deal with the

female members of his community interpret his interest in these kinds of women to be an advocacy for truly promiscuous or non-repentant behavior, Matthew adds the exception to the divorce prohibition (Matt 19:3–9).[48]

Herod's Birthday Party (Matt 14:1–12)

Unlike Luke, Matthew preserves a dramatization of the events surrounding the death of John the Baptist, material he receives from Mark. Here Matthew inherits an account of a dinner party which fits a more typical Greco-Roman symposium scene. Matthew's redaction of this birthday party scene further indicates his more egalitarian stance regarding meals. Matthew's redaction places the blame for the incident firmly upon Herod and allows for the presence of Herodias at the meal. Matthew's redaction of Mark 6:14–29 also reveals his interest in maintaining a strong link between John and Jesus.

Matthew begins by identifying Herod with the more accurate title ὁ τετραάρχης.[49] This distinguishes Herod Antipas from Herod the Great.[50] Omitted are the references to the military officers (χιλίαρχοι) and upper-class Galileans (οἱ πρῶτοι τῆς Γαλιλαίας; Mark 6:21) which helped characterize the party as a men's symposium in Mark. Thus, Matthew does not seem interested in using this story (as does Mark) to contrast the behavior of the overlord Herod to that of the servant-king Jesus.[51]

In 14:2, Matthew has Herod immediately connect Jesus with John the Baptist. The possibility that Jesus is Elijah or another prophet is reserved by Matthew until 16:13–14.[52] This is another

---

relationship between Jesus and John in Q. Enough suspicion has been raised here, however, to merit further close attention to the possibility of including Luke 7:29–30/Matt 21:31–32 as part of Q 7 in some form.

[48] I.e., that women may be divorced on account of "unchastity" (πορνεία) (v. 9). Matthew here omits the woman's right to file divorce proceedings. Only the man's right to divorce is mentioned.

[49] As does Luke (9:7). See Albright and Mann, *Matthew*, 175; Willoughby Allen, *A Critical and Exegetical Commentary on the Gospel According to St. Matthew* (Edinburgh: T. and T. Clark, 1965), 157; Schweizer, *Matthew*, 317. For an opposing view, see Gundry, *Matthew*, 285

[50] Matthew retains the title βασιλεύς in v. 9 (Gundry, *Matthew*, 285).

[51] See pp. 93–95 and Freyne, *Galilee, Jesus and the Gospels*, 36–37.

[52] Allen, *Matthew*, 159; Freyne, *Galilee, Jesus and the Gospels*, 73, n. 7; Gundry,

example of the close association Matthew makes between Jesus and John. Moreover, here John's disciples report the turn of events to Jesus (14:12). This added clause gives the impression that John's disciples have been sent to Jesus by John[53] and suggests that, after John's death, the disciples of John were incorporated into Jesus' group.[54] Among these would no doubt be the "tax-collectors and prostitutes" who are said to have "believed John" in Matthew 21:31–32.[55] Once again Matthew implies that Jesus and John are connected by means of a shared group of followers.[56] Given the use of πόρναι in Matthew 21:31–32, we must conclude that Matthew intends his readers to realize that some of Jesus' followers are women.[57]

Matthew's rendition of the actual dinner also allows for the inclusion of women and removes the burden of guilt from Herodias. The daughter of Herodias does not need to "enter" (εἰσέρχομαι) (so Mark) because she is already "in the midst" (ἐν τῷ μέσῳ) of the partygoers. Nor does the young girl need to "go out" (ἐξέρχομαι) of the party to find her mother. Since this is not necessary, it can be assumed that her mother is present.[58] Herodias becomes a natural guest of her brother-in-law, since she is not portrayed as having already married Herod, and she is not assumed here to have apartments in the royal palace (14:3; cf. Mark 6:19).[59] For example, her young daughter is called "the daughter of Herodias" not the daughter of Herod (14:6).[60] Furthermore, Matthew omits the remark that Herodias was unable to kill John (Mark 6:19) and ignores her subsequent resentment of John's opposition to her second marriage. In Matthew, it is Herod who resents John's objection to a marriage which Herod intends, and it is Herod who wants John dead (14:3–

Matthew, 285.

[53] Freyne, *Galilee, Jesus and the Gospels*, 73, n. 7; John P. Meier, "John the Baptist in Matthew's Gospel," *JBL* 99 (1980): 383–405.

[54] Gundry, *Matthew*, 289.

[55] Luke also records that "tax-collectors" came to John for baptism (Luke 3:12–13). It may also be argued on the basis of Luke 7:29–30 that a certain number of people, including tax-collectors, were a part of John's circle and eventually joined that of Jesus. See pp. 125–30.

[56] Gundry, *Matthew*, 289; Schweizer, *Matthew*, 317.

[57] Luke, on the other hand, wants to obscure this. See pp. 130–33.

[58] Gundry, *Matthew*, 286–89.

[59] Ibid., 286–87.

[60] This is following the better reading for Mark 6:22a. See Metzger, *Textual Commentary*, 89.

5).[61] In Matthew, Herod is not John's protector who only reluctantly gives into the whims of his new, vindictive mate, as in Mark (6:20); rather, he instigates the events leading to John's death. Thus, Matthew shifts the guilt for the death of John from Herodias to Herod. Just as Herod the Great wished for the death of Jesus (Matt 2:1–18), here Herod Antipas seeks the death of John.[62] John and Jesus are further linked, and the women, now present for the meal, are exonerated in the process.[63]

The Feeding of Thousands, Including Women (Matt 14:13–21; 15:32–39)

Matthew's true openness to women in his community can be deduced from his mention of women in the crowds which benefit from the miraculous feedings. Of all the evangelists, only Matthew includes women in both of his feeding narratives. Men, women, and children gather to receive bread from Jesus via his disciples, giving these meals the ambiance of a large family celebration. Moreover, Matthew recasts these meals as Eucharistic feasts, and his wording alludes to the institution of the Lord's Supper in chapter 26. Matthew's feeding stories look forward to the messianic banquet, which he characterizes as a wedding banquet (Matt 22:1–14), the kind of family affair for which even unmarried virgins prepare (25:1–13). Thus, of all the Synoptics, only Matthew allows for the egalitarian presence of women in public meals, not only within the time of the Jesus movement, but within the context of Matthean church gatherings.

---

[61] Albright and Mann, *Matthew*, 176; Gundry, *Matthew*, 286–87; Schweizer, *Matthew*, 317–18.

[62] Albright and Mann, *Matthew*, 176; Gundry, *Matthew*, 286–87; Jack Dean Kingsbury, *Matthew* (Philadelphia: Fortress Press, 1977), 5; Schweizer, *Matthew*, 317–18.

[63] Matthew also includes another glimpse of an upper-class woman, whom he also casts in a more sympathetic light, that being the wife of Pilate (27:19). This may be due to his interest in the upper classes in general, as well as his interest in women. See Michael H. Crosby, *House of Disciples. Church, Economics and Justice in Matthew* (Maryknoll, N.Y.: Orbis Books, 1988), who considers the Matthean community to be relatively urban and wealthy, as does Kingsbury, *Matthew*. For a discussion of this more recent consensus on the urban origin of Matthew in Syrian Antioch, see Donald Senior, *What Are They Saying About Matthew?* (New York: Paulist Press, 1983), 13–14.

The first feeding miracle opens with a reference to the lateness of the hour, "when evening came" (ὀψίας δὲ γενομένης; 14:15). This characterizes the scene as an evening meal and associates the feeding with the Lord's Supper or Eucharist. The reference to the late hour also occurs in the opening to the Last Supper in Matthew 26:20. In fact, Matthew's abbreviation of the Markan feeding narratives further emphasizes the allusions to the Eucharist already present in Mark.[64] Matthew also here emphasizes the "crowds" (ὄχλοι; 14:13, 14, 15, 19) that gather for the meal, which foreshadows the eventual numbers that will join the Eucharistic feasts of the church.[65] Jesus, like the host of the Lord's Supper, "takes" (λαμβάνω), "blesses" (εὐλογέω), "breaks" (κλάω), and "gives" (δίδωμι) the bread, which the disciples then distribute to the crowds. This vocabulary will be repeated at the institution of the Lord's Supper in Matthew 26:26–29.[66] Since the Lord's Supper does not include fish, Matthew repeatedly deemphasizes its presence in this scene (14:16, 20).[67]

Not only is this a gathering foreshadowing the Eucharists of the Matthean community, but Matthew also characterizes this meal as a large family meal, not a symposium just for men as in Mark. Matthew omits the arrangement of the men "symposia by symposia" (συμπόσια συμπόσια; Mark 6:39). Instead, in this feeding scene, "men" (ἄνδρες), "women" (γυναῖκες) and "children" (παιδία; 14:21) all "recline" (ἀνακλίνω; 14:19) together for the meal. The mixture of the sexes here and the mention of men, women, and children gathering together to eat a meal suggest that the Greek words ἄνδρες and γυναί could be translated as "husbands" and "wives."[68] Thus, the crowds represent the church, which is here likened to a household, reminiscent of the "holy family" of Joseph (ἀνήρ), Mary (γυνή), and Jesus (παῖς), found in chapters 1—2 of the Gospel.[69] A household would also include

---

[64] Many commentators acknowledge that the Matthean scenes are cast as Eucharists. This is best clarified by Heinz Joachim Held, "Matthew as Interpreter of the Miracle Stories," in *Tradition and Interpretation in Matthew*, Günther Bornkamm et al. (Philadelphia: Westminster Press, 1963), 187; See also Albright and Mann, *Matthew*, 178–79; Gundry, *Matthew*, 291; Lachs, *Rabbinic Commentary*, 241; Luz, "Disciples in the Gospel According to Matthew," 105; Schweizer, *Matthew*, 319.

[65] Gundry, *Matthew*, 291.

[66] Albright and Mann, *Matthew*, 179; Gundry, *Matthew*, 293. This terminology may also reflect rabbinic table procedure. See Lachs, *Rabbinic Commentary*, 241.

[67] Held, "Matthew as Interpreter," 185–86; Gundry, *Matthew*, 293–94.

[68] Gundry, *Matthew*, 295; Crosby, *House of Disciples*, 115.

[69] For Joseph as "husband" (ἀνήρ) see Matt 1:19; Mary as "wife" (γυνή) see

servants.[70] Noting this identification of the church as a household in Matthew 14:21, Robert Gundry remarks: "Thus Matthew portrays the crowds as the church, a gathering of Christian families."[71] The Matthean community is not gathering together for orgiastic symposia, but is rather reclining for a religious family meal more akin to a Jewish Passover celebration or a wedding feast, both of which always included women and children.[72]

This apologetic interest is related to Matthew's redaction of the feast parable and his addition of the parable of the ten virgins. In 22:1–14, Matthew likens the coming messianic banquet to a marriage feast given by a king. In the ancient world, women and children commonly attended such parties, even during times when respectable women did not attend other kinds of public dinners.[73] Wedding celebrations were an exception, being family gatherings with a more limited guest list. Even young unmarried women were allowed to attend these banquets, although the adult women and young virgins were often seated separately and at times wore veils.[74] Given this background, it is significant that the special Matthean material contains the parable of the ten virgins (Matt 25:1–13). In this parable, the coming messianic feast is also likened to a wedding, a dinner for which even young unmarried virgins prepare. The young

---

1:20, 24; Jesus, by implication is "child" (παῖς or τὸ παιδίον) (2:2, 8, 9, 11, 13–14, 20–21). Gundry, *Matthew*, 295; Crosby, *House of Disciples*, 115; Jack Dean Kingsbury, "The Title 'Son of David' in Matthew's Gospel," *JBL* 95 (1976): 591–602, esp. 594–96.

[70] Could παιδίων in Matt 14:21 be "servants"?

[71] Gundry, *Matthew*, 295.

[72] If the Last Supper is thought to be a Passover meal, which would include women, it is Matthew who is thus the most likely Gospel which may assume the presence of women in the final meal of Jesus and his disciples. See Joachim Jeremias, *The Eucharistic Words of Jesus*, (New York: Charles Scribner's Sons, 1966), 41–62 and concluding remarks below. Given Matthew's characterization of the feedings, in this regard the Gospel of Matthew fits well into the context of early Christian groups which were accused of promiscuous behavior at evening meals. See pp. 75–78.

[73] That the Talmud prohibited women from reclining at weddings is a prohibition too late to be relevant to the first century. Jeremias is therefore incorrect in assuming that women would not have been present (Joachim Jeremias, "Lampades in Matthew 25:1–13," *Soli Deo Gloria: New Testament Studies in Honor of William Childs Robinson*, ed. J. McDowell Richards [Richmond, Va.: John Knox Press, 1968], 86). Elizabeth Waller is correct to challenge Jeremias on this point ("Mt 25:1–13: The Parable of the Ten Virgins," *Proceedings of the Eastern Great Lakes Biblical Society* 1 (1981): 85–109, esp. 91. See pp. 26, 29–30.

[74] See pp. 26, 29–30.

women in this parable parade down a public street at night in an urban area,[75] and their procession is reminiscent of those conducted in the worship of Hellenistic deities.[76] The closest parallel to the language of this story appears in the Jewish *Joseph and Asenath* from Egypt.[77] Thus, Matthew constructs a story in which women figure prominently, appearing at night on public streets and proceeding to a festive meal which looks forward to the messianic banquet. In spite of their behavior, Matthew still calls them virgins, although he may intend for the reader to understand them to be hired servants.[78] In any case, the parable does not indicate that their behavior is inappropriate. The women are parading to a familial gathering. The meal portrayed in the feeding narrative is a similar kind of public meal, and it too looks forward to this messianic banquet.[79] Women attend the meals around Jesus, and subsequently the Eucharistic feasts of the Matthean community, not because they are truly promiscuous,

---

[75] Joachim Jeremias, *Rediscovering the Parables* (New York: Charles Scribner's Sons, 1966), 136; idem, "Lampades," 85. Waller questions the urban setting Jeremias gives the parable (Waller, "Ten Virgins," 97–98).

[76] Waller, "Ten Virgins," 98.

[77] Young Asenath is similarly attended by a group of virgins, who rise to inquire after their mistress, whose door is then found shut (*Joseph and Asenath* 10). These young women, however, are definitely slaves. The text is now dated first century BCE through the second century CE. See translation and notes by C. Burchard, in *The Old Testament Pseudipigrapha*, vol. 2, ed. James H. Charlesworth (Garden City, N.Y.: Doubleday, 1985), 177–247; Waller, "Ten Virgins," 100–101.

[78] As in *Joseph and Asenath* 10. This is similar to Matthew's handling of Mary in Matt 1—2 (Waller, "Ten Virgins," 95). Mary is the only other woman designated "virgin" in the Gospel. "Virgin" may here merely designate a young unmarried woman (for example, even one who may have been married previously, but is now widowed) (J. Massingberd Ford, "The Meaning of 'Virgin,' " 298; Waller, "Ten Virgins," 96). Jeremias expresses discomfort with the image of the parable, which he argues cannot be true to life (Jeremias, *Rediscovering*, 136; idem, "Lampades," 85). What ancient Near Eastern family would allow their daughters to behave in such a manner? Compounding the problem is the fact that the young women here perform a task usually given to men. Young girls attend the bride, not the bridegroom. Bridegrooms are attended by men (Waller, "Ten Virgins," 86, 92, 105, n. 56; 107, n. 47). Gundry suggests that the Ten Virgins may be maidservants or slaves (*Matthew*, 501). This would buttress Waller's comparison of the parable's terminology with the language in *Joseph and Asenath* 10. If they are meant to be hired for the wedding party (in a similar manner to slave women hired for a funeral, see Waller, "Ten Virgins," 98), then their being out in the open is not an issue. The verbal similarities between the story of Tamar's rape and this parable which is cited by Waller are tantalizing, given the listing of Tamar in the genealogy in ch. 1 ("Ten Virgins," 99). If these women are meant to be slaves, then their "going in" to the wedding feast corresponds to the entering into the kingdom of God by the πόρναι in 21:31–32.

[79] Albright and Mann, *Matthew*, 179; Gundry, *Matthew*, 292.

but because the church is like a family or a large household which joins together for festive meals, even nocturnal ones.[80] Hence Matthew's addition to the divorce prohibition becomes more explicable. Women in the Matthean community still may be divorced for true promiscuity (πορνεία; Matt 19:9), but this would not include attendance at public religious meals.

Matthew also records the feeding of the four thousand. This second scene also allows for the presence of "women" (γυναῖκες) and "children" (παιδία) in a similarly familial grouping (Matt 15:32–39).[81] Again, Eucharistic language is present, and Jesus as the host of the Lord's Supper, "takes" (λαμβάνω), "blesses" (εὐλογέω), "breaks" (κλάω), and "gives" (δίδωμι) the bread to be distributed to the crowds by the disciples.[82] In chapter 15, however, Jesus is in Gentile territory, and the crowds in this instance are Gentiles rather than Jews.[83] As in Mark, the second feeding narrative follows the story of the Syro-Phoenician woman, who in Matthew is called a Canaanite. After Jesus allows for the healing of a Gentile girl, he is pictured as feeding an entire Gentile group.[84] Again, the large numbers of those fed foreshadows and symbolizes the large numbers that will eventually join the church. In this case Gentile members are represented, which includes women proselytes and their children. Matthew here, as in 14:13–21, depicts an open, egalitarian, and inclusive household meal. Thus, all will be welcomed to the table fellowship of the Matthean community, whether they be Jew or Gentile, slave or free, young or old, male or female.

---

[80] See Crosby, *House of Disciples* and concluding remarks below.

[81] It is difficult to decide between the two readings for Matt 15:38: (1) γυναικῶν καὶ παιδίων (attested by B C L W f[13] Maj and numerous others) and (2) παιδίων καὶ γυναικῶν (attested to by ℵ D Θ f[1] lat, and by Coptic and Syriac versions. Variant (1) is supported by a wide variety of witnesses, (2) by primarily Western text types. The phrase "children and women," would have been unusual and is more likely to have caused scribes to alter it to "women and children." However, given the weighty external evidence, the editors of the UBS still cautiously adopt variant (1). They rate their decision with only a {D}. See Metzger, *Textual Commentary*, 41.

[82] Albright and Mann, *Matthew*, 189; Gundry, *Matthew*, 321; Held, "Matthew as Interpreter," 187; Schweizer notes the repeated emphasis on the bread (*Matthew*, 330).

[83] Gundry, *Matthew*, 319ff. Schweizer notes the Gentile location of the second feeding, but doubts that a contrast with the Jewish location of the first feeding is meant (*Matthew*, 332).

[84] Gundry, *Matthew*, 320–22.

The Canaanite Woman (Matt 15:21–28)

Spliced in between the two feeding miracles, Matthew continues to follow Markan order by repeating the story of the Syro-Phoenician woman.[85] Given the addition of women and children to the feeding narratives, particularly the second feeding of Gentiles in 15:29–38, Matthew's intention to highlight this story as one which concerns a woman and her child (who are also Gentiles) cannot entirely be discounted.[86] Unlike Mark, Matthew did have before him another miracle story involving a Gentile,[87] yet here he still keeps Markan order. Thus, set between the feeding of the five thousand and the feeding of the four thousand, the story of the Syro-Phoenician woman sets a precedent within the ministry of Jesus for including Gentiles—even women Gentiles—in church meals.

Matthew begins his narrative by further connecting this section to the preceding discussion of Jewish dietary laws (15:1–20) by means of a continuative καί (15:21).[88] Matthew adds "and Sidon" to the Markan "Tyre"[89] (v. 21b), the "districts" (τὰ μέρη) of which Jesus "withdraws into" (ἀναχωρέω with εἰς). Hence, in Matthew Jesus actually enters Gentile territory, rather than merely remaining on its outskirts as in Mark.[90] The way in which Matthew refers to "Tyre and Sidon" recalls even more stereotypical language concerning sinful cities worthy of God's judgment in Jewish biblical tradition.[91] The woman who approaches Jesus in Gentile territory is here called

---

[85] Luke's Gospel does not contain a section of material from this point in Mark (Mark 6:45—7:26), which deals with Jesus and Gentiles. Luke's decision to omit the story of the Syro-Phoenician woman may be part of a larger decision. See Ringe, "Gentile Woman's Story," 154, n. 2.

[86] In contrast to Gundry, *Matthew*, 317. Although one could argue that both feedings involve women and children, the combination of Matthew's addition of the women in 14:20–21 and 15:37–38 makes the gender of the Gentile woman in 15:21–28 more noticeable.

[87] The Centurion's son from Q (Matt 8:5–13); Schweizer, *Matthew*, 329.

[88] Gundry, *Matthew*, 313.

[89] The addition of καί Σιδῶνος to Mark 7:24 probably arose by means of assimilation from Matt 15:21. The shorter text of Mark 7:24 is supported by Western and Caesarean text types. See Metzger, *Textual Commentary*, 95.

[90] Albright and Mann, *Matthew*, 187; Gundry, *Matthew*, 310. Schweizer argues the Greek could also indicate that Jesus went in the direction of Gentile territory (*Matthew*, 330).

[91] See p. 98, esp. n. 73. See also Matt 11:21–22; Derrett, "Law in the New Testament," 164; Gundry, *Matthew*, 310; Schweizer, *Matthew*, 330.

a Canaanite, rather than "Syro-Phoenician." This is an outdated identification, since there were no "Canaanites" by the first century.[92] Nonetheless, Matthew must have some reason for choosing it. First, "Canaanite woman" (γυνὴ Χαναναία) recalls at least two of the women accused of harlotry in Matthew's genealogy, Tamar and Rahab, both Canaanites.[93] Moreover, given Israel's struggle with temple prostitution assimilated from Canaanite religious ritual, Canaanite women have a strong connection with prostitution and sexual sin in Jewish biblical tradition.[94] Furthermore, Matthew sets the scene more naturally out in the open,[95] which might heighten the impropriety of the woman's actions.[96] Thus, even more clearly in Matthew than in Mark[97] Jesus is portrayed as ministering to a woman associated with harlotry, a "sinner."[98]

As the woman approaches, she immediately begs for mercy and calls Jesus by the messianic title, "Son of David" (υἱὸς Δαυίδ; 15:22). This title is reserved in Matthew for healing miracles.[99] In combining "Son of David" with the title "Lord" (κύριε), the Canaanite

---

[92] Lachs, *Rabbinic Commentary*, 248. Albright and Mann suggest that Carthaginian peasants at the time of Augustine still called themselves "Canaanites" (*Matthew*, 187). Derrett argues that the reference to "Canaanite" comes from a Matthean use of Judg 1:5–7, in which King Adoni–bezek (a Canaanite) places other kings under his table to scavenge for crumbs after first cutting off their thumbs and big toes ("Law in the New Testament," 173).

[93] See pp. 150–51.

[94] A perusal of the Hebrew prophets would easily support this. Commentators mention the distinction between Jews and Canaanites in the Hebrew Bible, but miss the relevance of that distinction with regard to Canaanite *women*. See for example comments by Gundry, *Matthew*, 310; Schweizer, *Matthew*, 330.

[95] Allen, *Matthew*, 168; Hasler, "The Incident," 459.

[96] Ringe, "A Gentile Woman's Story," 70.

[97] See pp. 95–102.

[98] A few scholars connect the Canaanite woman to the group "sinners" and note her impropriety. See Mark C. Thompson, "Matthew 15:21–28," *Int* 35 (1981): 279–84, esp. 282; Burkill, "The Syro-Phoenician Woman," 177; Ringe understands this clearly, as she writes, "No Jewish man, especially one with a religious task or vocation, expected to be approached by a woman (Jew or Gentile), except perhaps by one of the many lone *women reduced to prostitution* to support themselves" ("A Gentile Woman's Story," 70, italics mine). Ringe also calls the Canaanite woman "the poorest of the poor and most despised of the outcasts—a Gentile woman on her own before God and humankind" ("A Gentile Woman's Story," 72). Likewise, Anderson recognizes the marginality of the Canaanite Woman. She is "alone with no indication of an embedded status in a patriarchal family" ("Gender and Reading," 11).

[99] Kingsbury, *Matthew*, 54; Jack Dean Kingsbury, *Matthew: Structure, Christology and Kingdom* (Philadelphia: Fortress Press, 1975), 108–9; Kingsbury, "The Title 'Son of David,' " 592, 598.

woman makes what amounts to a confession of faith—even before Jesus grants her request.[100] Her faith in Jesus as the Messiah is contrasted with the lack of belief among many Jews, particularly the Pharisees featured at the beginning of chapter 15.[101] The association of the woman with harlotry allows her to be easily compared to the πόρναι who also "believe" and enter the messianic kingdom before the Pharisees (Matt 21:31–32).[102]

After the woman acknowledges Jesus as Lord and Messiah, crying out (κράζω) she beseeches Jesus to cast a demon from her daughter. Her tone annoys the disciples (15:23). At first, Jesus simply ignores the woman and speaks only to his disciples, who tell him to "send her away." This does not imply that they want him to grant her request, but merely that he rid them of her annoying presence.[103] Jesus' lack of direct response to the woman makes his first reaction to her even more rude than it is portrayed in Mark.[104] At first Jesus says nothing at all. Subsequently, Jesus gives only a flat refusal: "I was sent only to the house of Israel" (15:24). This refusal alludes to Matthew 10:5–6, where Jesus limits his ministry to the Jews.[105] In spite of his refusal, the woman persists, kneeling in worship (προσκυνέω) before Jesus, again calling him "Lord" (κύριε; 15:25).[106] Jesus' next reply (still spoken to the disciples, not to the woman) does not even refer to the sequential priority of the Jews (who are to be fed "first" in the Markan version [Mark 7:27]), which would imply that the Gentiles might at least be "fed" second. Only the negative remark remains, "It is not good (καλός) to take the children's bread

---

[100] Gundry, *Matthew*, 311; Kingsbury, "The Title 'Son of David,' " 600–601.

[101] See Matt 15:1ff. Kingsbury writes of the Matthean use of the title 'Son of David,' that those who use the title " 'see' and 'confess' what Israel and its leaders do not, viz., that he is the Davidic Messiah promised and sent to this people by God" ("The Title 'Son of David,' " 601). This is also true in the case of the Canaanite woman, in that "even a Gentile woman will see what Israel will not" ("The Title 'Son of David,' " 601). Also at issue would be the dietary laws which separate Jews and Gentiles (Albright and Mann, *Matthew*, 188; Gundry, *Matthew*, 311–12).

[102] See pp. 152–58.

[103] Ringe, "Gentile Woman's Story," 65. Lachs suggests the opposite (*Rabbinic Commentary*, 248), as does Gundry, *Matthew*, 312.

[104] Ringe, "Gentile Woman's Story," 69; Schweizer, *Matthew*, 329.

[105] Allen, *Matthew*, 169; Gundry, *Matthew*, 313–14.

[106] Her supplication also reflects the language of the Psalms (Gundry, *Matthew*, 313–14). G. R. O' Day suggests that Matthew patterns this entire story after a lament psalm. See "Surprised by Faith: Jesus and the Canaanite Woman," *Listening* 24 (1989): 290–301.

and give it to the dogs" (15:26).[107] Again, the woman and her child
are the "little dogs" (κυνάρια). In Matthew the term "dogs" is unques-
tionably a derogatory designation for Gentiles.[108]

In spite of Jesus' rude remarks and continued refusal the woman
agrees with him. Matthew adds the word "yes" (ναί) to the woman's
reply (15:27).[109] With the addition of ναί, the woman's reply becomes
an agreement with Jesus' statement, not the clever rebuttal that it
seems in Mark.[110] Matthew thus tempers the image of the woman's
similarity to a witty courtesan.[111] The "children" (so Mark) have been
replaced with "masters" (κύριοι), which relates the table in question
to the "Lord's" (i.e., Jesus').[112] The woman affirms that she and her
daughter are included within the household of the new movement,
even though Jesus' ministry was to be only on behalf of the "household" (οἶκος) of Israel. By requesting the healing of her daughter, the
woman requests "scraps of bread" from a table, a phrase which alludes
to the "scraps" collected after the miraculous feedings, which are in
turn symbolic of Eucharistic feasts held by the new "household," the
church.[113]

Finally, Jesus relents; however, he relents not because of the
woman's witty argumentation but because of her great faith which
persists in spite of his rudeness and repeated refusals: "O woman,
great is your faith! Be it done for you as you desire" (15:28). Matthew's heightening of Jesus' refusal accentuates the great faith of the
woman.[114] It is the great faith of the woman which justifies the
extension of the Matthean mission to the Gentiles and their inclu-

---

[107] Gundry, *Matthew*, 314; Held, "Matthew as Interpreter," 198; Schweizer,
Matthew, 329.

[108] Allen, *Matthew*, 169; Derrett, "Law in the New Testament," 165, n. 3;
Lachs, *Rabbinic Commentary*, 249; Ringe, "Gentile Woman's Story," 68. See pp.
100–101, n. 86. Gundry does not consider the remark derogatory (*Matthew*, 315).

[109] Again, the addition of ναί to Mark 7:28 is due to assimilation from the
Matthean parallel. See Metzger, *Textual Commentary*, 95; Gundry, *Matthew*, 315.

[110] Derrett, "Law in the New Testament," 171; Gundry, *Matthew*, 315; Held,
"Matthew as Interpreter," 199; Ringe, "Gentile Woman's Story," 66.

[111] See pp. 101–2.

[112] Gundry, *Matthew*, 316.

[113] Anderson, "Gender and Reading," 15; Crosby, *House of Disciples*; Gundry,
Matthew, 316.

[114] Albright and Mann, *Matthew*, 187; Gundry, *Matthew*, 313; Held, "Matthew
as Interpreter," 198; Jerome H. Neyrey, "Decision Making in the Early Church. The
Case of the Canaanite Woman (Matt 15:21–28)," *ScEs* 33 (1981): 373–78, esp. 375;
O' Day, "Surprised by Faith"; Ringe, "Gentile Woman's Story," 71.

sion in the meals of the church.[115] The "great faith" of this woman is held up as an example for members of the Matthean community, many of whom have "little faith" (ὀλιγοπιστία).[116]

The Woman Who Anoints Jesus at a Meal (Matt 26:6–13)

Matthew also includes, with select changes, the story of the woman who anoints Jesus.[117] Matthew omits from Mark the parallel story of the poor widow who gives "everything" (Mark 12:41–44) and underscores the cost of the perfume in the anointing scene proper.[118] This may reflect his wealthy urban provenance.[119] The identification of the ointment as "spikenard" drops out, and the oil is here called "very expensive" (βαρύτιμος; Matt 26:7).[120] Likewise, the actual detail

---

[115] The faith of the centurion also leads to the healing of his son/servant (Matt 8:5–13). Thus, it is the faith of these Gentiles, as well as the exceptions made by Jesus on their behalf, which justify the inclusion of Gentiles in the Matthean community. See Albright and Mann, *Matthew*, 188; Allen, *Matthew*, 169; Burkill, "Syro-Phoenician Woman," esp. 175–77; Derrett, "Law in the New Testament," 171; Gundry, *Matthew*, 313; Hasler, "The Incident," 461; Held, "Matthew as Interpreter," 193ff.; Kingsbury, *Matthew*, 51; Neyrey's entire article suggests that this story was used to justify the evangelization of Gentiles in spite of the limitation of Jesus' ministry to Jews ("Decision Making in the Early Church"). See Ringe, "Gentile Woman's Story," 68; Schweizer, *Matthew*, 330; Smart, "Jesus, the Syro-Phoenician Woman," 470.

[116] On the theme of faith in Matthean miracle stories, Luz remarks, "When Matthew repeatedly orients the healings to the theme of 'faith,' he is certainly speaking to the community about their faith, or their need of it" (Luz, "Disciples in the Gospel According to Matthew," 107).

[117] See pp. 102–6; 121–30. Ronald F. Theimann comments that the close relationship between the Markan anointing and the Matthean one leads scholars to neglect Matthean redaction of this story. Few scholars mention the Matthean version in articles on the pericope; Schüssler Fiorenza does not discuss Matthew's text at all in her opening discussion of *In Memory of Her* ("The Unnamed Woman at Bethany," *TToday* 44 (1987): 179–88, esp. 183 and n. 11). There is little interest in Matthew's portrayal of women. Theimann remarks, however, that "The female followers of Jesus play a more prominent role in Matthew's Gospel than is usually recognized" (p. 181). He notes the lone article on women in Matthew's Gospel, that of Anderson, "Gender and Reading" ("The Unnamed Woman," 181, n. 8).

[118] Gundry, *Matthew*, 519–20; Elizabeth E. Platt, "The Ministry of Mary of Bethany," *TToday* 34 (1977): 29–39, esp. 31.

[119] See p. 160, n. 63. Gundry notes that it may be on account of Matthew's status as a publican (*Matthew*, 520).

[120] Following the editors of the UBS, the reading βαρύτιμου should be preferred over πολυτίμου. It is supported by B W and Byzantine text types, and by the Matthean insertion of βαρύς in Matt 23: 4, 23 (Allen, *Matthew*, 268; Gundry,

of the cost of the ointment ("over 300 denarii" [Mark 14:5]) is short-
ened to "a large sum" or "for much" (πολλοῦ; Matt 26:9). Matthew
also stresses and clarifies the connection of the anointing to the burial
of Jesus (Matt 26:12).[121] Plainly, the requisite anointing for burial is
properly done by the unnamed woman in chapter 26. In Matthew
the women do not take spices to the tomb (Matt 28:1).[122]

By clarifying the connection between the anointing and the
burial, a connection which the unnamed woman understands, Matthew draws attention to the disciples' lack of understanding at the
meal. Matthew writes that the "disciples" (μαθηταί; Matt 26:8) silently object to the woman's deed, Mark makes an indefinite reference to "some."[123] It is therefore the woman, not the disciples, who
understands the true nature of Jesus' messiahship (i.e., that he is to
die).[124] In this instance, it is the woman who understands Jesus'
previous discussions of his upcoming Passion. The other disciples,
even Peter, will continue to waver in their faith.[125] Moreover,
Matthew emphasizes that the woman's action is a "work" (or
"deed" [ἔργον]) done on behalf of Jesus: "She has done a good work
[ἔργον καλόν] for me [εἰς ἐμέ]" (Matt 26:10).[126] This links the

---

Matthew, 520).

[121] David Daube, "The Anointing at Bethany and Jesus' Burial," *ATR* 32
(1950): 186–99, esp. 193ff.; Elliott, "The Anointing of Jesus," 107; Legault, "Anointings in Galilee and Bethany," 142; Platt, "Mary of Bethany," 31; Theimann, "The
Unnamed Woman," 183.

[122] Albright and Mann, *Matthew*, 315; Daube, "The Anointing at Bethany,"
193; Elliott, "The Anointing of Jesus," 106; Theimann, "The Unnamed Woman,"
183.

[123] Albright and Mann, *Matthew*, 314; Gundry, *Matthew*, 520; Schweizer,
Matthew, 487.

[124] Anderson, "Gender and Reading," 17–18; Theimann, "The Unnamed
Woman," 183.

[125] The portrayal of the disciples in Matthew is a topic of debate. Suffice it for
now to say that Matthew does not portray the disciples as completely lacking
understanding, as he often omits Markan references to their lack of belief. Moreover,
they are often made to understand aspects of Jesus' teaching which they at first fail to
grasp by Jesus' own instruction. However, at the same time the disciples are often
characterized as those with "little faith." It is the women who remain faithful until
the time of Jesus' crucifixion and wait patiently at the tomb. This is in contrast to the
men who are unable to stay awake while Jesus prays in the garden and desert him after
his arrest. Even Peter denies that he knows Jesus (and he does so to two female slaves).
See Theimann, "The Unnamed Woman," 180–83; Luz, "Disciples in the Gospel
According to Matthew," 107; Mark Sheridan, "Disciples and Discipleship in Matthew and Luke," *BTB* 3 (1973): 235–55, esp. 247ff. and discussion below.

[126] Matthew gives emphasis to the woman's action as a "work" by moving the

woman's deed to the good "works" of Jesus/Wisdom (Matt 11:19),[127] and relates her deed to Christian service (διακονία).[128] All service in the community is inadvertently done on behalf of Jesus (Matt 25:23–46). Peter's mother-in-law (Matt 8:14–15) and the group of women around Jesus (Matt 27:55–56) are the only others who minister (διακονέω) directly to Jesus himself.[129] All who exemplify this kind of service are women, including the unnamed woman who anoints Jesus. Accordingly, Matthew emphasizes the genuineness of this woman's discipleship,[130] just as he emphasized the "faith" (πίστις) of the Canaanite woman (Matt 15:21–28) and the πόρναι who "believe" (πιστεύω), in contrast to others who do not (Matt 21:31–32).

Furthermore, given the inclusion of women in other meal scenes, the anointing story in Matthew acquires additional significance in the context of his Gospel. There is no reason to suppose that this woman is not part of the dining company. The indignation expressed by others at the meal is not on account of her mere presence, but is truly in this case on account of the waste of the perfume. The unnamed woman's presence at the meal is accepted, and her action is held up as an example to all. Thus, the deed of this woman exemplifies the essence of the message of Matthew's entire Gospel.[131] Wherever "this Gospel [i.e., Matthew's][132] is preached,"

---

reference to ἔργον forward. See Grassi, *Hidden Heroes*, 77; Gundry, *Matthew*, 521.

[127] Matthew changed Q's ending to the "Children in the Marketplace" pericope by substituting "works" for "children" (τέκνα). In Matthew, Wisdom's "deeds" refer back to the miracles done by Jesus in chs. 5—7, 8—9 and 10. See Cotter, "Children in the Marketplace," 292–93; Kloppenborg, *Formation of Q*, 110, n. 36. Matthew's frequent use of ἔργον leads Gundry to remark, "Above all, Matthew emphasizes the doing of good works before men (*sic*)" (*Matthew*, 6–7). Crosby notes on this pericope: "People are blessed (11:6) when their work imitates Jesus' works (11:2) by being directed to resource the needs of others (25:31–46)" (*House of Disciples*, 118).

[128] Grassi, *Hidden Heroes*, 76–77. Crosby notes in this pericope that "good works" are those which meet the needs of others in the Matthean community. Thus the "good work" of the woman is in response to a projected need of Jesus, i.e., to be anointed for his burial (*House of Disciples*, 118).

[129] See pp. 172–77.

[130] Crosby, *House of Disciples*, 118.

[131] Ibid., 119.

[132] In a final addition, Matthew modifies the two occurrences of the word "gospel" with "this." See Grassi, *Hidden Heroes*, 78; Gundry, *Matthew*, 522; Theimann, "Unnamed Woman," 184–85. In Matthew the term "gospel" refers to that which Jesus preaches, particularly the "gospel of the Kingdom" which is to be preached "throughout the whole world" (see Matt 4:23; 9:35; 10:1) (Kingsbury, *Matthew: Structure*,

this story may be recalled "in memory of her" rather than Jesus (Matt 26:13).

The Women Who Follow and Serve (Matt 27:55–56)

Like the other Synoptics, Matthew includes a reference to the women who are present for Jesus' crucifixion. Matthew records that "many women" watched the crucifixion from a distance. This behavior contrasts that of the men, who flee following the arrest. Like Mark, Matthew records that these women "followed" (ἀκολουθέω) and "ministered" (διακονέω) to Jesus. Matthew enhances the position of these women as disciples.

Matthew begins by moving to the fore Mark's comment that a large group of women gathered for the crucifixion: "There were also many women (γυναῖκες πολλαί) there, looking on from afar" (27:55). Here Matthew moves πολλαί forward from Mark 15:41b.[133] Matthew underscores the position of these women by using an emphatic αἵτινες in place of the Markan αἵ.[134] These are the same women "who had followed [ἀκολουθέω] Jesus from Galilee, ministering [διακονέω] to him" (27:55b). Among these many women are those named Mary Magdalene, Mary the mother of James and Joseph, and the mother of the sons of Zebedee (27:56).[135] That they followed Jesus "from" (ἀπό) Galilee (not "in" [ἐν] as in Mark 15:41) does not necessarily limit their time with Jesus to his journey to Jerusalem.[136] Women

---

Christology and Kingdom, 128ff.). However, Theimann points out that the memorial to the woman spoken of in 26:13 is accomplished when Matthew's *Gospel narrative* reaches the whole world. Given the egalitarian emphasis found only in Matthew's Gospel, I agree. Kingsbury also writes in regard to the use of "this gospel" in 26:13: "In 26:13 we have evidence that in Matthew's community the term 'gospel' embraces not merely traditions of logia of Jesus but traditions of narratives about him as well. In light of this, we have good reason to believe that in the mind of Matthew the expression 'the [this] Gospel of the Kingdom' can properly be explicated only in terms of the subject matter of the entire document" (*Matthew: Structure, Christology and Kingdom*, 130–31).

[133] Allen, *Matthew*, 297; Gundry, *Matthew*, 578; Schweizer, *Matthew*, 517.

[134] Gundry, *Matthew*, 578.

[135] Matthew omits the reference to Salome and changes Joses to Joseph. The "mother of James and Joseph" is Mary, the mother of Jesus (Gundry, *Matthew*, 579).

[136] Gundry suggests that Matthew's emphasis serves to underscore the nature of Christian ministry (*Matthew*, 578); Schweizer argues that the women only join Jesus for the journey to Jerusalem (*Matthew*, 518).

have been with Jesus and his disciples at meals throughout the narrative; consequently, there is no reason to suggest that Matthew intends by this choice of preposition to exclude them from the period of the Galilean ministry.

Ἀκολουθέω, a technical term in Matthew for the activity of a disciple,[137] characterizes the women here as "followers" of Jesus (i.e., as disciples).[138] This interpretation of Matthew's use of ἀκολουθέω to refer to the women is supported by the ascensive use of καί in 27:57: "When it was evening, there came a rich man from Arimathea, named Joseph, who was *also* a disciple [μαθητεύω] of Jesus."[139] The "also" continues a thought from the previous sentence and thus refers back to the immediately mentioned group, the women in 27:55–56. Joseph of Arimathea is a disciple, as are the women who "follow" Jesus in the fashion of disciples. Likewise, the women are models of discipleship in that they "minister" (διακονέω) to Jesus. Because all ministry (διακονία) and Christian service are inadvertently directed toward Jesus (Matt 25:31–46), these women serve as examples of Matthean ministry.[140] In this regard, they are like other women in the narrative who have "ministered" to Jesus, such as Peter's mother-in-law (Matt 8:14–15) and the unnamed woman who anoints Jesus (Matt 26:6–13).[141] The large numbers of women pictured here and the presence of women throughout his narrative suggest that it is unrealistic that Matthew intends by his choice of words for the reader to assume that they all are Jesus' personal servants.[142] Moreover, if

---

[137] Many scholars contend that in Matthew the term ἀκολουθέω consistently carries the metaphorical meaning "to come or go after a person as his disciple." See discussion by Sean Freyne, *The Twelve: Disciples and Apostles. A Study in the Theology of the First Three Gospels* (London and Sydney: Sheed and Ward, 1968), 159ff.; Jack Dean Kingsbury, however, attempts to distinguish between metaphorical meanings of ἀκολουθέω and the simple meaning of literal accompaniment ("The Verb *Akolouthein* as an Index of Matthew's View of His Community," *JBL* 97 [1978]: 56–73).

[138] So Crosby, *House of Disciples*, 114–15; Gundry, *Matthew*, 578ff.; Theimann, "The Unnamed Woman," 182;

[139] So A. H. McNeile, *The Gospel According to St. Matthew* (London: Macmillan and Co.; New York: St. Martin's Press, 1961), 426. I concur. Others presuppose that the καί here is ascensive, but it does not affect their subsequent discussions of the women. See Gundry, *Matthew*, 580; Schweizer, *Matthew*, 517; Anderson makes this suggestion (following McNeile), but rejects it ("Gender and Reading," 20).

[140] See previous section pp. 174–76.

[141] Grassi, *Hidden Heroes*, 78–79.

[142] In contrast to Anderson, "Gender and Reading," 19. Here Anderson somewhat reluctantly follows Kingsbury who writes: "In 27:55, Matthew, like Mark (15:41), employs *akolouthein* in the literal and local sense of accompaniment from

those who are to be disciples are to "follow" Jesus to the point of "taking up" their cross (Matt 16:24ff.), it is noteworthy that only the women follow Jesus to the cross; the rest of the disciples do not.[143] Neither are the women frozen with fear at the tomb (Matt 28:8); rather they worship the risen Lord without doubt and joyfully report the resurrection (Matt 28:8–9).[144] The rest of the disciples will worship, but some will doubt (Matt 28:17).[145] Such an attitude of worship which recognizes Jesus as "Lord" is a hallmark of true discipleship in Matthew's Gospel.[146]

This analysis of the women in Matthew 27:55–56 fits well within Matthew's broader concept of "discipleship." Although scholars have suggested that the category of "disciples" excludes women,[147] many now suggest that the Matthean understanding of "disciples" encompasses a larger group than previously thought.[148] In particular, the group of "disciples" is not limited to the Twelve.[149] True, women

---

place to place.... The appended notation that they were 'waiting on him' is not meant to characterize them as disciples of Jesus in the strict sense of the word but instead explains why they had been in his company" ("The Verb *Akolouthein* as an Index of Matthew's View of His Community," *JBL* 97 [1978]: 61). So also Albright and Mann who translate διακονέω "looked after" in Matt 28:55 (*Matthew*, 349). Matthew's emphasis is in contrast to the "ministry" of the women in Mark, who do seem to be primarily "table servants." Still, even in Mark, these female "servants" are examples of discipleship for the Markan community (See ch. 3).

[143] If the "ministry" of the women is limited to the journey to the cross (Anderson, "Gender and Reading," 19; possibly Gundry, *Matthew*, 579), then they are here depicted as "an example of Christian ministry to the persecuted" (Gundry, *Matthew*, 579). The point that the women are an example of Christian ministry remains. See also Theimann, "The Unnamed Woman," 182.

[144] Gundry, *Matthew*, 590–91; Cynthia Jarvis, "Matthew 28:1–10," *Interpretation* 42 (1988): 63–68, esp. 64.

[145] Theimann, "The Unnamed Woman," 181, n. 7.

[146] Ibid., 181.

[147] Anderson, "Gender and Reading," 20; Kingsbury, *"Akolouthein,"* 61.

[148] This perspective views the "disciples" as a character group rather than a number limited to the Twelve or to men. See Crosby, *House of Disciples*, 114; Freyne, *The Twelve*, 152ff., 186ff.; Luz, "Disciples in the Gospel According to Matthew," 99–101; Sheridan, "Disciples and Discipleship," 247ff.; Theimann, "The Unnamed Woman," 108–83. Anderson, while she limits the "disciples" to a smaller all-male group, discusses the options ("Gender and Reading," 20–21). A recent discussion of μαθητής in Matthew may be found in Michael J. Wilkins, *The Concept of Disciple in Matthew's Gospel as Reflected in the Use of the Term* Μαθητής (Leiden: Brill, 1988).

[149] Luz notes that the total affect of Matthean redaction is to reduce the total references to "the Twelve." According to Luz, Matthew is aware of the identification of "the Twelve" with the disciples, but it is unimportant to him ("Disciples in the Gospel According to Matthew," 99); Schweizer suggests there is a distinction between

are not called "disciples" in Matthew,[150] but in a more general sense, women do meet the criteria for being "disciples," a larger group also identified as the "little ones"[151] as well as "brothers and sisters."[152]

First, women are depicted in Matthew as appropriately calling Jesus by the christological title "Lord" (κύριος). This is a frequent title used by "disciples" in Matthew's narrative.[153] The Canaanite woman calls Jesus by this title (Matt 15:22, 25). Moreover, women also offer Jesus the worship which corresponds to such a title and are depicted "worshipping" (προσκυνέω) at Jesus' feet (Matt 15:25; 28:9). By worshipping Jesus in this manner, they also show themselves to be his true disciples.[154] Furthermore, women such as the Canaanite woman are held up as examples of "faith" (πίστις). The "courtesans" (πόρναι) who join Jesus' following from John's are also those who "believe" (πιστεύω) and therefore enter the kingdom of God (Matt 21:31–32). Such "belief" or "faith" (πίστις) is a primary quality of a disciple in Matthew,[155] as is the acceptance of the "kingdom" (βασιλεία).[156] Indeed, the great faith of these women is sometimes contrasted to the "little faith" (ὀλιγοπιστία) of the male disciples.[157]

---

the Twelve of the historical past in Matthew's narrative and a secondary notion that these historical "disciples" are examples for Matthew's church. Thus, through the "transparency" of the disciples, the Matthean church is disclosed ("Matthew's Church," 136–37); Sheridan assumes this throughout "Disciples and Discipleship."

[150] Anderson, "Gender and Reading," 20; Kingsbury, "Akolouthein," 61.

[151] Freyne, The Twelve, 165ff. Luz, "Disciples in the Gospel According to Matthew," 110–11; Eduard Schweizer, "Matthew's Church," in The Interpretation of Matthew, ed. Graham Stanton (Philadelphia: Fortress Press; London: SPCK, 1983), 129–55, esp. 138–39; Sheridan, "Disciples and Discipleship," 250–51.

[152] The plural ἀδελφοί may be accurately translated "brothers and sisters." This is particularly true in Mark and Matthew, considering Mark 3:34 and Matt 12:49. In Matthew Jesus points to "the disciples" and declares, "Here are my mother and my brothers! For whoever does the will of my Father in heaven is my brother, and sister, and mother" (Matt 12:49–50; NRSV). On the identification of the group "disciples" with "brothers" in Matthew, see Freyne, The Twelve, 158, 167; Luz, "Disciples in the Gospel According to Matthew," 109–10; Overman, Matthew's Gospel, 135; Schweizer, "Matthew's Church," 138–39; Sheridan, "Disciples and Discipleship," 249, n. 15.

[153] Freyne, The Twelve, 163–64; Sheridan, "Disciples and Discipleship," 246–48.

[154] Sheridan, "Disciples and Discipleship," 246–47.

[155] Luz, "Disciples in the Gospel According to Matthew," 107; Sheridan, "Disciples and Discipleship," 247ff.; Theimann, "The Unnamed Woman," 181.

[156] Freyne, The Twelve, 153; Luz, "Disciples in the Gospel According to Matthew," 109.

[157] Freyne, The Twelve, 199, 202–4; Theimann, "The Unnamed Woman," 180–81.

Unlike others in the narrative, women also live out their faith in that they "minister" (διακονέω) to Jesus. Such self-giving "service" (διακονία) is also a primary concern of Matthean discipleship.[158] Finally, women, like the men, are given a place at the dinner table, the classic location of learning (μανθάνω/μαθητεύω) in the ancient world.[159] The "disciples" in Matthew are considered a "transparent" group to be equated with Christians in Matthew's community.[160] It may therefore be argued that Matthew's category of discipleship allows for a degree of egalitarian treatment of the women in that community as well.

Such egalitarianism is consistent with the most current scholarly characterization of Matthew's community. In recent years, it has been suggested that Matthew adheres to an anti-hierarchical, egalitarian ecclesiology.[161] All disciples are disciples equally—even Peter, being the "first among equals."[162] The notion of Matthew's non-hierarchical stance is derived primarily from 23:8–12:

> But you are not to be called rabbi, for you have one teacher [διδάσκαλος], and you are all students [ἀδελφοί]. And call no one your father on earth, for you have one Father—the one in heaven. Nor are you to be called instructors, for you have one instructor, the Messiah. The greatest among you shall be your servant [διάκονος]; All who exalt themselves will be humbled, and all who humble themselves will be exalted (NRSV).

---

[158] Matt 18:1ff.; 23:6ff.; Grassi, *Hidden Heroes*, 76–77; Overman, *Matthew's Gospel*, 136ff.

[159] See pp. 17–19, 138.

[160] Luz, "Disciples in the Gospel According to Matthew." Luz writes: "The verb *matheteuō* functions as transparency to make discipleship in the Gospel illuminate the evangelist's own day" (p. 109). Although Sheridan cautions against completely identifying the disciples in Matthew with the Matthean Christian community, he considers the Matthean disciples to be "exemplary for Christians" ("Disciples and Discipleship," 249). Overman concurs with Luz on the "transparency" of the disciples in his book, *Matthew's Gospel and Formative Judaism*, 124ff. Schweizer also sees the disciples as "transparent" for the Matthean church ("Matthew's Church," 136–37).

[161] Freyne, *The Twelve*, 206; E. Krentz, "Community and Character: Matthew's Vision of the Church," Paper presented at national meeting of the SBL, New Orleans, La., November 1990; Dennis Duling, "Response to Krentz" (with modifications); Overman, *Matthew's Gospel*, 122ff.; Schweizer, "Matthew's Church," 139ff.; Sheridan, "Disciples and Discipleship," 251–52.

[162] Jack Dean Kingsbury, "The Figure of Peter in Matthew's Gospel as a Theological Problem," *JBL* 98 (1979): 67–83, esp. 71; Overman, *Matthew's Gospel*, 136.

Thus, Matthew advocates a church structure which does not depend on developed ecclesiastical orders or church hierarchy.[163] Rather, Matthew's community is modeled after a "household." However, this Matthean "household," in spite of the social stratification associated with such a structure, allows for a degree of egalitarianism.[164] The Matthean church is made up of "little ones" who are all equally disciples, all equally capable of "following" Jesus. Even those who are leaders in the community must seek to be as the "least" of the "little ones."[165] Even leaders remain "learners."[166] In his recent book, *Matthew's Gospel and Formative Judaism*, Overman writes: "Leaders, teachers and other positions are all a part of the Matthean community. Ideally, Matthew would have the members fulfill their roles in a way that does not disrupt the egalitarian spirit which should pervade the community."[167] Thus, there is a tension within Matthew's ecclesiology, given his egalitarian ideology, that coexists with the identification of his community with the structure of a household.

At the end of Matthew's Gospel, the entire world is to be "discipled."[168] Thus, the Eleven are instructed to "Go therefore and make disciples [μαθητεύω] of all nations [πάντα τὰ ἔθνη]" (Matt 28:19). "All nations" clearly includes Gentiles. Since Gentile women associated with harlotry foreshadow this future influx of Gentile "disciples" at the very beginning of Matthew's Gospel (Matt 1:1–16),[169] it is unquestionable that women are included in the perimeter of Matthean discipleship proclaimed at the end.[170]

---

[163] So Krentz; Overman, *Matthew's Gospel*, 122ff.; Schweizer, "Matthew's Church," 139ff.; Sheridan, "Disciples and Discipleship," 251–52.

[164] Crosby, *House of Disciples*.

[165] Freyne, *The Twelve*, 165–66; Schweizer, "Matthew's Church," 138–39; Sheridan, "Disciples and Discipleship, 251–52.

[166] Freyne, *The Twelve*, 206; Overman, *Matthew's Gospel*, 134ff.; Sheridan, "Disciples and Discipleship," 251.

[167] Overman, *Matthew's Gospel*, 124.

[168] Ibid., 128; Schweizer, "Matthew's Church," 141.

[169] So Theimann, "The Unnamed Woman," 186. See also pp. 147–52.

[170] Ibid., 185. Freyne asserts that "In trying to discover Matthew's ideas on discipleship, the best starting point is the manifesto at the end of his gospel" (*The Twelve*, 152). (See also 153–54).

Women and Meals in Matthew's Gospel: Some Conclusions

This analysis of the Gospel of Matthew, which takes into consideration women and meal imagery in his narrative, produces striking results. Matthew, the Gospel considered the most andro-centric of the four, is the only Synoptic Gospel which portrays women reclining with men for meals. Only in Matthew are women allowed a place at the table. Women and children join the men for the miraculous feedings, which Matthew characterizes as Eucharistic feasts enjoyed by the Matthean church. Thus, Matthew portrays an egalitarian community which gathers together for meals like a household and awaits the messianic banquet. Even the future kingly meal with the Messiah is akin to a wedding, the kind of family celebration for which even young unmarried women prepare. Women who "follow" Jesus meet the Matthean criteria for discipleship, and many are even held up as examples of true faith and Christian service.

The slander leveled against ancient religious and philosophical groups which enjoyed mixed gender dining underscores Matthew's mention of the presence of women accused of promiscuity as members of Jesus' own group and, by inference, his own. Only Matthew embraces such sectarian slander and records that Jesus' group inherits "courtesans" who were previously disciples of John the Baptist. Furthermore, Matthew includes Gentile women associated with harlotry in his genealogy and later narratives. "Sinners," a group including women, join Jesus and his disciples for meals. Given that early Christian groups were often accused of welcoming promiscuous women and suspected of partaking of lecherous nocturnal "love feasts," Matthew's bold affirmation of the presence of "sinners" and "courtesans" among Jesus' dining company is a significant rhetorical statement. By doing so it is possible that Matthew further betrays his penchant for an anti-hierarchical egalitarian ecclesiology, an ecclesiology which likens the church to an equal gathering of "little ones" or a household of "brothers and sisters." Matthew's understanding of the church as a "household" does not result in an emphasis on traditional gender roles. Thus, his call to disciple "all nations" is gender and class-inclusive.

Finally, there is reason to suspect that Matthew might have inherited this egalitarian aspect of his ecclesiology from an earlier source, namely Q. The pericope concerning "courtesans" comes from a layer of tradition that deals with the relationship of Jesus to John.

If there is indeed a trajectory from Q to Matthew which allows for the merging of the Q community into Matthew's own,[171] then part of Matthew's "own" traditions might have included the characterization of Jesus and John as Cynics who welcomed women into their circles. Future scholarship on Q 7 may well shed light on the possibility that Q included a reference to "courtesans." Thus, the observation that Matthew includes women in his meal scenes and embraces the term "courtesans" (πόρναι) for women in his community could have great significance not only for Matthean studies generally, but for studies of the historical Jesus as well.

---

[171]As is now suggested. James M. Robinson, "The Q Trajectory: Between John and Matthew via Jesus," in *The Future of Early Christianity. Essays in Honor of Helmut Koester*, ed. Birger A. Pearson (Minneapolis: Fortress Press, 1991), 173–94.

Conclusion

The presence and position of women in early Christian communities have been of great concern to biblical scholars during the past decade. The Synoptic Gospels in particular have been analyzed as to their perspective on women. Behind this endeavor lies the more modern controversy over the proper place of women in the contemporary church. Many modern Christian women still look to the New Testament for scriptural confirmation of a genuine religious call to ministry. This has led many Christian exegetes to emphasize the uniqueness of the Christian creed, "In Christ there is neither Jew nor Greek, neither slave nor free, neither male nor female" (Gal 3:28) to support the modern call of women to ministerial orders. Thus, the place of women in early Christianity suggested by New Testament books like the Synoptics is perceived by many to be the result of a uniquely Christian message which superseded an earlier, more restrictive Jewish code. According to this reconstruction, Hellenistic patriarchalism encroached upon this specifically Christian egalitarianism. This work challenges this reconstruction of women's place in early Christian groups and locates both the impetus of early Christian egalitarianism, as well as the erosion of that ethic, outside of Christianity altogether. The controversy over the place and position of women among early Christian communities is the result of larger social and economic forces affecting all of Greco-Roman society, including Hellenistic Judaism.

In order to substantiate my explanation of the presence of women in early Christian groups, I first investigated changes taking place in the meal customs of Greco-Roman women. Social anthropological studies show that meal customs are resistant to change; as a result, fluctuations in those customs indicate an ongoing social renovation at a basic level of a society. Meal customs during the Greco-Roman period were indeed undergoing change, so that women were beginning to attend public meals with men, a behavior previously associated with prostitutes and slaves. This is an example of women's increased access during this period to the "public" sphere usually reserved for men according to ancient Greek social ideology. Although the "liberation" of ancient women was somewhat limited in scope, this freedom of movement of Greco-Roman women produced a kind of social criticism that emphasized ideal or "private" women's roles. Thus, women who attended public meals with men were labeled "promiscuous" or "public." This means that the presence of women in meetings of free association in early Christian communities and the language used to describe them, although noteworthy, are neither extraordinary nor unique. There were several religious and philosophical groups during the Hellenistic era apart from Christianity who welcomed women to their meals, and in turn received criticism for doing so. Notable among egalitarian philosophical groups include the Cynics, Epicureans, and the Stoics. Other religious groups open to women's participation include Hellenistic Judaism and the Isis religion.

Thus, Jewish groups were by no means unaffected by Greco-Roman meal customs or the fluctuations in the meal practices of Greco-Roman women. Jewish festive meals follow the pattern of all Greco-Roman meals, with a formal δεῖπνον followed by a συμπόσιον used in most cases for liturgical practices. This is true for the group at Qumran as well as for the Therapeutae described by Philo. Even Jewish Passover liturgy reflects this Greco-Roman meal structure and requires that Jewish women be present and recumbent next to their husbands for the meal. Sirach, the Hellenistic Jewish document written in Jerusalem around 180 BCE, in an extensive discussion of banquet etiquette, warns against dining with a neighbor's wife. Finally, the fortress of Herod at Machaerus contains two dining rooms side-by-side, one for men and one for women. That means that upper-class Jewish women may indeed have attended public meals with their husbands, but they sat separately, as was often the case for many Greco-Roman women. Furthermore, both Philo and Josephus show a concern to portray Jewish women as respectable in meal situations. The first section of this study establishes that not only were Greco-Roman meal customs pervasive and undergoing change, but that other religious and philosophical groups besides Christianity, including Judaism, were equally affected by the changing meal customs of the Hellenistic world.

In a second section, this study demonstrates that the Synoptic Gospels themselves reflect both the fluctuations in Greco-Roman meal etiquette and an awareness that a social mixture of men and women for meals was at odds with Greco-Roman propriety. The Gospels reveal their familiarity with Greco-Roman meal customs and reflect Greco-Roman literary banquet themes. As a collection, the Synoptics present several positionings on the issue of women and gender-inclusive table practice.

Of all the Synoptics, Mark is the least concerned for the impropriety of the scenes involving women in his narrative, in spite of the fact that the majority of women in Mark's Gospel fit the "public" or "promiscuous" literary stereotype. Women appear as a sub-group of Jesus' disciples. Women are healed and receive exorcism. They are present at the cross and the tomb. Moreover, Mark describes the women who accompany Jesus as being present for meals, both as servants and as participants in the scene created by the slander that Jesus "eats and drinks" with "tax-collectors and sinners." Such a characterization reflects typical depictions of those known for banqueting with "promiscuous" women and pimps.

Although aware that his depictions evoke such slanderous clichés, Mark's storytelling reveals other concerns, such as Jewish/Gentile relations or the significance of Jesus' death and discipleship. Mark uses scenes involving stereotypically "promiscuous" women to underscore other theological points. Women "follow" and "serve" Jesus, yet their accompaniment receives little comment on Mark's part and is subtly incorporated into Mark's larger theme of discipleship. The woman's anointing of Jesus in the context of a meal is not objected to on account of its impropriety but its cost. Jesus at first rejects the request of the Syro-Phoenician woman not because she is "promiscuous," but because she is a Gentile. The Pharisees object to Jesus' "eating and drinking with tax-collectors and sinners" not because the group includes women, but because it includes ritually unclean Gentiles. Mark's redirection of his audience's attention to other theological matters also obscures the undercurrent of scandal in these scenes involving women, and thus, the concern for Greco-Roman propriety, though not emphasized, is not totally absent from Mark's Gospel.

Women, although present, are never explicitly depicted as reclining with men for meals.

Surprisingly, of all the Gospels writers, Luke upholds the traditional, submissive role for Greco-Roman women. Women appear in large numbers in both his Gospel and in Acts, and women are identified as the wealthy patrons who financially support Jesus' movement. Along with respectable Hellenistic women, Luke portrays lower-class slaves and repentant prostitutes as responding favorably to Jesus' message. In spite of their lower social position, however, Luke never calls any of the women around Jesus "prostitutes." Moreover, throughout his narrative Luke consistently avoids depicting women as reclining with men for meals. Luke's vocabulary limits women to actual "table service" or charitable giving, while excluding them from ministerial "service," a role reserved for men. His literary strategy involving "possessions" brings the women, along with the rest of the community, under the male leadership of Peter and the Twelve. Although Luke probably knew of women leaders of house churches, his portrayal of the conflict between Mary and Martha discourages women from seeing their role in the community as being equal to that of men. Rather, Mary is extolled for acting out the silent, submissive role of a Greco-Roman matron; she sits quietly at the feet of Jesus for a meal. Thus, Luke's portrayal of women in the context of meals indicates his sensitivity to literary traditions which connected women to public meals or banquets. Hence, women and "sinners" do not recline with Jesus for meals in the Gospel of Luke.

Even more surprising than Luke's maintenance of traditional Greco-Roman values, however, is Matthew's portrayal of women. Matthew, considered the most androcentric of all the Synoptics, is the only Gospel which portrays women reclining with men for meals. Only in Matthew are women allowed an equal place at the table. Women and children join the men for the miraculous feedings, meals Matthew characterizes as Eucharistic family feasts. Thus, Matthew portrays an egalitarian community which awaits the messianic banquet, a family affair for which even unmarried women prepare. The women who "follow" Jesus meet the Matthean criteria for discipleship, and other women in the story are held up as examples of true faith and Christian service. Furthermore, Matthew allows for the presence of women identified as "courtesans" among the followers of Jesus. "Sinners," a group which in Matthew includes women, join

183

Jesus and his disciples for meals. To foreshadow this development, Matthew includes women accused of harlotry within Jesus' own legal ancestry. In spite of the larger controversy over the "public" behavior of Greco-Roman women, Matthew affirms the presence of women accused of promiscuity among the followers of Jesus. Thus, in Matthew, the characterization of the church as a family or "household" does not result in an emphasis on ideal gender roles. Matthew's ecclesiology is gender-inclusive, as well as somewhat anti-hierarchical. There is reason to suspect that Matthew inherits this gender-inclusivity from earlier Gospel traditions.

Finally, several insights may be gained from examining women and meals in the Gospels. First, Greco-Roman ideas about meal propriety helped both to shape the identity of the Synoptic communities and to determine the position of women in these early Christian groups. This should not be surprising; recent research indicates that early Christian groups gathered around meals for their public worship and discourse. It is logical then that the evangelists' ideas about meals would also reflect their ideas about the place of women in their communities. Mark allows for the presence of women, but is not overly concerned about them. Luke encourages large numbers of women converts, but wishes to limit the behavior of women according to Greco-Roman ideals. Matthew encourages an open and egalitarian community in which women and men recline together for meals. Thus, the development of early Christian groups into communities "at table" greatly influenced the position of women in the Synoptic communities.

Second, ample evidence from the Gospels confirms the presence of women among the earliest converts to Christianity. At an early layer of the Gospel tradition Jesus is slandered for his table practice, which includes the presence of "tax-collectors and sinners" for meals, and features "wine-bibbing" and "gluttony." Such characterizations reflect stereotypical slander used against those known for dining with "promiscuous" or "liberated" women. Other religious and philosophical groups were criticized in like manner for including women in socially mixed public meals. The children of the marketplace pericope from Q also highlights those who acknowledge Jesus and John by "wailing" and "piping," both activities of women and slaves hired for banquets and funerals. There is also reason to suspect that Q might have included a reference to the presence of "courtesans" among Jesus' followers, which would further connect Jesus to

Greco-Roman Cynicism. By incorporating these kinds of materials, the evangelists reveal the roots of their communities in earlier groups which featured corporate meals involving a social mixture of sexes. This may be particularly true in Matthew's case. Therefore it is Matthew who may be more in line with earlier Jesus movements insofar as his table etiquette is concerned.

Third, the results of this study should advance our general understanding of women in early Christianity and the New Testament. The controversy over women is not to be considered unique to Christianity. Rather, texts in the New Testament like the Gospels reflect varying positions on a larger Greco-Roman social controversy. Moreover, the earlier Gospel materials lean toward a more egalitarian direction, supporting Schüssler Fiorenza's reconstruction of the Jesus movement as a "discipleship of equals." One could argue that the early Christian concept of leadership as "table-service" was modeled after a social role often delegated to women. Those Christian communities still concerned with the biblical witness as the determining factor in modern definitions of a woman's proper place in the home and church should be cautious in overestimating the significance of ideal Greco-Roman women's roles for universal Christendom.

Fourth, by illustrating that the presence of women in early Christian groups was not due to a specifically Christian ideology, a major problem in current Christian feminist hermeneutics is solved. It is not necessary to devalue Hellenistic Judaism in order to appreciate the inclusivity and egalitarianism of early Christianity. On the contrary, it is more than likely that convivial inclusivity was one aspect of religious and social life that early Christianity shared with Hellenistic Jews, who were also accused of welcoming numerous women converts to their synagogues—women who were also accused of promiscuity. Jewish women were among those who joined men for public meals, particularly for the formal Passover seder. The conservative trend which affected Jewish women's lives as seen in later rabbinic writings, usually read back into the first century as being indicative of first-century Jewish ideology, is rather a reflection of the same conservative domestication of morals that affected Christian groups of the same period. The motivation toward convivial egalitarianism among both Jews and Christians and the conservative resurgence that emphasized ideal women's roles are neither specifically Jewish nor Christian, but Greco-Roman. Should this thesis gain acceptance, then the tendency among Christian exegetes towards an anti-Judaic hermeneutic should be curtailed. Moreover, this analysis demonstrates that the most *Jewish* Christian of the Synoptic Gospels betrays the most egalitarian ecclesiology.

Finally, should the major tenets of this thesis gain acceptance, its wider implications are far-reaching. This study focused on the participation of women in early Christian groups. However, should that participation merely reflect a more general proclivity for Christian groups to participate in the wider Hellenistic mentality of their times, this has broader implications for the entire question of the social constituency of early Christianity. The presence of other segments of Greco-Roman society within Christian groups will need renewed analysis in light of these more general observations. For example, explanations for the predominance of slaves and freed-people in early Christian groups, often attributed to the attractiveness of doctrines fundamental to Christian theology, will need reassessment. The social significance of major categories of even Pauline theology may need additional review. For scholars concerned with the variety of social issues faced by early Christian communities, there is much work to be done.

Bibliography

Ancient Authors

Athenaeus. *Deipnosophists*. Translated by Charles Burton Gulick. *Athenaeus. The Deipnosophists*. LCL; London: William Heinemann; New York: G. P. Putnam's Sons, 1933–1959.

Carmina Priapea. Translated by Howard M. Jackson and Susan A. Zenger. "*Carmina Priapea*. Roman Poems in Honor of Priapus. The Latin Text and English Translation with Text-Critical and Expository Commentary." Unpublished manuscript.

Cicero. *Letters*. Translated by W. Glynn Williams. *Cicero. The Letters to His Friends*. LCL; Cambridge, Mass.: Harvard University Press; London: William Heinemann, 1952.

_____. *Speeches*. Translated by R. Gardner. *Cicero. The Speeches: Pro Caelio, De Provinciis, Consularibus, Pro Balbo*. LCL; Cambridge, Mass.: Harvard University Press; London: William Heinemann, 1958.

_____. *The Verrine Orations*. Translated by L. H. G. Greenwood. *Cicero. The Verrine Orations*. LCL; London: William Heinemann; New York: G.P. Putnam's Sons, 1928.

Clement of Alexandria. *The Teacher*. Text Otto Stählin. *Clemens Alexandrinus*. Leipzig: J. C. Hinrichs'sche Buchhandlung, 1936. Translated by *Ante-Nicene Fathers*. Vol. 2. Edited by A. Cleveland Coxe. Grand Rapids, Mich.: Eerdmans, 1962.

Cornelius Nepos. Translated by John C. Rolfe. *Cornelius Nepos*. LCL; London: William Heinemann; New York: G. P. Putnam's Sons, 1929.

Dio Chrysostom. *Orations*. Translated by J. W. Cohoon. *Dio Chrysostom*. LCL; Cambridge, Mass.: Harvard University Press; London: William Heinemann, 1961.

Eunapius. Translated by Wilmer Cave Wright. *Philostratus and Eunapius, The Lives of the Sophists*. LCL; London: William Heinemann; Cambridge, Mass.: Harvard University Press, 1968.

The Greek Anthology. Translated by W. R. Paton. *The Greek Anthology.* LCL; Cambridge, Mass.: Harvard University Press; London: William Heinemann, 1953.

Josephus. *Antiquities.* Translated by H. St. J. Thackeray et al. *Josephus.* LCL; Cambridge, Mass.: Harvard University Press; London: William Heinemann, 1958–1965.

Juvenal. *Satires.* Translated by Rolfe Humphries. *The Satires of Juvenal.* Bloomington and London: Indiana University Press, 1974.

Lucian. *Dialogues of the Courtesans.* Translated by M. D. Macleod. *Lucian.* LCL; Cambridge, Mass.: Harvard University Press; London: William Heinemann, 1961.

Martial. *Epigrams.* Translated by Walter C. A. Ker. *Martial. Epigrams.* LCL; Cambridge, Mass.: Harvard University Press; London: William Heinemann, 1947–50.

Minucius Felix. *Octavius.* Translated by Jo-Ann Shelton. *As the Romans Did. A Source Book in Roman Social History.* Oxford: Oxford University Press, 1988.

Philo of Alexandria. Translated by F. H. Colson et al. *Philo.* LCL; Cambridge, Mass.: Harvard University Press; London: William Heinemann, 1929–1962.

Philostratus. *Life of Apollonius of Tyana.* Translated by F. C. Conybeare. *Philostratus. Life of Apollonius of Tyana.* LCL; Cambridge, Mass.: Harvard University Press; London: William Heinemann, 1960.

Plutarch. *Moralia.* Translated by F. C. Babbitt et al. *Plutarch's Moralia.* LCL; Cambridge, Mass.: Harvard University Press; London: William Heinemann, 1927–1969.

Sallust. Translated by J. C. Rolfe. *Sallust.* LCL; London: William Heinemann; Cambridge, Mass.: Harvard University Press, 1971.

Seneca, the Elder. *Declamations.* Translated by M. Winterbottom. *The Elder Seneca. Declamations.* LCL; Cambridge, Mass.: Harvard University Press; London: William Heinemann, 1974.

Sirach. Text *Septuaginta.* Stuttgart: Deutsche Bibelgesellschaft, 1979. Translated by *The Oxford Annotated Apocrypha.* Edited by Bruce M. Metzger. New York: Oxford University Press, 1965.

Tacitus. *Germania.* Translated by William Peterson. *Tacitus. Dialogus, Agricola, Germania.* LCL; London: William Heinemann; New York: G. P. Putnam's Sons, 1925.

Vitruvius. *On Architecture.* Translated by Frank Granger. *Vitruvius. On Architecture.* LCL; Cambridge, Mass.: Harvard University Press; London: William Heinemann, 1956.

Modern Authors

Abrahams, I. "Publicans and Sinners." In *Studies in Pharisaism and the Gospels,* 54–61. New York: KTAV Publishing House, 1967.

Achtemeier, Elizabeth. "The Impossible Possibility: Evaluating the Feminist Approach to Bible and Theology." *Interpretation* 42 (1988): 45–57.

Achtemeier, Paul J. *Mark. A Proclamation Commentary.* Philadelphia: Fortress Press, 1986.

_____. "The Origin and Function of the Pre-Markan Miracle Catenae." *Journal of Biblical Literature* 91 (1972): 198–221.

_____. "Toward the Isolation of Pre-Markan Miracle Catenae." *Journal of Biblical Literature* 89 (1970): 265–91.

Adams, Margaret G. "The Hidden Disciples. Luke's Stories about Women in his Gospel and in Acts." D.Min. diss., San Francisco Theological Seminary, 1980.

Albright, W. F. and C. S. Mann. *Matthew.* Anchor Bible; Garden City, N.Y.: Doubleday, 1971.

Allberry, C. R. C., ed. *A Manichaean Psalmbook.*, part 2. Stuttgart: W. Kohlhammer, 1938.

Allegro, John M. "The Wiles of the Wicked Woman." In *Discoveries in the Judean Desert.* Vol. 5, 82–84. Oxford: Oxford University Press, 1968.

Allen, Willoughby. *A Critical and Exegetical Commentary on the Gospel According to St. Matthew.* Edinburgh: T and T Clark, 1965.

Amaru, Betsy Halpern. "Portraits of Biblical Women in Josephus' Antiquities." *Journal of Jewish Studies* 39 (1988): 143–70.

Anderson, Janice Capel. "Matthew: Gender and Reading." *Semeia* 28 (1983): 3–27.

Archer, Lèonie J. "The 'Evil Woman' in Apocryphal and Pseudepigraphical Writings." In *Proceedings of the Ninth World Congress of Jewish Studies. Jerusalem, August 4–12, 1985*, 239–46. Jerusalem: World Union of Jewish Studies, 1986.

_____. *Her Price is Beyond Rubies. The Jewish Woman in Graeco-Roman Palestine.* JSOT Suppl. 60; Sheffield: JSOT Press, 1990.

_____. "The Role of Jewish Women in the Religion, Ritual and Cult of Graeco-Roman Palestine." In *Images of Women in Antiquity*, 273–87. Edited by Averil Cameron and Amélie Kuhrt. Detroit, Mich.: Wayne State University Press, 1983.

Arthur, Marylin. " 'Liberated Women:' The Classical Era." In *Becoming Visible*: *Women in European History*, 60–89. Edited by Renate Bridenthal and Claudia Koonz. Boston: Houghton Mifflin, 1977.

Augsten, M. "Lukanische Miszelle." *New Testament Studies* 14 (1968): 581–83.

Aune, David E., ed. *Greco-Roman Literature and the New Testament.* Atlanta, Ga.: Scholars Press, 1988.

_____. "Septem Sapientium Convivium." In *Plutarch's Ethical Writings and Early Christian Literature*, 51–105. Edited by Hans Dieter Betz. Leiden: Brill, 1978.

Bahr, Gordon J. "The Seder of Passover and the Eucharistic Words." *Novum Testamentum* 12 (1970): 181–202.

Baker, Aelred. "One Thing Necessary." *Catholic Biblical Quarterly* 27 (1965): 127–37.

Balch, David L. *Let Wives be Submissive: The Domestic Code in 1 Peter.* SBL Monographs 26; Chico, Calif.: Scholars Press, 1981.

Balsdon, J. P. V. D. *Romans and Aliens.* Chapel Hill: University of North Carolina Press, 1979.

_____. *Roman Women. Their History and Habits.* London: The Bodley Head, 1962.

Barrow, R. H. *Slavery in the Roman Empire*. New York: Barnes and Noble; London: Methuen and Co., 1968.

Bartchy, S. Scott. "Table Fellowship with Jesus and the 'Lord's Meal' at Corinth." In *Increase in Learning: Essays in Honor of James G. Van Buren*, 45–61. Edited by Owens and Hamm. Manhattan, Kans.: Manhattan Christian College Press, 1979.

Beavis, Mary Ann. "Women as Models of Faith in Mark." *Biblical Theology Bulletin* 18 (1988): 3–9.

Becker, Wilhelm Adolf. *Charicles. or Illustrations of the Private Life of the Ancient Greeks*. London: Longmans Green and Co., 1895.

Bergquist, Birgitta. "Sympotic Space: A Functional Aspect of Greek Dining Rooms." In *Sympotica. A Symposium on the Symposion*, 37–65. Edited by Oswyn Murray. Oxford: Clarendon Press, 1990.

Best, Edward. "Cicero, Livy, and Educated Roman Women." *Classical Journal* 65 (1970): 199–204.

Best, Ernest. *Disciples and Discipleship: Studies in the Gospel According to Mark*. Edinburgh: T and T Clark, 1986.

_____. *Following Jesus: Discipleship in the Gospel of Mark*. JSOT Suppl. 4; Sheffield: JSOT Press, 1981.

_____. "The Role of the Disciples in Mark." *New Testament Studies* 23 (1977): 377–401.

Betz, Hans Dieter. "Jesus as Divine Man." In *Jesus the Historian. Written in Honor of Ernest Cadman Caldwell*, 114–33. Edited by F. Thomas Trotter. Philadelphia: Westminster Press, 1968.

Beydon, F. "A temps nouveau, nouvelles questions. Luc 10, 38–42." *Foi et Vie* 88 (1989): 25–32.

Beyer, H. W. "διακονέω, κτλ." *Theological Dictionary of the New Testament*. Vol. 2, 81–93. Edited by G. Kittel. Grand Rapids, Mich.: Eerdmans, 1968.

Bird, Phyllis A. "The Harlot as Heroine: Narrative Art and Social Presupposition in Three Old Testament Texts." *Semeia* 46 (1989): 119–39.

Bjorndahl, Sterling. "Thomas 61–67: A Chreia Elaboration Pattern." New Testament Seminar, Claremont, California, Feb. 2, 1988.

Blümner, Hugo. *The Home Life of the Ancient Greeks*. New York: Cooper Square Publishers, 1966.

Boardman, John. "*Symposion* Furniture." In *Sympotica. A Symposium on the Symposion*, 122–31. Edited by Oswyn Murray. Oxford: Clarendon Press, 1990.

Boldrey, Richard and Joyce Boldrey. *Chauvinist or Feminist? Paul's View of Women*. Grand Rapids, Mich.: Baker Book House, 1976.

Bookidis, Nancy. "Ritual Dining in the Sanctuary of Demeter and Kore at Corinth: Some Questions." In *Sympotica. A Symposium on the Symposion*, 86–94. Edited by Oswyn Murray. Oxford: Clarendon Press, 1990.

Bornkamm, Günther et al. *Tradition and Interpretation in Matthew*. Translated by Percy Scott. Philadelphia: Westminster, 1963.

Brawley, Robert L. *Luke–Acts and the Jews: Conflict, Apology and Conciliation*. SBL Monograph Series 33; Atlanta, Ga.: Scholars Press, 1987.

Brendel, Otto J. "The Scope and Temperament of Erotic Art in the Greco-Roman World." In *Studies in Erotic Art*, 3–108. Edited by T. Bowie and C. V. Christenson. New York and London: Basic Books, 1970.

Bridenthal, Renate and Claudia Koonz, eds. *Becoming Visible: Women in European History*. Boston: Houghton Mifflin, 1977.

Brodie, Thomas L. "Luke 7:35–50 as Internalization of 2 Kings 4:1–37: A Study in Luke's Use of Rhetorical Imitation." *Bib* 64 (1983): 457–85.

Brooten, Bernadette J. "Early Christian Women and Their Cultural Context: Issues and Method in Historical Reconstruction." In *Feminist Perspectives on Biblical Scholarship*, 65–91. Edited by Adela Yarbro Collins. Chico, Calif.: Scholars Press, 1985.

_____. "Jewish Women's History in the Roman Period: A Task for Christian Theology." *Harvard Theological Review* 79 (1986): 22–30.

_____. *Women Leaders in the Ancient Synagogue. Inscriptional Evidence and Background Issues*. Brown Judaic Studies 36; Chico, Calif.:Scholars, 1982.

Brown, Raymond E. *The Birth of the Messiah. A Commentary on the Infancy Narratives in Matthew and Luke*. New York: Doubleday, 1977.

_____. "The Role of Women in the Fourth Gospel." *Theological Studies* 36 (1975): 688–99.

Brown, Raymond E. et al. *Mary in the New Testament*. Philadelphia: Fortress Press; New York: Paulist Press, 1978.

Bullough, Vern and Bonnie Bullough. *Prostitution. An Illustrated Social History*. New York: Crown Publishers, 1978.

Bultmann, Rudolf. *History of the Synoptic Tradition*. Translated by John Marsh. Oxford: Basil Blackwell, 1963.

Burkill, T. A. "The Historical Development of the Story of the Syrophoenician Woman (Mark 7:24–31)." *Novum Testamentum* 9 (1967): 161–77.

_____. "The Syrophoenician Woman: The Congruence of Mark 7:24–31." *Zeitschrift für die Neutestamentliche Wissenschaft* 57 (1966): 23–37.

Burkitt, F. C. "Mary Magdalene and Mary, Sister of Martha." *Expository Times* 42 (1930–31): 157–59.

Burrus, Virginia. *Chastity as Autonomy. Women in the Stories of the Apocryphal Acts*. Lewiston, New York: E. Mellen Press, 1987.

Cameron, Averil. "Neither Male or Female." *Greece and Rome* 27 (1980): 60–68.

_____. "Redrawing the Map: Early Christian Territory After Foucault." *Journal of Roman Studies* 76 (1986): 266–71.

Cameron, Averil and Amélie Kuhrt, eds. *Images of Women in Antiquity*. Detroit, Mich.: Wayne State University Press, 1983.

Cameron, Ron. " 'What Have You Come Out to See?' Characterizations of John and Jesus in the Gospels." *Semeia* 49 (1990): 35–69.

Cantarella, Eva. *Pandora's Daughters. The Role and Status of Women in Greek and Roman Antiquity*. Translated by Maureen B. Fant. Baltimore and London: Johns Hopkins University Press, 1987.

Carcopino, Jérôme. *Daily Life in Ancient Rome. The People and the City at the Height of the Roman Empire*. Translated by E. O. Lorimer. New Haven and London: Yale University Press, 1940.

Castner, Catherine J. "Epicurean Hetairai as Dedicants to Healing Deities?" *Greek, Roman and Byzantine Studies* 23 (1982): 51–57.

Catchpole, David. "The Fearful Silence of the Women at the Tomb: A Study in Markan Theology." *Journal of Theology for Southern Africa* 18 (1977): 3–10.

Charlesworth, James H., ed. *The Old Testament Pseudipigrapha*. Vol. 2. Garden City, N.Y.: Doubleday, 1985.

Clouse, Bonnidell and Robert G. Clouse. *Women in Ministry: Four Views*. Downers Grove, Ill.: InterVarsity Press, 1989.

Cohen, Shaye J. D. "Women in the Synagogues of Antiquity." *Conservative Judaism* 34 (1980): 23–39.

Cole, Susan G. "Could Greek Women Read and Write?" In *Reflections of Women*, 219–45. Edited by Helene P. Foley. New York, London, and Paris: Gordon and Breach Science Publishers, 1981.

Collins, Adela Yarbro, ed. *Feminist Perspectives on Biblical Scholarship*. Chico, Calif.: Scholars Press, 1985.

Cooper, Frederick. "Dining in Round Buildings." In *Sympotica. A Symposium on the Symposion*. 66–85. Edited by Oswyn Murray. Oxford: Clarendon Press, 1990.

Corley, Kathleen E. "*Noli Me Tangere*: Mary Magdalene in the Patristic Literature." SBL Pacific Coast Region, Claremont, Calif., March 1989.

_____. "Salome." *International Standard Bible Encyclopedia*. Vol. 4, 286. Grand Rapids, Mich.: Eerdmans, 1988.

_____. "Salome Traditions in the Early Church." Unpublished manuscript.

_____. "Silence in the Context of Ascent and Liturgy in Gnostic Texts." New Testament Seminar, Claremont Graduate School, Claremont, Calif., 1987.

_____. "Were the Women Around Jesus Really Prostitutes? Women in the Context of Greco-Roman Meals." *Society of Biblical Literature 1989 Seminar Papers*, 487–521. Edited by David Lull. Atlanta, Ga.: Scholars Press, 1989.

_____. "Women's Inheritance Rights in Antiquity and Paul's Metaphor of Adoption." New Testament Seminar, Claremont Graduate School, Claremont, Calif., 1988.

Cotter, Wendy J. "The Parable of the Children in the Marketplace (Q (Lk) 7:31–35); An Examination of the Parable's Image and Significance." *Novum Testamentum* 29 (1987): 289–304.

Countryman, L. Wm. "Patrons and Officers in Club and Church." *Society of Biblical Literature 1977 Seminar Papers*, 135–43. Edited by P. J. Achtemeier. Missoula, Mont.: Scholars Press, 1977.

Crosby, Michael H. *House of Disciples. Church, Economics and Justice in Matthew*. Maryknoll, N.Y.: Orbis Books, 1988.

Csillag, Pal. *The Augustan Laws on Family Relations*. Budapest: Academiai Kiado, 1976.

Daly, Mary. *Beyond God the Father: Toward a Philosophy of Women's Liberation*. Boston: Beacon Press, 1973.

_____. *Gyn/Ecology: The Metaphysics of Radical Feminism*. Boston: Beacon Press, 1978.

_____. *Pure Lust*. Boston: Beacon Press, 1984.

D'Angelo, Mary Rose. "Images of Jesus and the Christian Call in the Gospels of Luke and John." *Spirituality Today* 37 (1985): 196–212.

_____. "Women in Luke–Acts: A Redactional View." *Journal of Biblical Literature* 109 (1990): 441–61.

"The Danvers Statement." Wheaton, Ill.: Council in Biblical Manhood and Womanhood, November 1988.

D'Arms, John. "The Roman *Convivium* and the Idea of Equality." In *Sympotica. A Symposium on the Symposion*, 308–20. Edited by Oswyn Murray. Oxford: Clarendon Press, 1990.

Davies, Stevan L. *The Revolt of the Widows. The Social World of the Apocryphal Acts.* Carbondale and Edwardsville: So. Illinois University Press; London and Amsterdam: Feffer and Simons, 1980.

D'Avino, Michele. *The Women of Pompeii.* Translated by M. H. Jones and L. Nusco. Napoli: Loffredo, 1967.

Daube, David. "The Anointing at Bethany and Jesus' Burial." *Anglican Theological Review* 32 (1950): 186–99.

Deissmann, Adolf. *Light From the Ancient East.* Translated by L. R. M. Strachan. London: Hodder and Stoughton, 1927.

Delobel, J. "L'onction par la pécheresse: La composition littéraire de Lc. VII, 36–50." *Ephemerides Theologicae Lovanienses* 42 (1966): 415–75.

de Meeûs, X. "Composition de Lc, XIV et genre symposiaque." *Ephemerides Theologique Lovanienses* 37 (1961): 847–70.

De Melo, C. M. "Mary of Bethany the Silent Contemplative." *Review for Religious* 48 (1989): 690–97.

Dentzer, Jean-Marie. "Aux origines de l'iconographie du banquet couché." *Revue archéologique* 2 (1971): 215–58.

Dermience, A., "La péricope de la Cananéene, (Mt 15, 21–28). Rédaction et théologie." *Ephemerides Theologicae Lovanienses* 58 (1982): 25–49.

Derrett, J. Duncan M. *Law in the New Testament.* London: Darton, Longman and Todd, 1970.

_____. "Law in the New Testament: The Syrophoenician Woman and the Centurion of Capernaum." *Novum Testamentum* 15 (1973): 161–86.

Dewey, Joanna. *Disciples of the Way: Mark on Discipleship.* Women's Division, Board of Global Ministries, UMC, 1976.

Donahue, John R. "Tax–collectors and Sinners: An Attempt at Identification." *Catholic Biblical Quarterly* 33 (1971): 39–61.

Donini, Ambrogio. "The Myth of Salvation in Ancient Slave Society." *Science and Society* 15 (1951): 57–60.

Douglas, Mary. "Deciphering a Meal." In *Myth, Symbol and Culture*, 61–81. Edited by C. Geertz. New York: W. W. Norton and Co., 1971.

Douglas, Mary and Michael Nicod. "Taking the Bisquit: The Structure of British Meals." *New Society* 30 (1974): 744–47.

Downing, F. Gerald. *Christ and the Cynics: Jesus and Other Radical Preachers in First-Century Tradition.* JSOT Manuals 4; Sheffield: Sheffield Academic Press, 1988.

_____. *Jesus and the Threat of Freedom.* London: SCM Press, 1987.

Duff, A. M. *Freedmen in the Early Roman Empire.* N.Y.: Barnes and Noble, 1958.

Dunn, James D. G. "Pharisees, Sinners and Jesus." In *The Social World of Formative Christianity and Judaism. Essays in Tribute to Howard Clark Kee*, 264–89. Edited by J. Neusner et al. Philadelphia: Fortress Press, 1988.

Elliott, J. K. "The Anointing of Jesus." *Expository Times* 85 (1973–74): 105–7.

Ellis, E. Earle. *The Gospel of Luke.* London and Edinburgh: Thomas Nelson, 1966.

Elshtain, Jean Bethke. *Public Man, Private Woman. Women in Social and Political Thought.* Princeton, N.J.: Princeton University Press, 1981.

Espérandieu, Emile. *Recueil général des bas-reliefs. statues et bustes de la Gaule romaine.* Vols. 6 and 8. Paris: Imprimerie Nationale, 1919 and 1922.

Farmer, William R. "Who are the 'Tax-Collectors and Sinners' in the Synoptic Tradition?" In *From Faith to Faith: Essays in Honor of Donald G. Miller on his 70th Birthday,* 167–74. Edited by D. Y. Hadidian. Pittsburgh, Penn.: Pickwick Press, 1979.

Fee, Gordon D. " 'One Thing Needful?' Luke 10:42." In *New Testament Textual Criticism: Its Significance for Exegesis. Essays in Honour of Bruce M. Metzger,* 61–75. Edited by Eldon Jay Epp and Gordon Fee. Oxford: Clarendon Press, 1981.

Fehr, Burkhard. "Entertainers at the *Symposion:* The *Akletoi* in the Archaic Period." In *Sympotica. A Symposium on the Symposion,* 185–95. Edited by Oswyn Murray. Oxford: Clarendon Press, 1990.

Finley, M. I. "The Silent Women of Rome." In *Aspects of Antiquity: Discoveries and Controversies,* 129–42. New York: Viking Press, 1968.

Fiorenza, Elisabeth Schüssler. *Bread Not Stone: The Challenge of Feminist Biblical Interpretation.* Boston: Beacon Press, 1984.

—————. *In Memory of Her: A Feminist Reconstruction of Christian Origins.* New York: Crossroad, 1983.

—————. "Theological Criteria and Historical Reconstruction: Martha and Mary; Luke 10:38–42." *Colloquy* 53. Berkeley, Calif.: Center for Hermeneutical Studies in Hellenistic and Modern Culture, 1987.

—————. "The Will to Choose or Reject: Continuing Our Critical Work." In *Feminist Interpretation of the Bible,* 125–36. Edited by Letty M. Russell. Philadelphia: Westminster Press, 1985.

Fischel, Henry A. "Studies in Cynicism and the Ancient Near East: The Transformation of a *Chria.*" In *Religions in Antiquity, Essays in Memory of Erwin Ramsdell Goodenough,* 372–411. Edited by J. Neusner. Leiden: Brill, 1968.

Fitzmyer, Joseph A. *The Gospel According to Luke.* Garden City, N.Y.: Doubleday, 1981–85.

Flammer, Barnabas. "Die Syro-Phoenizerin: Mk 7:24–30." *Theologische Quartalschrift* 148 (1968): 463–78.

—————. "The Syro-Phoenician Woman (Mk 7:24–30)." *Theology Digest* 18 (1970): 19–24.

Flanagan, Neal M. "The Position of Women in the Writings of St. Luke." *Marianum* 40 (1978): 288–304.

Flender, Helmut. *St. Luke, Theologian of Redemptive History.* Philadelphia: Fortress Press, 1967.

Foley, Helen P., ed. *Reflections of Women in Antiquity.* New York, London, and Paris: Gordon and Breach Science Publishers, 1981.

Forbes, Clarence A. "The Education and Training of Slaves in Antiquity." *Proceedings of the American Philological Association* 86 (1955): 321–60.

Ford, J. Massingberd. "The Meaning of 'Virgin.' " *New Testament Studies* 12 (1966): 293–99.

Fowler, Robert M. *Loaves and Fishes. The Function of the Feeding Stories in the Gospel of Mark.* SBL Dissertation Series 54; Chico, Calif.: Scholars Press 1981.

Fowler, W. Warde. *Social Life at Rome in the Age of Cicero.* New York and London: Macmillan and Co., 1909.

Frank, Tenney. *Life and Literature of the Roman Republic*. Berkeley and Los Angeles: University of California Press, 1956.

Freyne, Sean. *Galilee, Jesus and the Gospels: Literary Approaches and Historical Investigations*. Philadelphia: Fortress Press, 1988.

_____. *The Twelve: Disciples and Apostles. A Study in the Theology of the First Three Gospels*. London and Sydney: Sheed and Ward, 1968.

Freed, Edwin D. "The Women in Matthew's Genealogy." *Journal for the Study of the New Testament* 29 (1987): 3–19.

Freidländer, Ludwig. *Roman Life and Manners Under the Early Empire*. Translated by A. B. Gough. London: George Routledge and Sons; New York: E. P. Dutton and Co., 1909.

Garlan, Yvon. *Slavery in Ancient Greece*. Translated by Janey Lloyd. Ithaca and London: Cornell University Press, 1988.

Gibson, J. "Οἱ Τελῶναι καὶ αἱ Πόρναι." *Journal of Theological Studies* 32 (1981): 429–33.

Glotz, Gustave. *Ancient Greece at Work: An Economic History of Greece from the Homeric Period to the Roman Conquest*. New York: Alfred Knopf, 1926.

Goody, Jack. *Cooking, Cuisine and Class. A Study of Comparative Sociology*. Cambridge: Cambridge University Press, 1982.

Grassi, Joseph A. *The Hidden Heroes of the Gospels. Female Counterparts of Jesus*. Collegeville, Minn.: Liturgical Press, 1989.

_____. "The Secret Heroine of Mark's Drama." *Biblical Theology Bulletin* 18 (1988): 10–15.

Grimal, Pierre. *Love in Ancient Rome*. Norman and London: University of Oklahoma Press, 1986.

Guelich, Robert A. *Mark 1—8:26. Word Biblical Commentary*, 34A. Dallas, Tex.: Word Books, 1989.

Gundry, Robert H. *Matthew: A Commentary on His Literary and Theological Art*. Grand Rapids, Mich.: Eerdmans, 1982.

Hallett, Judith P. *Fathers and Daughters in Roman Society. Women and the Elite Family*. Princeton, N.J.: Princeton University Press, 1984.

_____. "The Role of Women in Roman Elegy: Counter-Cultural Feminism." In *Women in the Ancient World: The Arethusa Papers*, 241–62. Edited by John Peradotto and J. P. Sullivan. Albany, N.Y.: State University of New York Press, 1984.

Hanson, A. T. "Rahab the Harlot in Early Christian Tradition." *Journal for the Study of the New Testament* 1 (1978): 53–60.

Hasler, J. Ireland. "The Incident of the Syrophoenician Woman (Matt. 15:21–28; Mark 7:24–30)." *Expository Times* 45 (1933–34): 459–61.

Hauck, F. and S. Schulz. "πόρνη, κτλ." *Theological Dictionary of the New Testament*. Vol. 6, 579–95. Edited by G. Kittel. Grand Rapids, Mich.: Eerdmans, 1968.

Hedrick, Charles W. "Narrator and Story in the Gospel of Mark: Hermeneia and Paradosis." *Perspectives in Religious Studies* 14 (1987): 239–58.

Heffern, Andrew D. "The Four Women in Matthew's Genealogy of Christ." *Journal of Biblical Literature* 31 (1912): 68–81.

Held, Heinz Joachim. "Matthew as Interpreter of the Miracle Stories." In *Tradition and Interpretation in Matthew*, 165–299. Günther Bornkamm et al. Philadelphia: Westminster Press, 1963.

Hock, Ronald F. "The Greek Novel." In *Greco-Roman Literature and the New Testament*, 127–46. Edited by David E. Aune. Atlanta, Ga.: Scholars Press, 1988.

_____. *The Social Context of Paul's Ministry. Tentmaking and Apostleship*. Philadelphia: Fortress Press, 1980.

_____. "The Will of God and Sexual Morality: 1 Thessalonians 4:3–8 in its Social and Intellectual Context." Paper presented at the SBL Annual Meeting, New York, 1982.

Hoïstad, Ragnar. *Cynic Hero and Cynic King*. Uppsala: Carl Bloms, 1948.

Holst, Robert. "The One Anointing of Jesus: Another Application of the Form-Critical Method." *Journal of Biblical Literature* 95 (1976): 435–46.

Hopkins, Keith. *Conquerors and Slaves*. Cambridge: Cambridge University Press, 1977.

Hopkins, M. K. "The Age of Roman Girls at Marriage." *Population Studies* 19 (1965): 309–27.

Horsley, G. H. R. "Invitation to the *Kline* of Sarapis." *New Documents Illustrating Early Christianity*. Vol. 1, 5–9. Macquarie University, Australia: The Ancient History Documentary Research Centre, 1981.

_____. "The Purple Trade, and the Status of Lydia of Thyatira." *New Documents Illustrating Early Christianity*. Vol. 2, 25–32. Macquarie University, Australia: The Ancient History Documentary Research Centre, 1982.

_____. "Reclining at the Passover Meal." *New Documents Illustrating Early Christianity*. Vol. 2, 75. Macquarie University, Australia: The Ancient History Documentary Research Centre, 1982.

Hurley, James B. *Man and Woman in Biblical Perspective*. Grand Rapids, Mich.: Zondervan, 1981.

Ingram, John Kells. *A History of Slavery and Serfdom*. London: Adam and Charles Black, 1895.

Irvin, Dorothy. "The Ministry of Women in the Early Church: The Archaeological Evidence." *Duke Divinity School Review* 45 (1980): 76–86.

Jackson, Howard M. "The Death of Jesus in Mark and the Miracle from the Cross." *New Testament Studies* 33 (1987): 16–37.

James, M., ed. *The Apocryphal New Testament*. Oxford: Clarendon Press, 1963.

Jarvis, Cynthia A. "Matthew 28:1–10." *Interpretation* 42 (1988): 63–68.

Jeremias, Joachim. *The Eucharistic Words of Jesus*. New York: Charles Scribner's Sons, 1966.

_____. *Jerusalem in the Time of Jesus*. Philadelphia: Fortress Press, 1969.

_____. "Λαμπαδάδες in Matthew 25:1–13." In *Soli Deo Gloria: New Testament Studies in Honor of William Childs Robinson*, 83–87. Edited by J. McDowell Richards. Richmond, Va.: John Knox, 1968.

_____. *New Testament Theology*. New York: Charles Scribner's Sons, 1971.

Johnson, Luke T. *The Literary Function of Possessions in Luke–Acts*. SBL Dissertation Series 39; Chico, Calif.: Scholars Press, 1977.

_____. "The New Testament's Anti-Jewish Slander and the Conventions of Ancient Polemic." *Journal of Biblical Literature* 108 (1989): 419–41.

Johnson, Marshall D. *The Purpose of the Biblical Genealogies with Special Reference to the Setting of the Genealogies of Jesus*. Cambridge: Cambridge University Press, 1969.

Johnston, E. B. "Jezebel." *International Standard Bible Encyclopedia*. Vol. 2, 1057–59. Grand Rapids, Mich.: Eerdmans, 1975.

Jones, A. H. M. "Slavery in the Ancient World." In *Slavery in Classical Antiquity*. Edited by M. I. Finley. Cambridge; W. Heffer and Sons, 1960.

Judge, E. A. *The Social Pattern of the Christian Groups in the First Century*. London: Tyndale Press, 1960.

Kantzer, Kenneth S. "Problems Inerrancy Doesn't Solve." *Christianity Today* 31 (Feb. 20, 1987): 14–15.

Karris, Robert J. *Luke: Artist and Theologian. Luke's Passion Account as Literature*. New York; Mahwah; Toronto: Paulist Press, 1985.

Kee, Howard Clark. *Community of the New Age: Studies in Mark's Gospel*. Philadelphia: Westminster Press, 1977.

_____. *Miracle in the Early Christian World: A Study in Sociohistorical Method*. New Haven and London: Yale University Press, 1983.

Keuls, Eva C. *The Reign of the Phallus: Sexual Politics in Ancient Athens*. New York: Harper and Row, 1985.

Kiefer, Otto. *Sexual Life in Ancient Rome*. New York: Barnes and Noble, 1953.

Kilgallen, John J. "John the Baptist, the Sinful Woman, and the Pharisee." *Journal of Biblical Literature* 104 (1985): 675–79.

Kingsbury, Jack Dean. "The Figure of Peter in Matthew's Gospel as a Theological Problem." *Journal of Biblical Literature* 98 (1979): 67–83.

_____. *Matthew*. Proclamation Commentaries. Philadelphia: Fortress Press, 1978.

_____. *Matthew: Structure, Christology and Kingdom*. Philadelphia: Fortress Press, 1975.

_____. "The Title 'Son of David' in Matthew's Gospel." *Journal of Biblical Literature* 95 (1976): 591–602.

_____. "The Verb *Akolouthein* as an Index of Matthew's View of His Community." *Journal of Biblical Literature* 97 (1978): 56–73.

Kittel, G. "ἀκολουθέω, κτλ." *Theological Dictionary of the New Testament*. Vol. 1, 210–16. Edited by G. Kittel. Grand Rapids, Mich.: Eerdmans, 1968.

Knockaert, A. "Structural Analysis of the Biblical Text (Lk 10:38–42)." *Lumen Vitae* 33 (1978): 471–81.

Klassen, William. "Musonius Rufus, Jesus and Paul: Three First-Century Feminists." In *From Jesus to Paul. Studies in Honor of Francis Wright Beare*, 185–206. Edited by P. Richardson and J. Hurd. Ontario: Wilfred Laurier University Press, 1984.

Kloppenborg, John S. *The Formation of Q: Trajectories in Ancient Wisdom Collections*. Philadelphia: Fortress Press, 1987.

Klosinski, Lee E. "Meals in Mark." Ph.D. diss., The Claremont Graduate School, 1988.

Kopas, Jane. "Jesus and Women: Luke's Gospel." *TToday* 43 (1986): 192–202.

_____. "Jesus and Women in Mark's Gospel." *Review for Religious* 44 (1985): 912–20.

Kraemer, Ross S. "Hellenistic Jewish Women: The Epigraphical Evidence." *SBL 1986 Seminar Papers*, 183–200. Edited by Kent Richards. Atlanta, Ga.: Scholars Press, 1986.

_____. "Monastic Jewish Women in Graeco-Roman Egypt: Philo Judaeus on the Therapeutrides." *Signs* 14 (1989): 342–70.

Kraemer, Ross and Cornell West. "Review: In Memory of Her." *Religious Studies Review* 11 (1985): 1–9.

Krentz, E. "Community and Character: Matthew's Vision of the Church." Paper presented at the Annual Meeting of the SBL, New Orleans, November 1990.

Lachs, Samuel Tobias. *A Rabbinic Commentary on the New Testament. The Gospels of Matthew, Mark and Luke.* Hoboken, N.J.: KTAV Publishing House; New York: Anti-Defamation League of B'nai B'rith, 1987.

Lagrand, James. "How was the Virgin Mary 'Like a Man'? A Note on Mt 1:18b and Related Syriac Texts." *Novum Testamentum* 22 (1980): 97–107.

Laland, E. "Marthe et Marie. Quel message l' église primitif lisait-elle dans ce récit? Luc 10, 38–42." *Bibel et Vie chrétienne* 76 (1967): 29–43.

Lambert, Jean C. "An 'F Factor'? The New Testament in Some White, Feminist, Christian Theological Construction." *Journal of Feminist Studies in Religion* 1 (1985): 93–113.

Lattimore, Richmond *Themes in Greek and Latin Epitaphs.* Illinois Studies in Language and Literature 28; Urbana: University of Illinois Press, 1942.

Lefkowitz, Mary R. "Invective Against Women." In *Heroines and Hysterics*, 32–40. New York: St. Martin's Press, 1981.

Lefkowitz, Mary R. and Maureen B. Fant. *Women's Life in Greece and Rome. A Source Book in Translation.* Baltimore, Md.: Johns Hopkins University Press, 1982.

Légasse, S. "Jésus et les prostituées" *Revue théologique de Louvain* 7 (1976): 137–54.

Legault, André. "An Application of the Form-Critique Method to the Anointings in Galilee (Lk 7: 36–50) and Bethany (Mt 26: 6–13; Mk 14:3–9; Jn 12:1–8)." *Catholic Biblical Quarterly* 16 (1954): 131–45.

Licht, Hans. *Sexual Life in Ancient Greece.* New York: Barnes and Noble, 1953.

Lieberman, Saul. *Greek in Jewish Palestine. Studies in the Life and Manners of Jewish Palestine in the II–IV Centuries C.E.* New York: Jewish Theological Seminary of America, 1942.

Lightman, Marjorie and William Zeisel. "Univira: An Example of Continuity and Change in Roman Society." *Church History* 46 (1977): 19–32.

Loades, Ann, ed. *Feminist Theology: A Reader.* London: SPCK; Philadelphia: Westminster Press, 1990.

Love, Stuart L. "Women's Roles in Certain Second Testament Passages: A Macrosocial View." *Biblical Theology Bulletin* 17 (1987): 50–59.

Lukinovich, Alessandra. "The Play of Reflections between Literary Form and the Sympotic *Deipnosophistae* of Athanaeus." In *Sympotica. A Symposium on the Symposion*, 263–71. Edited by Oswyn Murray. Oxford: Clarendon Press, 1990.

Luz, Ulrich. "The Disciples According to Matthew." In *The Interpretation of Matthew*, 98–128. Edited by Graham Stanton. Philadelphia: Fortress Press; London: SPCK, 1983.

_____. *Matthew 1—7. A Commentary.* Translated by Wilhelm C. Linss. Minneapolis: Fortress Press, 1989.

Lyne, R. O. A. M. *The Latin Love Poets From Catullus to Horace.* Oxford: Clarendon Press, 1986.

MacDonald, Dennis R. *The Legend and the Apostle. The Battle for Paul in Story and Canon.* Philadelphia: Westminster Press, 1983.

Mack, Burton L. *A Myth of Innocence.* Philadelphia: Fortress Press, 1988.

Mack, Burton L. and Vernon K. Robbins. *Patterns of Persuasion in the Gospels.* Sonoma, Calif.: Polebridge Press, 1989.

MacMullen, Ramsay. "Women in Public in the Roman Empire." *Historia* 29 (1980): 208–18.

McMahan, Craig Thomas. "Meals as Type Scenes in the Gospel of Luke." Ph.D. diss., Southern Baptist Theological Seminary, 1987.

McNamara, Elmer A. "The Syro-Phoenician Woman." *AER* 127 (1952): 360–69.

McNeile, A. H. *The Gospel According to Matthew.* London: Macmillan and Co.; New York: St. Martin's Press, 1961.

Malbon, Elizabeth Struthers. "Fallible Followers: Women and Men in the Gospel of Mark." *Semeia* 28 (1983): 29–48.

_____. *Narrative Space and Mythic Meaning in Mark.* San Francisco: Harper and Row, 1986.

_____. "Τῇ οἰκίᾳ αὐτοῦ: Mark 2:15 in Context." *New Testament Studies* 31 (1985): 282–92.

Maly, Eugene H. "Women and the Gospel of Luke." *Biblical Theology Bulletin* 10 (1980): 99–104.

Mann, C. S. *Mark.* Anchor Bible. Garden City, N.Y.: Doubleday, 1986.

Marshall, I. Howard. *Luke: Historian and Theologian.* Exeter: Pasternoster, 1970.

Martin, Dale B. *Slavery as Salvation: The Metaphor of Slavery in Pauline Christianity.* New Haven and London: Yale University Press, 1990.

Martin, Josef. *Symposion. Die Geschichte einer literarischen Form.* Paderborn: Ferdinand Schöningh, 1931.

Maunder, C. J. "A Sitz im Leben for Mark 14:9." *Expository Times* 99 (1987): 78–90.

Maxey, Mima and M. F. Park. *Two Studies on the Roman Lower Classes.* New York: Arno Press, 1975.

Meeks, Wayne A. *The First Urban Christians. The Social World of the Apostle Paul.* New Haven and London: Yale University Press, 1983.

_____. "The Image of the Androgyne: Some Uses of a Symbol in Earliest Christianity." *History of Religions* 13 (1974): 165–207.

Meier, John P. "John the Baptist in Matthew's Gospel." *Journal of Biblical Literature* 99 (1980): 383–405.

Meltzer, Milton. *Slavery from the Rise of Western Civilization to the Renaissance.* New York: Cowles Book Co., 1971–72.

Metzger, Bruce M. *Textual Commentary on the Greek New Testament.* London and New York: United Bible Society, 1971.

Meyer, Marvin W. "Making Mary Male: The Categories 'Male' and 'Female' in the Gospel of Thomas." *New Testament Studies* 31 (1985): 554–70.

_____. "The Youth in Mark and the Beloved Disciple in John." In *Gospel Origins and Christian Beginnings. In Honor of James M. Robinson*, 94–105. Edited by James E. Goehring et al. Sonoma, Calif.: Polebridge Press, 1990.

_____. "The Youth in the Secret Gospel of Mark." *Semeia* 49 (1990): 129–53.

Michaelis, W. "μύρον, κτλ." *Theological Dictionary of the New Testament.* Vol. 4, 800–801. Edited by G. Kittel. Grand Rapids, Mich.: Eerdmans, 1968.

Mickelsen, Alvera, ed. *Women, Authority and the Bible.* Downers Grove, Ill.: Inter-Varsity Press, 1986.

Mollenkott, Elizabeth Ramey. *Women, Men and the Bible.* Revised edition. New York: Crossroad, 1988.

Moltmann-Wendel, Elisabeth. *The Women Around Jesus.* Translated by John Bowden. New York: Crossroad, 1982.

Motto, Anna Lydia. "Seneca on Women's Liberation." *Classical World* 65 (1972): 155–57.

Munro, Winsome. "The Anointing in Mark 14:3–9 and John 12:1–8." *SBL 1979 Seminar Papers.* vol. 1, 127–30. Edited by P. J. Achtemeier. Missoula, Mont.: Scholars Press, 1979.

_____. "Women Disciples in Mark?" *Catholic Biblical Quarterly* 44 (1982): 225–41.

_____. "Women Disciples. Light from Secret Mark." *Journal of Feminist Studies in Religion* 9 (1992): 47–64.

Murray, Oswyn. "The Greek Symposion in History." In *Tria Corda. Scritti in onore di Arnaldo Momigliano,* 257–72. Edited by E. Gabba. Biblioteca di Athanaeum 1; Como: New Press, 1983.

_____, ed. *Sympotica. A Symposium on the Symposion.* Oxford: Clarendon Press, 1990.

Myers, Ched. *Binding the Strong Man, A Political Reading of Mark's Story of Jesus.* Maryknoll, N.Y.: Orbis Books 1988.

Nathanson, Barbara H. Geller. "Reflections on the Silent Woman of Ancient Judaism and Her Pagan Roman Counterpart." In *The Listening Heart. Essays in Wisdom and the Psalms in Honor of Roland E. Murphy, O. Carm,* 259–79. Edited by Kenneth Hoglund et al. JSOT Suppl. 58; Sheffield: JSOT Press, 1987.

Neyrey, Jerome H. "Decision Making in the Early Church. The Case of the Canaanite Woman (Mt 15:21–28)." *Science et Espirit* 33 (1981): 373–78.

_____, ed. *The Social World of Luke–Acts: Models for Interpretation.* Peabody, Mass.: Hendrickson, 1991.

O' Day, G. R. "Surprised by Faith: Jesus and the Canaanite Woman." *Listening* 24 (1989): 290–301.

O' Rahilly, A. "The Two Sisters." *Scripture* 4 (1949): 68–76.

Osborne, Delores. "Women: Sinners and Prostitutes." Paper presented at the SBL Pacific Coast Region, Long Beach, California, April, 1987.

Osiek, Carolyn. "The Feminist and the Bible: Hermeneutical Alternatives." In *Feminist Perspectives on Biblical Scholarship,* 93–105. Edited by Adela Yarbro Collins. Chico, Calif.: Scholars Press, 1985.

Overman, J. Andrew. *Matthew's Gospel and Formative Judaism. The Social World of the Matthean Community.* Minneapolis: Fortress Press, 1990.

Parvey, Constance F. "The Theology and Leadership of Women in the New Testament." In *Religion and Sexism. Images of Woman in the Jewish and Christian Traditions,* 117–49. Edited by Rosemary Radford Ruether. New York: Simon and Schuster, 1974.

BIBLIOGRAPHY

Patterson, Orlando. *Slavery and Social Death: A Comparative Study*. Cambridge, Mass. and London: Harvard University Press, 1982.

Pellizer, Ezio. "Outlines of a Morphology of Sympotic Entertainment." In *Sympotica. A Symposium on the Symposion*, 177–84. Edited by Oswyn Murray. Oxford: Clarendon Press, 1990.

Peradotto, John and J. P. Sullivan, eds. *Women in the Ancient World: The Arethusa Papers*. Albany, N.Y.: State University of New York Press, 1984.

Perkins, Pheme. "Women in the Bible and Its World." *Interpretation* 42 (1988): 33–44.

Perrin, Norman. *Rediscovering the Teaching of Jesus*. New York and Evanston, Ill.: Harper and Row, 1967.

Pervo, Richard I. *Profit with Delight. The Literary Genre of the Acts of the Apostles*. Philadelphia: Fortress Press, 1987.

_____. "Wisdom and Power: Petronius' *Satyricon* and the Social World of Early Christianity." *Anglican Theological Review* 67 (1985): 307–25.

Petersen, Norman R. *Literary Criticism for New Testament Critics*. Guides to Biblical Scholarship; Philadelphia: Fortress Press, 1978.

Philsy, Sr. "Diakonia of Women in the New Testament." *Indian Journal of Theology* 32 (1983): 110–18.

Plaskow, Judith. "Christian Feminism and Anti–Judaism." *Cross Currents* 28 (1978): 306–9.

Platt, Elizabeth E. "The Ministry of Mary at Bethany." *TToday* 34 (1977): 29–39.

Plummer, Alfred. *The Gospel According to Luke*. New York: Charles Scribner's Son, 1925.

_____. "The Woman that was a Sinner." *Expository Times* 27 (1915–19): 42–43.

Pomeroy, Sarah B. *Goddesses, Whores, Wives, and Slaves: Women in Classical Antiquity*. New York: Schocken Books, 1975.

_____. *Women in Hellenistic Egypt. From Alexander to Cleopatra*. New York: Schocken Books, 1984.

Puzo, F. "Marta y María. Nota exégetica a Luc 10, 38–42 y 1 Cor 7, 29–35." *Estudios Eclesiásticos* 34 (1960): 851–57.

Quesnell, Quentin. "The Women at Luke's Supper." In *Political Issues in Luke–Acts*, 59–79. Edited by R. J. Cassidy and P. J. Scharper. New York: Orbis Books, 1983.

Quinn, Jerome D. "P46–The Pauline Canon?" *Catholic Biblical Quarterly* 36 (1974): 379–85.

_____. "Is Ῥαχάβ in Mt 1, 5 Rahab of Jericho?" *Biblica* 62 (1981): 225–28.

Ramaroson, L. "Le premier, c'est l'amour' (Lc 7, 47a)." *Science et Espirit* 39 (1987): 319–29.

Rathje, Annette. "The Adoption of the Homeric Banquet in Central Italy in the Orientalizing Period." In *Sympotica. A Symposium on the Symposion*, 279–88. Edited by Oswyn Murray. Oxford: Clarendon Press, 1990.

Ravens, D. A. S. "The Setting of Luke's Account of the Anointing: Luke 7, 2—8,3." *New Testament Studies* 34 (1988): 282–92.

Rawson, Beryl, ed. *The Family in Ancient Rome. New Perspectives*. Ithaca, N.Y.: Cornell University Press, 1986.

201

_____. "Family Life Among the Lower Classes at Rome in the First Two Centuries of the Empire." *Classical Philology* 61 (1966): 71–83.

Rengstorf, K. H. "ἁμαρτωλός, κτλ." *Theological Dictionary of the New Testament.* Vol. 1, 317–35. Edited by G. Kittel. Grand Rapids, Mich.: Eerdmans, 1968.

Richlin, Amy B. "Sources of Adultery at Rome." In *Reflections of Women in Antiquity*, 379–404. Edited by Helene P. Foley. New York; London; Paris: Gordon and Breach Science Publishers, 1981.

Ringe, Sharon H. "A Gentile Woman's Story." In *Feminist Interpretation of the Bible*, 65–72. Edited by Letty M. Russell. Philadelphia: Fortress Press, 1985.

Robbins, Vernon K. "Last Meal: Preparation, Betrayal and Absence." In *The Passion in Mark. Studies on Mark 14—15*, 21–40. Edited by Werner H. Kelber. Philadelphia: Fortress Press, 1976.

Robinson, James M. *The Problem of History in Mark and Other Markan Studies.* Philadelphia: Fortress Press, 1985.

_____. "The Q Trajectory: Between John and Matthew via Jesus." In *The Future of Early Christianity. Essays in Honor of Helmut Koester.* Pages 173–94. Edited by Birger A. Pearson. Minneapolis: Fortress Press, 1991.

Rosaldo, Michelle Zimbalist and Louise Lamphere, eds. *Women, Culture and Society.* Stanford, Calif.: Stanford University Press, 1974.

_____. "The Use and Abuse of Anthropology: Reflections on Feminism in a Cross-Cultural Understanding." *Signs* 5 (1980): 389–417.

Rousselle, Aline. *Porneia. On Desire and the Body in Antiquity.* Translated by Felicia Pheasant. Oxford: Basil Blackwell, 1988.

Ruether, Rosemary Radford. *Religion and Sexism: Images of Woman in the Jewish and Christian Traditions.* New York: Simon and Schuster, 1974.

_____. *Sexism and God-Talk: Toward a Feminist Theology.* London: SCM Press; Boston: Beacon Press, 1984.

_____. *Women-Church: Theology and Practice of Feminist Liturgical Communities.* New York: Harper and Row, 1985.

Ruether, Rosemary Radford and Eleanor McLaughlin, eds. *Women of Spirit: Female Leadership in the Jewish and Christian Traditions.* New York: Simon and Schuster, 1979.

Russell, Letty M., ed. *Feminist Interpretation of the Bible.* Philadelphia: Westminster Press, 1985.

_____. *Household of Freedom. Authority in Feminist Theology.* Philadelphia: Westminster Press, 1987.

Ryan, Rosalie. "The Women of Galilee and Discipleship in Luke." *Biblical Theology Bulletin* 15 (1985): 56–59.

Sakenfeld, Katherine Doob. "Feminist Perspectives on Bible and Theology. An Introduction to Selected Issues and Literature." *Interpretation* 42 (1988): 5–18.

Sanders, E. P. *Jesus and Judaism.* Philadelphia: Fortress Press, 1985.

Sanders, J. N. "Those Whom Jesus Loved." *New Testament Studies* 1 (1954): 29–41.

Sanger, William W. *The History of Prostitution.* New York: Arno Press, 1972.

Sargent, Rachel. "The Size of the Slave Population at Athens during the 5th and 4th c. Before Christ." *Studies in the Social Sciences.* 12.3. University of Illinois, Urbana, September 1924.

Scanzoni, Letha and Nancy Hardesty. *All We're Meant to Be. A Biblical Approach to Women's Liberation*. Waco, Tex.: Word Books, 1974.

Schaberg, Jane. *The Illegitimacy of Jesus. A Feminist Theological Interpretation of the Infancy Narratives*. San Francisco: Harper & Row, 1987.

Schaps, David. "The Women Least Mentioned: Etiquette and Women's Names." *Classical Quarterly* 27 (1977): 323–30.

Schierling, Marla J. "Women as Leaders in the Markan Communities." *Listening* 15 (1980): 250–56.

Schmidt, Thomas. *Hostility to Wealth in the Synoptic Gospels*. JSOT Suppl. 15; Sheffield: JSOT Press, 1987.

Schmitt, John J. "Women in Mark's Gospel." *Bible Today* 19 (1981): 228–33.

Schwank, B. "Neue Funde in Nabatäerstädten und ihre Bedeutung für die neutestamentliche Exegese." *New Testament Studies* 29 (1983): 429–35.

Schweizer, Eduard. *The Good News According to Luke*. Translated by David Green. Atlanta, Ga.: John Knox Press, 1984.

_____. *The Good News According to Mark*. Translated by Donald Madvig. Richmond, Va.: John Knox Press, 1970.

_____. *The Good News According to Matthew*. Translated by David Green. Atlanta, Ga.: John Knox Press, 1975.

_____. "Matthew's Church." In *The Interpretation of Matthew*, 129–55. Edited by Graham Stanton. Philadelphia: Fortress Press; London: SPCK, 1983.

Seeley, David. "Was Jesus like a Philosopher?" *SBL 1989 Seminar Papers*, 540–49. Edited by David Lull. Atlanta, Ga.: Scholars Press, 1979.

Selvidge, Marla J. "And Those who Followed Feared (Mark 10:32)." *Catholic Biblical Quarterly* 45 (1983): 396–400.

Senior, Donald. *What Are They Saying About Matthew?* New York: Paulist Press, 1983.

Shelton, Jo-Ann. *As the Romans Did. A Source Book for Roman Social History*. Oxford: Oxford University Press, 1988.

Sheridan, Mark. "Disciples and Discipleship in Matthew and Luke." *Biblical Theology Bulletin* 3 (1973): 235–55.

Simpson, A. R. "Mary of Bethany, Mary of Magdala and Anonyma." *The Expositor* 8 (1909): 307–18.

Smart, James D. "Jesus, the Syro-Phoenician Woman and the Disciples." *Expository Times* 50 (1939): 469–72.

Smith, Dennis E. "The Historical Jesus at Table." *SBL 1989 Seminar Papers*, 466–86. Edited by David Lull. Atlanta, Ga.: Scholars Press, 1979.

_____. "Social Obligation in the Context of Communal Meals: A Study of the Christian Meal in 1 Corinthians in Comparison with Graeco-Roman Communal Meals." Th.D. diss., Harvard Divinity School, 1980.

_____. "Table Fellowship as a Literary Motif in the Gospel of Luke." *Journal of Biblical Literature* 106 (1987): 613–38.

Smith, Dennis E. and Hal E. Taussig. *Many Tables: The Eucharist in the New Testament and Liturgy Today*. London: SCM Press; Philadelphia: Trinity Press International, 1990.

Smith, Jonathan Z. *Drudgery Divine. On the Comparison of Early Christianities and the Religions of Late Antiquity*. Chicago: University of Chicago Press, 1990.

_____. "Good News is No News: Aretalogy and Gospel." In *Christianity, Judaism and Other Greco-Roman Cults. Studies for Morton Smith at Sixty*. Part 1, 21–38. Edited by Jacob Neusner. Leiden: Brill, 1975.

Snyder, Graydon F. *Ante Pacem. Archaeological Evidence of Church Life Before Constantine*. Atlanta, Ga.: Mercer University Press, 1985.

Spitta, Friedrich. "Die Frauen in der Genealogie des Matt." *ZWT* 54 (1912): 1–8.

Stagg, Evelyn and Frank Stagg. *Woman in the World of Jesus*. Philadelphia: Westminster Press, 1978.

Stambaugh, John E. "Social Relations in the City of the Early Principate: State of Research." *SBL 1980 Seminar Papers*, 75–99. Edited by P. J. Achtemeier. Chico, Calif.: Scholars Press, 1980.

Steele, E. Springs. "Luke 11:37–54–A Modified Hellenistic Symposium?" *Journal of Biblical Literature* 103 (1984): 379–94.

Stein, S. "The Influence of Symposia Literature on the Literary Form of the Pesah Haggadah." *Journal of Jewish Studies* 8 (1957): 13–44.

Steinmetz, F.-J. "Jesus bei den Heiden: Aktuelle Überlegungen zur Heilung der Syrophönizierin." *Geist und Leben* 55 (1982): 177–84.

Stendahl, Krister. *The Bible and the Role of Women: A Case Study in Hermeneutics*. Philadelphia: Fortress Press, 1966.

Strack, H. L. and P. Billerbeck. *Kommentar zum Neuen Testament*. 6 vols. Munich: C. H. Beck, 1922–56.

Storch, W. "Zur Perikope von der Syrophönizierin (Mk 7,28 und Ri1,7)." *Biblische Zeitschrift* 14 (1970): 256–57.

Stroup, George W. "Between Echo and Narcissus: The Role of the Bible in Feminist Theology." *Interpretation* 42 (1988): 19–32.

Sudbrack, J. " 'Nur eines ist notwendig' (Lk 10, 42)." *Geist und Leben* 37 (1964): 161–64.

Summers, Walter C. *Select Letters of Seneca*. London: Macmillan and Co., 1926.

Swidler, Leonard. *Biblical Affirmations of Woman*. Philadelphia: Westminster Press, 1979.

_____. "Greco-Roman Feminism and the Origin of the Gospel." In *Traditio-Krisis-Renovatio aus theologischer Sicht. Festschrift für Winfried Zeller Zum 65. Geburtstag*, 41–55. Edited by Bernd Jaspert and Rudolf Mohr. Marburg: N. G. Elwert, 1976.

_____. *Women in Judaism. The Status of Women in Formative Judaism*. Metuchen, N.J.: Scarecrow Press, 1976.

Talbert, Charles H. *Reading Luke. A Literary and Theological Commentary on the Third Gospel*. New York: Crossroad, 1982.

Tannehill, Robert C. "The Disciples in Mark: The Function of a Narrative Role." In *The Interpretation of Mark*, 134–57. Edited by W. Telford. Philadelphia: Fortress Press; London: SPCK, 1985.

Tetlow, Elizabeth M. *Women and Ministry in the New Testament*. New York: Paulist Press, 1980.

Theimann, Ronald F. "The Unnamed Woman at Bethany." *TToday* 44 (1987): 179–88.

Theissen, Gerd. "Lokal—und Sozialkolorit in der Geschichte von der syrophönikischen Frau (Mk 7:24–30)." *Zeitschrift für die Neutestamentliche Wissenschaft* 75 (1984): 202–25.

_____. *The Miracle Stories of the Early Christian Tradition.* Translated by Francis McDonagh. Philadelphia: Fortress Press, 1983.

_____. *Sociology of Early Palestinian Christianity.* Translated by John Bowden. Philadelphia: Westminster Press, 1978.

Thompson, Mark C. "Matthew 15:21–28." *Interpretation* 35 (1981): 279–84.

Thurston, Bonnie Bowman. *The Widows. A Women's Ministry in the Early Church.* Minneapolis: Fortress Press, 1989.

Torjesen, Karen Jo. "Reconstruction of Early Christianity." In *Searching the Scriptures: A Feminist-Ecumenical Commentary and Translation.* Edited by Elisabeth Schüssler Fiorenza. New York: Crossroad, forthcoming.

_____. *When Women Were Priests.* Harper/Collins, forthcoming.

_____. "Tertullian's Political Eccesiology and Women's Leadership." *Studia Patristica* 21, ed. Elizabeth A. Livingstone. Leuven: Peeters Press, 1989, 277–82.

Toynbee, J. M. C. *Death and Burial in the Ancient World.* London: Thames and Hudson, 1971.

Treggiari, Susan. "Jobs for Women." *American Journal of Ancient History* 1 (1976): 76–104.

_____. "Libertine Ladies." *Classical World* 64 (1971): 196–98.

_____. *Roman Freedmen During the Late Republic.* Oxford: Clarendon Press, 1969.

_____. "Roman Social History: Recent Interpretations." *Social History* 8 (1975): 149–64.

Trible, Phyllis. *God and the Rhetoric of Sexuality.* Philadelphia: Fortress Press, 1978.

_____. *Texts of Terror. Literary-Feminist Readings of Biblical Narratives.* Philadelphia: Fortress Press, 1984.

Tucker, C. Wayne. "Women in the Manumission Inscriptions at Delphi." *Transactions of the American Philological Association* 112 (1982): 225–36.

Van Bremen, Riet. "Women and Wealth." In *Images of Women in Antiquity*, 223–42. Edited by Averil Cameron and Amélie Kuhrt. Detroit, Mich.: Wayne State University Press, 1983.

Veyne, Paul, ed. *A History of Private Life. I. From Pagan Rome to Byzantium*, Translated by Arthur Goldhammer. Cambridge, Mass.; London: Belknap Press of Harvard University Press, 1987.

Via, E. Jane. "Women in the Gospel of Luke." In *Women in the World's Religions: Past and Present*, 38–55. Edited by Ursula King. New York: Paragon House, 1987.

_____. "Women, the Discipleship of Service, and the Early Christian Ritual Meal in the Gospel of Luke." *St. Luke's Journal of Theology* 29 (1985): 37–60.

Vickers, Michael. *Greek Symposia.* London: The Joint Association of Classical Teachers, n.d.

Vidal-Naquet, Pierre. "Slavery and the Rule of Women in Tradition, Myth, and Utopia." In *Myth, Religion, and Society*, 187–200. Edited by R. L. Gordon. Cambridge: Cambridge University Press, 1981.

Völkel, Martin. "Freund der Zöllner und Sünder." *Zeitschrift für die Neutestamentliche Wissenschaft* 69 (1978): 1–10.

Waetjen, Herman C. "The Genealogy as the Key to the Gospel of Matthew." *Journal of Biblical Literature* 95 (1976): 205–30.

Walker, Wm. O. "Jesus and the Tax-Collectors." *Journal of Biblical Literature* 97 (1978): 221–38.

Waller, Elizabeth. "Mt 25:1–13: The Parable of the Ten Virgins." *Proceedings of the Eastern Great Lakes Biblical Society* 1 (1981): 85–109.

Wegner, Judith Romney. *Chattel or Person? The Status of Women in the Mishnah.* New York and Oxford: Oxford University Press, 1988.

Westermann, William. *The Slave Systems of Greek and Roman Antiquity.* Philadelphia: American Philosophical Society, 1955.

Wicker, Kathleen O' Brien. "First-Century Marriage Ethics: A Comparative Study of the Household Codes and Plutarch's Conjugal Precepts." In *No Famine in the Land. Studies in Honor of John L. McKenzie*, 141–53. Edited by James W. Flanagan and Anita Weisbrod Robinson. Missoula, Mont.: Scholars Press 1975.

_____. "Mulierum Virtutes." In *Plutarch's Ethical Writings and Early Christian Literature*, 106–34. Edited by Hans Dieter Betz. Leiden: Brill, 1978.

Wiedemann, Thomas. *Greek and Roman Slavery.* Baltimore, Md.: Johns Hopkins University Press, 1981.

Wilken, Robert L. *The Christians as the Romans Saw Them.* New Haven and London: Yale University Press, 1984.

Wilkins, Michael J. *The Concept of Disciple in Matthew's Gospel As Reflected in the Use of the Term Μαθητή.* Leiden: Brill, 1988.

Will, Elizabeth Lyding. "Women in Pompeii." *Archaeology* Sept/Oct (1979): 34–50.

Williams, Gordon Willis. "Terence." *Oxford Classical Dictionary*, 1044. Edited by N. G. L. Hammond and H. H. Scollard. Oxford: Clarendon Press, 1978.

Willis, Wendell Lee. *Idol Meat in Corinth. The Pauline Argument in I Corinthians 8 and 10.* SBL Dissertation Series 68; Chico, Calif.: Scholars Press, 1985.

Wire, Antoinette Clark. *The Corinthian Women Prophets. A Reconstruction Through Paul's Rhetoric.* Minneapolis, Minn.: Fortress Press, 1990.

Witherington, Ben. "On the Road with Magdalene, Joanna, and other Disciples—Luke 8:1–3." *Zeitschrift für die Neutestamentliche Wissenschaft* 70 (1979): 243–48.

_____. *Women and the Genesis of Christianity.* Cambridge: Cambridge University Press, 1990.

_____. *Women in the Earliest Churches.* Cambridge: Cambridge University Press, 1988.

_____. *Women in the Ministry of Jesus: A Study of Jesus' Attitudes to Women and their Roles as Reflected in His Earthly Life.* Cambridge: Cambridge University Press, 1984.

Wood, H. G. "The Use of Ἀγαπάω in Luke Viii (*sic*) 42, 47." *Expository Times* 66 (1954–55): 319–20.

Wright, F. A. *Martial. The Twelve Books of Epigrams.* Translated by J. A. Pott and F. A. Wright. London: George Routlege and Sons; New York: E. P. Dutton and Co., 1924.

Ziesler, J. A. "Luke and the Pharisees." *New Testament Studies* 25 (1978–79): 146–57.

Index of Modern Authors

Corley, K. E., 12, 43, 44, 65, 114
Cotter, W., 128, 129, 153, 155, 171
Countryman, L. W., 32
Crosby, M. H., 160–62, 164, 168, 171, 173, 174, 177
Csillag, P., 55
Culver, R., 4

Daly, M., 7
D'Angelo, M. R., 108, 109, 116, 122, 126, 128, 134, 135, 137, 141, 146
D'Arms, J., 28, 29
Daube, D., 122, 125, 170
Davies, S. L., 146
D'Avino, M., 46, 60
Deissmann, A., 91
DeLacey, P., 64
Delobel, J., 122–24, 127, 130, 145
de Meeûs, X., 123, 145
De Melo, C. M., 134, 136
Dentzer, J-M., 35
Dermience, A., 96
Derrett, J. D. M., 96, 97, 99, 100, 103–5, 122–25, 128, 165, 166, 168, 169
Dewey, J., 84, 85, 88, 105
Donahue, J. R., 89, 90
Donini, A., 33
Douglas, M., 20, 21
Dowing, F. G., 63
Duff, A. M., 13, 32, 50, 52, 58, 59, 100
Duling, D., 176
Dunn, J. D. G., 65, 89, 92

Einarson, B., 64
Elliott, J. K., 103, 105, 122, 123, 126, 170
Ellis, E. E., 109, 110, 118, 120, 122–25, 135, 138, 139, 144
Elshtain, J. B., 15, 16, 39
Epp, E. J., 134
Espérandieu, E., 35

Fant, M. B., 9, 10
Farmor, W. R., 89, 90
Fee, G. D., 134, 138–40
Fehr, B., 26
Ferguson, E., 68, 69
Finley, M. I., 43, 49
Fiorenza, E. S., 5–7, 14, 16, 31, 33, 84, 90, 96, 97, 100–103, 105, 110, 115, 117, 118, 122, 124, 133–44, 146, 169, 185
Firth, R., 20
Fishel, H. A., 100

Fitzmyer, J., 109–11, 115, 118–26, 133–39, 145
Flammer, B., 96–102
Flanagan, J. W., 62
Flanagan, N. M., 108, 109, 118, 119, 122, 134
Flender, H., 108
Foh, S. T., 4
Foley, H., 44, 56
Forbes, C. A., 33, 48, 52
Ford, J. M., 151, 163
Fowler, R. M., 94
Fowler, W. W., 8, 28, 30
Frank, T., 42
Freed, E. D., 149–51
Freidländer, L., 8, 25, 28–30, 34, 56, 59, 62
Freyne, S., 94, 95, 158, 159, 173–77

Gabba, E., 26
Gardner, R., 61
Garlan, Y., 48–51
Geertz, C., 20
Gibson, J., 89–91
Glotz, G., 50, 52
Goehring, J. E., 106
Goldhammer, A., 9
Goody, J., 20, 21
Gordon, R. L., 65
Gough, A. B., 8
Grassi, J. A., 84, 85, 96, 97, 103, 105, 108, 110, 111, 114, 115, 117, 122, 128, 171, 173, 176
Green, D. E., 157
Grimal, P., 38, 40, 42, 44, 53, 56, 57, 60
Guelich, R., 87, 88, 93, 96–102
Gundry, P., 5
Gundry, R. H., 153–74

Hadidian, D. Y., 89
Hallett, J. P., 10, 11, 13, 53
Hammond, N. G. L., 42
Hanson, A. T., 150
Hardesty, N., 5
Hasler, J. I., 96, 97, 99, 166, 169
Hauck, F., 40, 41
Hedrick, C. W., 84
Heffern, A. D., 149, 152
Held, H. J., 161, 164, 168, 169
Hock, R. F., 14, 27, 30, 33, 34, 40, 44, 60, 77, 91, 145
Hoglund, K. G., 66

Index of Ancient Sources